SHEILA

SHEILA

A biography of

Sheila Mary McClemans

OBE, CMG, SJM, BA, LLB

Lloyd Davies

OAM, LLB

Barrister at Law

To Peter Appel
with best wishes,
Lloyd Davies

Desert Pea Press

2000

Law at VIT Melbourne 29/11/02

Other books by Lloyd Davies:

Past Master (1980) and *The Lawyer and the Rhine Maiden* (1989) (short story collections)
Cult and Counter Cult (1984) (novel)
In Defence of My Family (1986) (autobiography)
(ed), *WA Duty Counsel Hand Book* (1st ed, 1974)

Published in Sydney by

Desert Pea Press
an imprint of The Federation Press
PO Box 45, Annandale, NSW, 2038.
71 John St, Leichhardt, NSW, 2040.
Ph (02) 9552 2200. Fax (02) 9552 1681.
E-mail: info@federationpress.com.au
Website: http://www.federationpress.com.au

National Library of Australia cataloguing-in-publication
Davies, Lloyd
Sheila: a biography of Sheila Mary McClemans

Bibliography
Includes index.
ISBN 1 876861 01 0

1. McClemans, Sheila Mary. 2. Australia. Royal Australian Navy. Women's Royal Australian Naval Service – Biography. 3. Lawyers – Western Australia – Biography. 4. Women lawyers – Western Australia – Biography. I. Title.

340.092

Typeset by The Federation Press, Leichhardt, NSW.
Printed by Ligare Pty Ltd, Riverwood, NSW.

Contents

To Sheila's faithful shipmates,
Iris Purnell and the late Mary Howard

Foreword

Moira Rayner

Achievement is not just a matter of will. There may be barriers which, with all the will in the world, cannot be surmounted to enter onto a "level playing field". One of the greatest mistakes a woman can make is to believe that merit and hard work will be rewarded. It is more complicated.

The law assumes that all human beings have the power to choose how they will live their lives. Society assumes that people are treated on their merits and desserts. That is why, when one person chooses to drive through a red light, they are punished for it, and when another works for high-profile and self-evidently charitable causes, she will probably receive some kind of award, eventually.

But, sometimes, society punishes people who did not have any, or the full range of, choices to make. A teenage car thief condemned to a life of poverty and neglect by his Aboriginality and his nation's racist history didn't have too many other decisions to make. When someone with real ability does not have the opportunity to use it, the choice made is not really "free", and society is not "fair".

Our legal system provides only a framework in which individuals can claim remedies if their rights are infringed. That is all very well for those who can use the framework. Those who cannot use systems that are denied to them in practice, because they are not designed with them in mind, can't claim "rights". They are alienated by the very system that we like to think protects them. Middle class children will ask a policemen the way when they get lost, but Aboriginal children simply find another way to get home.

Sheila McClemans was a brilliant naval officer and lawyer whose achievements were limited by the ignorance and mediocrity of the sexist and parochial society she graced. She was also a strong, passionate and deeply disciplined woman who would never have suggested, let alone complained of, anything of the kind, and who would probably be distressed that her colleagues and friends might perceive that she had been disadvantaged by the neglect or malice of others. She seems to have learned from her difficult childhood life never to complain, and to look for support from nobody but herself.

Sheila was the kind of woman who made it her business to support and advise other women entering into the legal profession, as she did me, without once mentioning the word "discrimination" or displaying (or encouraging the display of) frustration or anger at the constraints of the profession she loved. She was the kind of woman lawyer who did not, as I originally did not, support "women's" organisations, such as the formation of the Women Lawyer's Association in Western Australia in the early 1980s. She believed that the Western Australian Law Society was the proper vehicle for the expression of women's aspirations. She held those views even though it is probably now explicitly recognised that she should have been appointed to the Supreme Court Bench, and was not appointed only because she was a woman. Perhaps she, like me, would eventually have seen that women lawyers do benefit from combining their professional voices.

The practice of law, my careers mistress said when I went to see her about my choices at school, was "not very ladylike". Had it not been for that line, I might never have taken law seriously. A well-meaning fellow law student took me aside in my first year of law studies and warned me not to go into practice, because I, too, would "lose my femininity", and cited chain-smoking, pioneer practitioner Sheila, "Hard as Nails" McClemans, as a dreadful example not to follow. So I did.

Sheila did not describe herself as a "feminist" because she did not need to. A woman of such high achievements, and who was so conscious of the need to support other women, Sheila was a humanist and a human being, who was fully conscious of the systemic injustice of the community that enfolded her – or at least some aspects of it. She was certainly not backward in claiming for women the right to be treated with respect. Women barristers had been required, until she forced the issue to be re-considered, to robe in the "Ladies" – the lavatories – in the Supreme Court, for instance, because they were excluded from the men-only Robing Room.

She would be delighted, now, at the range of brilliant young women entering into law. She would no doubt be astonished that they should continue to suffer discrimination and block-headed disparagement from the dinosaurs of legal practice, and not yet have taken their place at the pinnacle of the profession.

Though anti-discrimination laws came into effect well and truly after her public working life was over, I have no doubt that Sheila understood at least the justice of the fundamental principles. Anti-discrimination laws are human rights laws. They are meant to protect and promote the rights of all human beings to be treated with respect for their innate dignity as human beings – whatever shape or strength or beauty or colour of their bodies; wherever they were born and whom their parents might have been; whether they have or haven't procreated and the structure of their living arrangements; and whatever they believe.

Sheila McClemans was often denied the respect due to her, though never complained about it. She lived through a time when the law was still described as "an unsuitable profession" for women. Australian courts, those well-known bastions of human rights protection – well, at times they are now – opined that women had never been, and therefore never could be, lawyers: thus, the word "person" in the Legal Practitioners Act did not include women.[1]

It is timely to write about Sheila's life, not only because of the intense interest in "equality before the law" and the prejudice of some judges affecting women, but because there is a resurgence of culpable blindness. The barriers of prejudice and superstition and old custom deprive society of its greatest asset, diversity, and individuals of their fundamental right, to strive and to achieve to the best of their ability.

Sometimes these barriers are, as they were in Sheila's case, explicit, even if they are expressed obliquely. Some years ago, I considered a Horacek cartoon to make a point in an equal opportunity newsletter which I reluctantly decided not to use: a man behind a desk saying to a female, clearly an applicant for a job, "Not

1 It is interesting to note how the term "person" is now taken to mean "woman", as a result of our attempts to create non-discriminatory language.

because you're a woman of course, but because you can't urinate standing up".[2]

Far more often, however, discrimination arises from unwritten rules that are so hard to challenge because they seem "fair" because they apply to everybody. These "indirectly discriminatory" rules and practices are not easy to identify because they make no apparent distinction between different classes or groups of people. These are the rules which failed to recognise the outstanding merit of Sheila McClemans as a naval officer, as a manager, and as a jurist.

Many of the rules, practices and structures of society are indirectly discriminatory. They grew from assumptions about people because of their sex, or where they were born, or what they looked like. Many industrial practices grew up because "the worker" is presumed to be a man. These rules tend to feel "right" and are difficult to challenge because they fit dominant cultural norms. Appointments to senior judicial office, for instance, are actually made on the recommendations of referees.

Practices grow up, such as an unwritten rule that the successful applicant should be a member of a particular club or simply a particular social set where his – less often, her – "merits" are displayed and approved. These indirectly discriminatory practices need to be identified, named and changed. Sheila did it by her life, but never by asking for anything for herself.

Sheila McClemans stood up for the rights of other women, while underplaying the magnitude of her own obstacles. She would never have asked for special treatment, and when denied even an equal opportunity soldiered on. She was a hero. We need to know about her life. She was tough – not as "Nails" as she was disparagingly described by some of her male peers – but resilient. She was compassionate, and she was funny, courageous and kind. If she and others of her time had not demanded "equal opportunity", I would never have practised law, and many women today would not even have economic independence.

Thanks to those women who got laughed at, belittled, overlooked and joked about. The women of today don't have to

2 I recently heard the old "but we haven't got any women's toilets so they can't work here" excuse offered, again, as a reason for excluding women from an industry. The old attitudes refuse to die easily.

prove, any more, that they are "mature enough" to vote; that they do not become homicidal maniacs according to the phase of the moon, pre-menstrual tension, motherhood or lactation, any more than men become irresponsible brutes according to their testosterone count.

Women like Sheila McClemans have demanded respect for all of us. I do not apologise for calling myself a feminist, as Sheila did not do. There are many brands of feminism, including women who want to work at home with their children, and women who want to live only with women, and women who just want to get on with their chosen careers, without having to act a role. People like me, who "made it" in a man's profession, did it because we knew that being excluded was wrong, and because we had the self-esteem to demand a right. We got that confidence from the acts and writings of other women, and because people fought for international guarantees of human rights, and because enlightened women and men fought for anti-discrimination laws and policies, and because of the trail-blazers who made it so much easier for us. I'm proud that I follow in Sheila McClemans' footsteps.

Acknowledgements

I am grateful to the Law Society of Western Australia for the research grant made to me through its Public Purposes Trust Fund and for its continuous assistance and encouragement over the 10-year gestation period of this work.

I must also thank the archival staffs of Perth Modern School, the University of Western Australia and the Guild of Undergraduates for the material relating to Sheila's student years. Of particular value has been Sheila's *Oral History Memoir* compiled by Christine Shervington. The University of Western Australia Press has also given me invaluable advice and guidance concerning the content of this work.

A number of patient and obliging librarians have been most generous with their time in assisting my researches at the following institutions: Battye and Alexander Libraries, Cottesloe – Peppermint Grove Municipal Library, UWA Library, Supreme Court Library, Industrial Court Library and the Public Library of Victoria. I am thankful to them all for this.

Naval background material was supplied by the staffs of the Australian War Museum, Canberra, the Naval Museum at Flinders Bay and the Victorian office of the Australian Archives. The Western Australian office of the Australian Archives supplied a printout of the history of the Canteens Services Trust fund. I am grateful to them all for this assistance.

Historians also have been invaluable. These include the late Professor Alexander and the late Sir Paul Hasluck who kindly directed me to his work *Mucking About* and gave me his blessing to use some brief passages about his school days at Perth Modern School which immediately preceded Sheila's. Sir Paul's blessing was kindly confirmed by his son and literary heir, the Hon Justice Nicholas Hasluck. Jon Faine supplied me with valuable histories of gender discrimination through the ABC's *Law Report* and its printed compilation *Taken on Oath* (Federation Press, 1992). Jon also referred me to Mary Anne Noone of La Trobe University who was the principal source of the material I have used for my account of the history of the Australian Legal Aid Office and the present crisis in legal aid. Michael Hess and Charlie Fox directed me to the feminist history sources which enabled me to find my point of view – an essential ingredient, it seems, for contemporary biographies. Dianne and Ron Davidson followed them up with invaluable source material about the Women's Service Guilds and the Mirror newspaper. It was Ron who provided me with the report of Sheila' first Supreme Court criminal trial.

My principal feminist mentor was, and is, Moira Rayner whose Foreword adds much authority to this book. During my many visits to Melbourne to confer with my WRAN authorities, Moira brought to life the many feminist truths outlined in the historical sources. Because she often generously provided me with bed and breakfast during my visits, we had plenty of opportunity to consider the law's unkindness to women and to women lawyers, in particular.

My principal WRAN sources were the late Mary Howard and Iris Purnell both of whom lived in Melbourne and spent many patient hours recalling their wartime memories of Sheila. They devoted many more patient hours reading and correcting the drafts of my manuscript. I am especially indebted to Mary for driving me to Flinders Naval Depot to visit the Naval Museum and to put some life and visual image into the history of that 1943 initial training course. Margaret Curtis-Offer's short history of the WRANS was also of great value, as were her letters to me. Sadly, I missed her on my one visit to Sydney and she died before I could get back there again.

My other naval adviser was Arthur Cooper whose diary of the voyage on *Shropshire* and of the London Victory March was a rich source of information. I am most grateful for his permission to use his photograph of that grand occasion. Pamela Johnson, in response to my press appeal, told me where to find them all. Ex-WRANS from all over Australia wrote to me with snippets of information. Old school friends and workmates from the days of Sheila's youth responded similarly to this press item. I thank them all for their accounts of Sheila's vibrant youth.

Many lawyers were most generous with their time and advice. Loris Wood's short handwritten history of the Legal Aid Scheme saved me many hours of research. His inside knowledge and recollection of his co-operation with Sheila in her Law Society and Legal Aid days was a major contribution to this book. I also thank

Sir Francis Burt for his reminiscences and, particularly, for his eloquent obituary which enabled me to conclude my book on a grand note. Fred Robinson supplied very useful information about Mary Kingston and kindly read and advised upon some of my early drafts. The Honourable Ian Medcalf, Leo Wood, John O'Halloran, Sir John Lavan, the late Jim Smythe, Ivan Vodanovich and the many others whose names appear in the text and the footnotes deserve equal thanks for their time and patience in granting me interviews and digging up material.

Family members – Judith Collett, the late Paddy McFadyen, Colin Sanders, Neil, Ethel and Lesley Kenworthy – have been most helpful in providing family history and glimpses of Sheila's private life. They have also been generous with photographs and treasured documents. Michael Wright has been exceedingly generous with financial support. I thank them all.

And finally I thank the workers: Constance Morgan, Mrs Tyler, Jo Hawkins, Beryl Bruce and Veronica Kviesis. Sheila lived for her work and their record of her days at the coalface made a fundamental contribution. I conclude by thanking my own staff of one – my wife, Jo – who manned the telephone and took scores of messages from all the people mentioned above as well as many more, who would have been mentioned if I had kept a proper record, and who attended to countless other details which is the uncomplaining lot of every writer's partner.

List of illustrations

1

THE FORERUNNERS

The *Oxford Dictionary* defines "establishment" as "an organised body of men maintained for a purpose". This definition is peculiarly apt for the legal establishment, being eloquently suggestive of its blend of executive and judicial power with the Masonic network of a profession, heavily biased towards wealth and privilege and – until recently – exclusively male.

The legal establishment even has its own honours system for professional excellence. These are: admission to a major partnership, appointment as Senior Counsel (QC or KC according to the gender of the reigning monarch) and elevation to the judiciary. Such rewards cannot be taken for granted, however, as the profession is dominated by congenital conservative traditions and failure to conform can bring denial of the usual accolades. The establishment of Western Australia denied all three to one of the State's most able practitioners, an outstanding advocate and administrator who was, as well, a decorated war-time commander, Sheila Mary McClemans OBE, CMG, SJM, BA, LLB (Hons) – in private life Mrs Sheila Kenworthy.

Sheila's aberration was to be born a female at a time and in a place when that entailed many disadvantages both by convention and law – particularly within the legal profession itself. Many members of the profession resented the intrusion of women. Their right to practise law had been won, by the enactment of the *Women's Legal Status Act* 1923 (WA), only five years before Sheila commenced her law course. That right had been won through determined campaigns by women who preceded her – campaigns waged in Parliament, in court, and in the public arena.[1]

The legal establishment had officially made clear its hostility to female lawyers in 1904 in the leading authority of *In re Edith Haynes* (1904) 6 WAR 209. In this case the unsuccessful applicant, Edith Haynes, was the 26-year-old niece of an eminent lawyer-politician, RS Haynes QC, MLC. Edith Haynes commenced a five-year course as an articled clerk with her uncle in November 1900, hoping at the end of her service to be admitted to practise as a lawyer.

Serving articles and passing the Barristers Board exams were the only way a young person could become a lawyer in Western Australia until the University inaugurated the Faculty of Law in 1928. Before commencing service the clerk had to enter into a deed of articles with his legal master, pay stamp duty of £10, and file the deed with the Barristers' Board together with an application for admission as a law student for the qualifying examinations conducted by the Board.

The articled clerk was not paid any wage during the five-year period of service, indeed most were required to put up a substantial premium to compensate the principal for his time and trouble in teaching the clerk the law.[2] The clerk was expected to work while he learned, and spent many hours of drudgery doing clerical tasks and running errands to the courts, government departments and the offices of other practitioners. The system effectively ensured that only the sons of the wealthy could afford to enter the profession, a high proportion of those coming from established legal families.

---

1 According to a broadcast of the ABC programme *The Law Report* on 12 August 1997, women currently comprised 30 percent of legal practitioners. There were, however, widespread complaints of gender discrimination, the most important being the so-called "glass ceiling" – the practical exclusion of women from the higher categories of employment. These complaints were given judicial status by Justice Gaudron, speaking at the inaugural meeting of Australian Women Lawyers in Melbourne on 20 September 1997, in which she accused legal institutions of being "hostile to women" and operating "on rules developed on the playing fields of Eton" (*West Australian*, September 1997, p 28) and by Justice Christine Wheeler who, on 31 July 1998, complained of a judicial "old boys' network" in a lecture at Edith Cowan University (*Brief*, Vol 25, Law Society of Western Australia, 1998, Pt 10, p 7).

2 In contrast, see the May 1997 issue of the *WA Law Society Bulletin* (Vol 1, Issue 5) detailing the minimum conditions of employment for an articled clerk which include (*inter alia*) an annual wage of $17,264.00, four weeks' annual leave, long service leave, parental leave and 6 percent employer contribution to superannuation.

There is no record of any female having sought or been offered legal articles in Western Australia before Edith Haynes. It seems likely that her uncle actively encouraged her to act as a pioneer in the field. A member of the Legislative Council from 1886 to 1902, Haynes QC was a radical thinker for his time, he had led an campaign for the 8-hour-day, marching at the head of a procession through Perth. He had also campaigned unsuccessfully in Parliament against capital punishment and had spoken and voted in support of women's franchise. His efforts in the latter cause were rewarded with the passage of an amendment to the State Constitution in 1899 by which women were eventually granted equal suffrage with men.

Once women won the vote it must have seemed that the way was open for sexual equality in all fields. It may well have given Haynes QC the confidence to encourage Edith to enter the law. There was some doubt as to whether women could be admitted as practitioners. Not only had it never been done before but s 14 of the *Legal Practitioners' Act* 1893 (WA) dealing with articled clerks contained (*inter alia*) the following provision:

> No person shall be articled to a practitioner unless and until he has satisfied the Board that he is of good fame and . . . [the section then proceeded to deal with the specified exams and payment of fees].

The exclusive use of the male pronoun *he* negatively reinforced the lack of precedent that any woman had ever been admitted to practise in any Common Law jurisdiction. There was also an unreported English decision, *Miss Cave*, in which the Lord Chancellor had refused to create such a precedent by allowing a woman to be admitted to practise.[3] The position appeared to have been clarified favourably in Western Australia by the *Interpretation Act* 1898 which provided that the expression "person" included both men and women, a situation which Parliament appeared to have re-enforced by amending the Constitution in 1899 to admit women to vote for Parliament. Nevertheless, the doubt still lingered.

---

3 The case of Miss Cave is referred to by Parker ACJ in *Re Edith Haynes* (1904) 6 WAR 209 at 211 but no reference is cited. It is also referred to (but not by name) by Haynes in his speech to his proposed amendment to the *Legal Practitioners' Act*, *Western Australian Parliamentary Debates*, Vol 17 (NS) p 450.

Haynes QC endeavoured to put the matter beyond all doubt on 18 September 1900 by introducing, in the Legislative Council, an amendment to the *Legal Practitioners' Act* which provided:

> From and after the passing of this Act any person of female sex who shall be qualified in other respects may be articled to a practitioner, and upon compliance with all the requirements of the principal Act . . . may be admitted as a practitioner.[4]

In speaking to his motion, Haynes found it necessary to counter two possible grounds of opposition. One was the resistance of the profession to any widening of the categories of admission to its restricted ranks; the other was the all-male profession's pervasive gender bias.

Haynes countered the first obstacle by calling upon members not to give the impression that the legal profession operated as a "closed borough" and minimising the economic threat posed by the admission of women:

> The result of this Bill will be – and I say this now for the benefit of members of the legal profession – not to at once deprive them of their livelihood because six or seven years must elapse before any female could be admitted . . . there will be no "rush" if I may be excused the expression. . . A woman who desires to be admitted will have to pass a matriculation . . . or some equal examination and afterwards serve five years without fee or reward in an office having the whole of that time behaved herself. . .[5]

He then spoke generally about the competence of women as employees and referred to the fact that women were already accepted as medical practitioners in Australia and overseas and that, in England, women were sitting on the London County Council and "exercising functions quite as important as the functions exercised by this House". He concluded with an appeal:

> Here, so far as the franchise is concerned, we have placed women on exactly the same footing as men, and what legal objection can there be to women practising as solicitors? If members of the legal profession are so week-kneed as to be afraid that in competition women may out run them, then, in Heaven's name, I appeal to members of

4 *Western Australian Parliamentary Debates*, Vol 17 (NS) p 450.

5 Ibid, p 450.

> the legal profession to pass the Bill, and let us have a stronger set of men practising law.[6]

No one spoke against the motion and it was carried by a majority of 13 to 8. The Bill was read for the first time in the Legislative Assembly on 2 October 1900 and came up again on 29 November 1900 when the Attorney-General moved that it be discharged on the ground that the Member who was in charge of it did not now wish to proceed with it, as his main contention had been conceded by the Barristers' Board admitting ladies to practise.[7]

It is puzzling why Haynes persuaded his niece to make her application to the Board before he had put beyond doubt her right to do so by ensuring the passage of his amendment to the Act. There is no Barristers' Board file relating to Edith Haynes. It is therefore not possible to discover when, in the sequence of the case, Edith lodged her application to the Board. It is only known from the head note in *Haynes* that the Board's letter of acceptance was dated 27 November 1900. The lodging of the application may have been some kind of tactical two-way bet on her uncle's part. Having had the Bill read for the first time in the Council he may have persuaded her to apply prior to the second reading debate with the thought that rejection by the Board would strengthen his argument. Perhaps he advised her to apply after the passage of the Bill through the Council to provide a potential argument for his supporters in the Assembly when the Bill came on for debate in that House.

In the event, the Board did accept Edith's application, two days before the Bill was withdrawn on 29 November. Why did not Haynes still press on with his amendment to put the matter beyond all doubt? Perhaps he was worried that he did not have the numbers in the Assembly to pass the Bill. There is a hint of such concern in his closing remarks in reply to the debate in the Council: "if in another place it meets with an adverse vote, we, at all events, will feel that we have done our duty".[8]

It may be significant, in this regard, that one member of the Assembly, Mr Frederick Illingworth MLA, opposed the withdrawal

---

6 Ibid, p 451.

7 Ibid, Vol 18, p 2052-3.

8 Ibid, Vol 17, p 453.

of the Bill, saying that the amendment proposed was of great importance to "a few people" and he hoped the government would take steps to amend "the small difficulty in the existing law".[9] This comment could have had sinister connotations. Mr Illingworth was a strong opponent of sexual equality. In the 1897 suffrage debate he made the assertion that: "the Creator who made [woman] has placed her in subjection; and woe be to the Parliament, or to the men who place her anywhere else".[10]

It seems possible that, in Illingworth's opinion, the "small difficulty" was the ambiguity in the *Legal Practitioners' Act*, which even admitted of the possibility that women were entitled to become lawyers. He could well have harboured the intention to move an amendment to make it indisputable that "person" meant "man" and "man" only.

Haynes certainly did not want the ambiguity clarified in that manner. He was fairly confident that, as a result of the operation of the *Interpretation Act*, "person" meant both "man" and "woman". In his speech in the Council he had said "that is the opinion pretty generally expressed [in the legal profession]".[11] As the Barristers' Board, consisting of some of the most learned minds in the profession, had agreed with him and had given their approval, he may have thought it wise to accept the position and not to push his luck by going on with the amendment.

The Secretary to the Barrister's Board, however, sounded a note of caution in the letter of 27 November, which acknowledged the lodging of Edith's documents:

> With reference to your application for admission as a law student, the same has been approved by the Board. I am directed, however, to warn you that although the Board is of opinion (with some doubt) that women are eligible for admission under the *Legal Practitioners Act* yet the Board cannot guarantee such admissions... It must be distinctly understood by you that you accept all risk of the Court eventually refusing your application.[12]

---

9 Ibid, Vol 18, p 2053.

10 Ibid, Vol 11, p 749-750.

11 Ibid, Vol 17, p 450.

12 Quoted by Parker ACJ in *Re Edith Haynes* (1904) 6 WAR 209 at 212.

Edith served articles in her uncle's office under the shadow of that doubt for almost four years until the time came to sit her intermediate examination. By this time the personnel of the Board had changed and so had its collective opinion. When Edith sought leave to sit for her exam, it rejected her on the ground that women were not entitled to be admitted as legal practitioners and there was thus no purpose in her sitting the examination.

There is no record of the reasoning which led the Board to differ from the decision of its predecessors although it is possible its members had become aware of the rejection of Australia's first female law graduate, Ada Evans, from practice in New South Wales in 1902. In that case, the Attorney-General of NSW had received advice from the judiciary that "person" meant "man" exclusively. The Board thus had a negative precedent to guide it. There is no reference, however, to the case of Ada Evans anywhere in *Haynes*.[13]

Haynes QC immediately applied to the Supreme Court of Western Australia for a writ of Mandamus to compel the Board to accept Edith's application to sit the examination. The summary of the arguments of counsel and the dicta of the judges recorded in *Haynes* are drearily technical. They give no hint that there was a human rights issue at stake. Even though Haynes QC argued his niece's case, there is no suggestion of any heart-felt appeal that women had the right to be treated as ordinary human beings. The nearest Haynes QC got to an appeal for equality was to cite that provision of the *Interpretation Act* 1898 (WA) which provided that the word "person" included women.

To be fair it should be remembered that he was addressing the Full Court on a question of law. Appeal judges are quite capable of countering high-minded rhetoric with such phrases as "We are not a jury Mr Haynes" or "We are concerned with law not with justice". It should also be remembered that he was confronting a Bench whose judgments produced the following gems of jurisprudence from Parker CJ:

---

13 The case of Ada Evans is not reported in any law report. It is summarised in two articles: Judith Allen, "Breaking into the Public Sphere"; and Daphne Kok, Joan O'Brien and Ruth Teale, "In the Office and at the Bar, Women in the Legal Profession" in J Mackinolty and H Radi (eds) *In Pursuit of Justice*, Hale & Iremonger, 1979, pp 111 and 182.

> The idea of women practising in the Supreme Court seems to me quite foreign to the legislation which has prevailed for the years past, not only here but in the mother country.[14]

and Burnside J:

> I think that the right of a woman to be admitted is a misnomer. The right to appear other than in person was first legalised very far back, before women were recognised in any legal capacity. The Common Law of England has never recognised the right of women to be admitted to the Bar.[15]

It was clearly a Bench which put servility to precedent before logic. It thus gave no thought to the possibility that the provision in the *Interpretation Act* defining "person" as both male and female might be an attempt to bring the law up to date and to give recognition to the many changes in the status of women which had occurred in the second half of the 19th century.

Another dictum of Burnside J is further indicative of this servility:

> It appears to me that we must also bear in mind that throughout the civilised world, so far as we know, we have not been able to ascertain any instances under the Common Law of the United States which is based on the Common Law of England, or of any instances in England or any British-speaking colony where the right of women to be admitted to the Bar has ever been suggested... When the Legislature in its wisdom confers the right on women, then we shall be pleased to admit them. But we must leave it to the Legislature to decide on the desirability or otherwise of such legislation.[16]

The judgment clearly demonstrates that their honours were men of their time. If no other jurisdiction admitted women why should Western Australia? The pioneering spirit, so strongly idealised in other fields, was not to be invoked when female rights were under consideration.

Edith did not appeal to the newly created High Court of Australia. It is possible Haynes QC realised it was a hopeless cause in the light of what had happened to Ada Evans in New South Wales

---

14 *Re Edith Haynes* (1904) 6 WAR 209 at 211.

15 Ibid, at 213.

16 Ibid.

and advised her against it. Perhaps it was Edith's own decision. Her subsequent career suggests that she became disenchanted with the law in the face of such treatment and gave up the fight.

It was open to Edith to remain in her uncle's office as an ordinary law clerk and put her four years experience to good use. Experienced law clerks are a valuable asset in any law office and in time can expect to be paid a respectable salary. Edith rejected this alternative. She left the firm and took a post as a clerk in the National Bank where she worked until retirement age. She never married and died in 1968 at the age of 92. Her nephew, RA Haynes, who carried on the family firm from 1940 to 1988, remembers her as a very dignified and independent lady and considers that she probably tired of being the person in the middle in her uncle's crusade.[17]

The struggle for recognition undoubtedly wore down Ada Evans in New South Wales. After a long campaign to achieve an appropriate alteration in the law through the enactment of the *Women's Legal Status Act* 1918 (NSW), she completed her articles and became the first woman to be admitted to the Bar in New South Wales on 12 May 1921 but, at almost 50 years of age, decided she was too old and never actually practised.[18]

The Barristers' Board expunged Edith Haynes from its records. It holds no file for her nor does her name appear anywhere in any book or document held in its archives. Fortunately, the case of *In re Edith Haynes* has assured her of a place in legal history – albeit as a casualty of a gallant but ill-fated expedition into hostile and unforgiving territory.

By 1904 Haynes QC had lost his seat in the Council and there seems to have been no one else either in the House or at the Bar willing to press amendments to the *Legal Practitioners' Act* to legalise the admission of women. The cause was taken over by the women's movement, which had provided the initial impetus in the campaign for female suffrage. This was a logical development of their general struggle for sexual equality.

---

17 In a personal interview.

18 Daphne Kok, Joan O'Brien and Ruth Teale, "In the Office and at the Bar, Women in the Legal Profession" in *In Pursuit of Justice*, Hale & Iremonger, 1979, p 182.

When an unjust anomaly in the law is exposed by a judicial decision it is usual for Parliament to respond with a law reform statute to right the injustice. This course was indicated by Burnside J in his dicta quoted above to the effect that when the legislature "in its wisdom" saw fit for women to become lawyers the court would be pleased to admit them. In that small colonial community, Burnside and his fellow judges would have been well aware of Haynes' manoeuvres to get his niece admitted by playing the legislature off against the Barristers' Board and were plainly not prepared to make new law to help him.

Parliament, however, did not see fit to revive the amendment to the *Legal Practitioners' Act* moved and then withdrawn by Haynes in 1900. It discussed several proposed amendments to the Act to broaden eligibility for admission for aspiring male practitioners in 1905 but no mention was made of any amendment to allow women to practise. This must be viewed as a significant indication of its political attitude and not a mere omission. Its significance is surely emphasised by the fact that Victoria and Tasmania had passed amendments to their equivalent Acts in 1903 and 1904 respectively and Ada Evans was engaging in a highly publicised campaign in NSW which had been the subject of humorous doggerel in the NSW press and which could have applied equally to the case of Edith Haynes:

> But the thirteen clucking, judges
> Shook their feathers out and swore
> That the only kind of persons
> They had ever seen before
> Were young men, young men only
> And they could not recognise
> That this earnest woman-student
> Was a person in their eyes.[19]

In view of its recent granting of women's suffrage it might have seemed reasonable to expect Western Australian politicians to be more tolerant towards the admission of female lawyers. Such reasoning, however, would ignore the history of the campaign for

---

19 *The Transmitter,* 17 May 1902, p 5, reprinted in *In Pursuit of Justice*, Hale & Iremonger, 1979, p 180.

women's suffrage in Western Australia and the devious reasons why Parliament eventually granted it.

The "votes for women" campaign had been waged throughout the 1890s with increasing tempo by political activists in the Women's Franchise Department of the Women's Christian Temperance Union, led by Janetta Griffiths Foulkes, and the Karrakatta Club, led by Lady Onslow (later a leading London suffragette) and Mrs Edith Cowan. It drew strength from similar campaigns throughout the English-speaking world and particular encouragement from the granting of female suffrage in New Zealand in 1893 and South Australia in 1894.

A motion to introduce female suffrage was presented in the Western Australian Legislative Assembly in 1893 by a liberal minded young lawyer, Walter James MLA, whose wife, Gwenyford, was prominent in the Karrakatta Club. The motion was defeated 11 to 17. A sample of the opposing arguments collated by the author, Peter Cowan, provides some idea of their intellectual poverty. TF Quinlan expressed the opinion that "Women like cats were best at home" and that his experience of ladies in municipal and other elections had been that they were "somewhat weak in mind". Alexander Forrest agreed with Quinlan that a woman's place was in the home. Premier Sir John Forrest and Mr HB Lefroy pointed out that there was a total lack of precedent to such a move. Attorney-General Septimus Burt QC condemned such a "stupendous alteration of the law" as being "too sudden".[20]

The opinion of Burt QC appears to have been ignored in a change of heart by Sir John Forrest when the issue was raised in 1899, again by Walter James, who moved an amendment to include women's suffrage as part of a Constitutional Act Amendment Bill. Sir John and the majority of his party on this occasion supported the motion and, with very little opposition, female suffrage became law.

According to Peter Cowan, this unexpected change of heart by the conservative government of the day was not caused by any radical mood swing towards sexual equality but was entirely due to the national move towards federation of the Australian States.

20 Quoted by Peter Cowan in his biography of his grandmother, Dame Edith Cowan: *A Unique Position*, University of Western Australia Press, 1980.

Sir John Forrest and the wealthy landowners whom he represented were opposed to federation, as was a sizeable proportion of voters in the Perth metropolitan area and the agricultural areas of the South West who displayed a strong feeling of resentment towards the Eastern States or the "T'othersiders" as the population of the rest of Australia was colloquially known in the West.

The gold rushes of the 1890s had introduced from the East a large population of unmarried males which was expected to support federation overwhelmingly in the coming referendum. Since the established population of the metropolitan and farming areas had a female population of approximately 50 percent who would reflect the xenophobia of their male partners, it was hoped women's suffrage would counter the pro-federation vote of the goldfields. In support of his opinion, Peter Cowan quotes the admission of Cocksworthy MLC that his vote was "purely for a conservative reason – to counteract the votes of the young men".[21] RS Haynes QC, in his contribution to the debate in genuine support of the principle of women's suffrage, was sarcastic about Forrest's turn-around and openly accused him using it as a tactic to counter the goldfield's vote.[22]

The granting of female suffrage did not create any automatic flow-on towards total sexual equality. In the early years of the 20th century, women in Western Australia still suffered many political disabilities despite the granting of the right to own property in 1892 and the suffrage in 1899. As well as being barred from practising law, they could not stand for Parliament, act as justices of the peace or sit on juries and their wage rate was much below the male rate. The women's movement of the time, therefore, had many campaign issues to confront. The urgent practical need for social reform, however, appears to have taken precedence over the struggle for political equality in the years immediately following the granting of the suffrage.

---

21 Ibid.

22 *Western Australian Parliamentary Debates* (NS) Vol 16 1899, p 952. For further discussion of the motives of Sir John Forrest and his supporters, see the first chapter of Dianne Davidson's history of the Women's Service Guilds of WA (Inc): *Women on the Warpath*, University of Western Australia Press, 1997.

This is not surprising. The social conditions of the poor and the powerless at that time were quite desperate. There was no children's hospital, no children's court, no maternity hospital, no unemployed or sickness benefit, no widow's pension, no family allowance, not even any public toilets for women. The plight of destitute children was a priority target for social reformers. This was publicised by a number of "baby farming" cases which were exposed from time to time in the courts. The most famous Australian case, that of *Makin v Attorney-General (NSW)* [1894] AC 57, is still a leading case in the law of evidence in Common Law countries. Mr and Mrs Makin, who were ultimately hanged for the murder of some 13 fostered babies, were less fortunate than their Western Australian equivalent, Mrs Alice Mitchell, who was imprisoned for the manslaughter of 40 babies left in her care and whom she starved to death.[23]

A campaign by the Children's Protection Society led by Edith Cowan and another prominent feminist, Bessie Rischbieth, achieved the passage of the State *Children's Act* in 1907, which established a separate Children's Court in 1908. Before this, children accused of criminal offences had to appear in the same courts as adults, before male judges and magistrates, and be lodged in adult lock-ups pending trial and sentence.

The establishment of the Children's Court was undoubtedly a victory of principle but hardly a shining example of progressive jurisprudence. Continued agitation by Cowan and Rischbieth and their followers led to an enquiry by a Select Committee of the Legislative Assembly which reported (*inter alia*):

> The Children's Court is a room scarcely large enough to swing a cat. Yet three or four officers work there and when the Court is sitting they have to take their work outside. . .
>
> Attached to the Children's Court is what is known as a detention ward – a small wooden building of two rooms 12 feet by 10 feet, and separated by a thin wooden partition . . . this institution is a disgrace to Western Australia and should be abolished immediately no matter what the cost.

---

23 *Report of The Department of Community Welfare of Western Australia (Sesqui-Centenary Edition)*, Government Printer, p 12.

> . . . There are no sanitary conveniences other than a commode in each room and the unfortunate children have to remain there all day and sleep as best they may at night. The caretaker stated he had as many as eight boys in the room for four days and nights. How they were packed in passes comprehension. It must have been a veritable "Black Hole".[24]

Other important practical campaigns proceeded contemporaneously with that for the Children's Court. These campaigns were not waged in isolation. In 1909 Edith Cowan took the lead in forming an organisation known as the Women's Service Guilds which began to provide common leadership for the various women's organisations concerned with social welfare and the rights of women and children. It was through the Women's Service Guilds that Bessie Rischbieth began to emerge as a leading female activist. Although it included in its objectives the achievement of the equality of women in all fields, the energy of the Guilds was concentrated on tackling immediate physical and practical problems.

It is perhaps significant that one of its first moves was to write to the Perth City Council for the appointment of a women's sanitary inspector to assist in establishing suitable "sanitary sites" for women and children in the city.[25] In 1910 it began its first major campaign for the establishment of a State maternity hospital, which ultimately succeeded with the opening of King Edward Memorial Hospital in Subiaco in 1915. Other campaigns during the first and second decades were for the establishment of free kindergartens, replacement of the inadequate Old Women's Home, improvement of the conditions of the female gaol inmates and amendments to the *Health Act* 1911 (WA) to cope with the spread of venereal disease.

The great significance of the Children's Court campaign was that it resulted in the first victory for women's legal status since the granting of female suffrage in 1899 – the right to be appointed as justices of the peace. Even before the establishment of the Court, Edith Cowan had called for the appointment of female justices of the peace, especially for service in the Children's Court. When the Court was established, a provision was made for the appointment of

---

24 Ibid, p 15.

25 Dianne Davidson, *Women on the Warpath*, University of Western Australia Press, 1997, p 31.

lay advisers to which position Edith Cowan was appointed but this was clearly inadequate. At the end of the 20th century, it is still true to say that women generally have much more experience in dealing with children than men and, consequently, a greater practical grasp of child psychology. In the early part of that century, this was overwhelmingly so. The care of pre-pubertal children was wholly allocated to women at home and very largely so at school. To entrust the assessment of the evidence of children entirely to middle-aged upper class males was a patent injustice.

A similar situation existed with the evidence of women, who were even more likely to be called upon to give evidence in the Children's Court than children, because it was the Children's Court which heard the bulk of the claims for custody, confinement expenses and maintenance on behalf of deserted wives and mothers of ex-nuptial children.

The male judiciary of the time came from the same professional and social stratum as the politicians who had made their contempt for the mentality of women so clear in the parliamentary debates upon female suffrage. Their attitude towards the evidence of women as well as children has been perpetuated in many classical judicial dicta such as:

> there is often very great temptation to a woman by making a false or exaggerated charge, and supporting it with minute details of a kind, which the female mind seems particularly adapted to invent . . . judges are in the habit of telling juries that it is not safe to convict the prisoner upon the unsupported statements of the woman. . .[26]

> Human experience has shown that in these courts girls and women do sometimes tell an entirely false story . . . for all sorts of reasons . . . and sometimes for no reason at all.[27]

More importantly, assessment of evidence was only part of the responsibility exercised by Children's Court magistrates. They had also to decide upon the penalties to be handed out to children – and this in days when whipping was a common from of punishment, whether children should be taken from the custody of their parents,

---

26 LJ Wills, *Principles of Circumstantial Evidence*, Butterworth Co, 1902, p 364. Cited critically by Deane J in *Longman v The Queen* (1989) 168 CLR 79 at 92.

27 Salmon LJ in *R v Henry* (1968) 53 Cr App R 150 at 153-154.

if so, to whom should they be entrusted, and, in maintenance cases, what should be the amount of the weekly payments. To appoint middle aged, upper class males to be the sole arbiters of the fortunes of women and children was yet another example of injustice.

Edith Cowan won her campaign for the appointment of women justices of the peace with the passage of *Justices Act Amendment Act* in 1919. The first 20 women justices were appointed in 1920. These included Edith Cowan and Bessie Rischbieth. Another nine were appointed the following year, among these was Sheila McClemans' mother, Ada Lucy McClemans, a close friend and supporter of Edith Cowan.

In 1920 close friends and supporters were of particular value to Edith Cowan. In that year Parliament granted women the right to stand for parliamentary election, professedly as a reward for their patriotic support on the home front during the Great War. Edith Cowan took advantage of this new liberty in 1921 and nominated for the Legislative Assembly seat of West Perth as a Nationalist (conservative) candidate in opposition to the official Nationalist candidate, Attorney-General Tom Draper.

Being an unofficial candidate Edith had no party machine to back her and had to rely upon the feminist movement for her campaign support. In better times she might have expected the Women's Service Guilds to throw its full weight behind her but in 1916, as the result of a factional struggle, she and another prominent activist, Dr Roberta Jull, had resigned from the leadership of the Women's Service Guilds and carried on their organisational work through the National Council of Women which did not have the grassroots support of the Guilds. Although they supported the same causes, she and Bessie Rischbieth had become arch rivals.[28]

In the event, it seems Edith was able to marshal sufficient friends and supporters to achieve victory. She was helped in this by the Labor Party declining to stand a candidate and advising its supporters to vote for her. On 11 March 1921, she created history by becoming the first Australian female Member of Parliament. Although she had her differences with the Women's Service Guilds, Edith fought to implement its policy in Parliament. A major plank of

28 Dianne Davidson, *Women on the Warpath*, University of Western Australia Press, 1997, pp 52-54.

that policy was to put to rights the wrong done to Edith Haynes in 1904 and to empower women to practise law. Edith Cowan achieved this by ensuring the passage of the *Women's Legal Status Act* 1923 (WA) which removed all legal barriers against women joining the professions.[29] The passage of this Act also had a strong personal interest for Ada McClemans. Her daughter Sheila had developed an ambition to practise law at an early age and, in the previous year at the age of 12, had entered Perth Modern School as a first step towards achieving that ambition.

Another important Act passed with Edith's strong support was the *Married Women's Protection Act* 1922 (WA). This gave women the right of easy access to magistrates' courts to seek summary orders for separation and maintenance against violent, adulterous or merely non-supportive husbands. It was a measure which women's organisations had urged for many years. Although Edith Cowan did not personally initiate the legislation, she got the blame for it.

In an outburst, prophetic of contemporary attacks upon the present *Family Law Act* 1975 (Cth), Mr Unmack, a local solicitor, complained in the Fremantle Court of Petty Sessions:

> The whole of the Acts dealing with these matters is in a state of absolute chaos, neither the Bench nor the Bar know where they are. . . This is the first effort of a woman legislator and it is much to be deplored.[30]

The *Married Women's Protection Act*, in addition to serving women generally, was a piece of legislation which would become a major source of professional work for the female lawyers who would eventually enter the profession as a result of the *Women's Status Act.*

Edith Cowan only held her seat for one term, being brought down by a number of adverse factors, some of her own making. In the 1924 elections, the National Party nominated a prominent lawyer, Mr TAL Davy, as its official candidate and mounted a strong campaign for his election. The Labor Party stood a candidate in opposition because Edith had failed to support it on an important social issue. In addition, Edith's feud with Bessie Rischbieth and the

29 The dates of equivalent enabling legislation in other States are: Victoria 1903, Tasmania 1904, Queensland 1905, South Australia 1911, NSW 1918.

30 Peter Cowan, *A Unique Position*, University of Western Australia Press, 1980.

women's Service Guild had reached the proportions of a public slanging match.[31] All these factors combined to cost her the seat.

The principal speaker at a grand valedictory function in Edith's honour was Ada McClemans. She recapitulated Edith's 30 years of service to social causes and branded her defeat as "a calamity and retrograde step".[32] It was a comment which recognised the fact that by the end of Edith Cowan's three years in Parliament the women's movement had achieved all its claims for legal status except the right of jury service.

The male establishment had very strong feelings about women and jury service. The strength of this feeling can be judged by the following contribution to the parliamentary debate by Mr RR Pilkington MLA: "I am opposed to women being on juries because at least once in every month no woman is quite sane".[33]

Male antipathy to female jurors was not confined to Western Australia. In 1913, the New South Wales *Evening News* proclaimed editorially in response to a campaign by the Progressive Women's Organisation:

> Nevertheless very few men consider women to possess the qualities which should distinguish the ideal juror. Men it is considered have a better sense of justice, a greater capacity to hear evidence compassionately and hear it impartially. Women, it is contended, are too apt to judge by instinct, a method which . . . is certain to work out unsatisfactorily on average.[34]

Western Australian women finally gained the right to jury service in 1957 – 25 years after Edith Cowan's death. At least Bessie Rischbieth lived to see it and to claim it as a victory for the Women' Service Guilds:

> In the Legislative Council on October 30th, 1957, a Full Gallery was present to hear Parliament pass the Bill. . . This culminated ten years' pressure by our members for equal jury service.[35]

31 Dianne Davidson, *Women on the Warpath*, University of Western Australia Press, 1997, pp 91-102.

32 Peter Cowan, *A Unique Position*, University of Western Australia Press, 1980.

33 Ibid.

34 J Mackinolty and H Radi (eds), *In Pursuit of Justice*, Hale & Iremonger, 1979, pp 112-3.

35 Bessie M Rischbieth, *March of Australian Women*, Paterson Brokensha Pty Ltd, 1964, p 34.

The granting of the right to jury service signified the achievement of full political equality for women in Western Australia. They were still a long way from the achievement of economic equality in industry, in the professions and in the home. They were even further from overcoming cultural inequality, the sexual "petty apartheid" – to borrow a South African term – which manifested itself in a multitude of minor discriminations and demeaning language which men applied to women and all their activities.

The final struggle for equality would be taken over by a new generation of women who called themselves, the Women's Liberation Movement and to whom historians would ascribe the title of "second wave feminists" to distinguish them from the forerunners or "first wave feminists" who stretched back in history from Bessie Rischbieth's generation all the way to 1792 when Mary Wollstonecraft published her seminal work, *The Vindication of the Rights of Women.*[36]

36 Judith A Allen, *Rose Scott: Vision and Revision in Feminism*, Oxford University Press, 1990, p 14.

2

FOUNDATIONS OF A CAREER

The proclamation of the *Women's Legal Status Act* in 1923 did not immediately generate an influx of women into the profession. The inspiration for the Act came from the women's movement not the lawyers, who showed no enthusiasm to encourage the admission of women. There was no pool of potential female lawyers available to seek admission because the decision in *Haynes* barred young women even from training for the law.

Even when the ban was lifted there was no "rush" to use Haynes QC's expression in his prophetic speech to the Legislative Council in 1900, quoted in Chapter 1. It was three years before the first woman applied for a position as an articled clerk. The pioneer applicant was Enid Russell, the daughter of a deceased solicitor. Her experience could well explain the reluctance of aspiring women lawyers to take advantage of the Act.

Enid Russell was born in 1904, the daughter of Charles Townsend Russell, a partner in the Perth legal firm of Haynes Robinson & Co. Russell died suddenly in 1911, being stricken with a heart attack while climbing the magnificent jarrah staircase of his office at 20 Howard Street, Perth.[1] Enid won a scholarship entrance to Perth Modern School from which she matriculated in 1923 at the age of 19. She had an ambition to become a lawyer like her father and, had she been a young man, the obvious course to take would have been to seek articles in her father's old firm as soon as she matriculated.

1 FM Robinson, from a personal interview. Deaths from heart attack among senior legal practitioners became so common over the years along that short, steep side-street between St George's Terrace and the Esplanade that the profession nick-named it "Coronary Hill".

Instead, she completed a secretarial course at a commercial college, got a job with the old firm as a humble typist and enrolled at the University as a part-time Arts student, graduating as a Bachelor of Arts in 1927.

She worked as a typist until 1926 when, her BA degree almost completed, she approached her father's old partner, RT Robinson KC, to change her status to that of an articled law clerk and inaugurate her five-year training period. Robinson KC was reluctant to agree to this and it was only "after some difficulty" that she was able to persuade him to article her.[2]

This, then, was the situation that faced young women considering a legal career in the 1920s, notwithstanding the passage of the *Women's Legal Status Act.* If a scholarship winner with three years' practical experience in a legal office and a University education had difficulty in obtaining articles from her father's old firm it can be imagined what were the prospects for the average young female school-leaver.

Enid Russell completed her articles and was admitted as a practitioner in March 1931, having, in the meantime, topped off her Arts degree with a Bachelor of Laws from the newly opened University Law School. She was the first locally qualified woman to be admitted as a practitioner in Western Australia. The old firm (which had by then become Robinson Cox & Wheatley) continued to employ her as a salaried practitioner until she left to travel overseas in 1934. She was not offered a partnership. She did not achieve that status until 1952 in the small country practice of Ball & Co – only six years before her death in 1958.

A measure of the legal profession's antipathy to female recruits is that it discouraged its own daughters from practising. Whereas, traditionally, a significant proportion of young men entering the law came from legal families, this was not the case with the early intake of women lawyers. According to the Law Society's journal, *Brief*, 33

---

2 "A Brief Biography of Enid Marjorie Russell BA LLB" by Sheila McClemans, published as Appendix IX to Enid Russell (completed posthumously and edited by FM Robinson and PW Nichols), *A History of The Law in Western Australia*, University of Western Australia Press, 1980. The words "after some difficulty" are Sheila's. She does not describe the nature of the difficulty but it seems reasonable to assume that it was gender bias on the part of Robinson KC or his partners.

women were admitted to practise between June 1930 and March 1969, but of these only four came from legal families.[3]

Although Enid Russell was the first locally trained female practitioner, she was not first to be admitted to practise. This distinction went to Alice Cummins, the daughter of a Kalgoorlie brewing family who was educated in South Australia and trained as a solicitor there. She was admitted to practise in Western Australia on 25 May 1930. Miss Cummins did not need to undergo a course of articles in Western Australia, her South Australian qualifications being accepted as sufficient.

The next three female admittees were Sheila McClemans, Margaret Battye and Molly Kingston. All three were fellow graduates of the newly established Faculty of Law at the University of Western Australia and were admitted together on 16 May 1933. At the date of her admission, Sheila was just 24 years of age, the date of her birth being 3 May 1909. She was born at the rectory, next door to Christ Church Claremont, where her father, Canon William Joseph McClemans, was the Rector.

Sheila's childhood ambition to study law was imprinted on her by a member of her father's congregation, a solicitor named John Forman. She described this process many years later as a guest writer for the Perth *Sunday Times*:

> When I was a very small girl and said I wanted to be a lawyer the only adult who took me seriously was John Campbell Forman. He did not know then that it was because of him that I first wanted to be a lawyer. He was a vestryman . . . and after vestry meetings he would come into our home and always had sweets in his pockets for children, and would tell them countless stories of most fantastic adventures. I knew in some obscure way he was a lawyer and thought that, when I grew up, I would like to be like him and have an endless supply of sweets and adventure stories for children. Mr Forman was an interesting man and had a profound sense of duty and service to others.[4]

Duty and service to others were held in high esteem in the McClemans household. The Canon, a Master of Arts from Trinity

---

3 *Brief*, Law Society of WA, 1984, Vol 12, No 8, p 9.

4 *Sunday Times*, Perth, 22.10.67, p 15.

College Dublin, had played a leading part in developing Anglican education in Western Australia as well as establishing two churches in the Eastern Goldfields and another in Nedlands early in the century.[5]

Ada McClemans had come to Western Australia from New Zealand as a child. Her father, William Walker, was a prominent engineer who had designed the water supply works at Milford Sound. His work had come to the notice of CY O'Connor, engineer-in-charge of the construction of the Mundaring Weir and the 700 kilometre overland pipe to carry fresh water to the Kalgoorlie goldfields. O'Connor visited Walker in New Zealand and persuaded him to join the Kalgoorlie project.

Walker embarked with his wife and four children in a sailing boat which took three months to arrive at Albany. En route the family was stricken by illness. One child died and was buried at sea, and Walker died soon after disembarking at Albany, leaving his family destitute. Fortunately, his widow was an accomplished pianist and singer and was able to keep her family alive by playing and singing at social functions.

Ada left school at 16 to help support her younger siblings. She chose nursing, one of the few careers then open to women. First year trainee nurses were paid only three shillings and sixpence for a seven-day week but were provided with uniforms and full board at the Perth Public Hospital. Because the minimum age for trainees was 21, Ada falsified her age to get in. This must have upset her as she had been brought up with strong Christian principles. It was, however, a matter of survival and it would not be the last time in her life that Ada would be forced to compromise her religious principles in order to survive.

Ada qualified as a nursing sister in 1902 and was sent to Geraldton where she met the Canon who was Rector of the local Anglican parish and whom she married on 3 January 1905. The Canon's parish included the Murchison goldfields which they were obliged to visit frequently and where Ada, as one of the few trained nurses in the area, was frequently called upon to nurse typhoid

---

5 F Alexander, *Four Bishops and Their See*, University of Western Australia Press, 1975, pp 87, 144, 147.

patients as well as coping with the constant daily demands put upon a Rector's wife. In addition to her pastoral and medical duties she also had to care for her two small daughters, Pauline, born in 1906, and Dorothy in 1908. According to family legend, Ada once had to quarantine herself in a typhoid ward for six weeks whilst a housekeeper tended the needs of her family.[6]

When he was transferred to Claremont in 1907, the Canon became involved once more in education. He was concerned that there was no Anglican boy's school with structural links to the Church. Hale School, founded by an Anglican bishop, had hitherto served the Anglican community but it was not part of the hierarchical structure. Upon the Canon's initiative, the Church founded Guildford Grammar School in 1909.

In 1910 he personally opened another school for boys, known as the Christ Church Preparatory School, on a block of land donated by a prominent Perth merchant, Alfred Sandover, on the western corner of the junction of Queenslea Drive and Stirling Highway – then called "The Perth-Fremantle Road". The church itself and adjacent rectory were across the street on the eastern corner. Initially the school had one classroom and nine day-boys. By the time the Canon joined the Australian Imperial Forces in 1915, it had expanded to two buildings and 120 boys, 35 of whom were boarders.[7]

In addition to founding Christ Church Grammar School, the Canon took an interest in a small Anglican girl's school, the Claremont High School, conducted by a Miss Parnell in the Christ Church parish hall, a small iron-roofed weather board structure adjoining the church on its eastern side. When the school out-grew the hall the Canon arranged its transfer to a larger building adjoining Christ Church Grammar School where it remained until 1928 when it was shifted to Mosman Park and renamed St Hilda's.[8]

---

6 Particulars of Ada's early family history were supplied by Mrs Paddy McFadyen (formerly Leschen née McClemans), Sheila's sole surviving sister, in a personal interview with the author.

7 *Chronicle*, Christ Church Grammar School, 1990, No 5, p 2.

8 Patricia Sharp and Laurie O'Hara, *A Goodly Heritage: Christ Church Claremort 1892-1992*, Anglican Parish of Claremont and Edith Cowan University Publication Services, 1992, p 38.

Besides involving herself in parish affairs as the Rector's wife, Ada McClemans joined in the activities of the local Women's Service Guild. When her husband formed the nucleus of his school she boarded several of the pupils at the rectory. She accepted this burden despite her own increasing family. The three older girls, Pauline, Dorothy and Sheila, were followed by Patricia (1911) and Quinta (1914).

Outwardly the McClemans family must have appeared a model of domestic excellence. Its paterfamilias was a tall lordly man with piercing blue eyes, thick dark hair parted in the middle above a wide, intelligent forehead, prominent nose and jutting jaw. These strong features are clearly shown in a photograph taken in 1915 in his chaplain's uniform. The eyes still gaze luminous and visionary from that old print.

It is easy to imagine the congregation entranced by those eyes throughout the eloquent sermons many had come long distances to hear. The Canon brought with him from Trinity the finest traditions of Irish oratory and he was also a considerable classical scholar. The combination bestowed upon his sermons a Ciceronic grandeur. The walls of the Rectory were lined with book-cases containing so many ancient scholarly tomes that his wife used to complain she could hear the silver fish eating them.[9]

Ada was a most efficient manager and the children were always well fed and clothed despite the frugality of her husband's stipend. She never allowed her good works to take precedence over caring for her family. In an oral history interview in 1982, Sheila described her childhood at the rectory as almost idyllic:

> Well I lived in a rectory because my father was Rector of Christ Church. I was one of five girls and the middle one, so we led a fairly cheerful childhood with lots of activity because of course we all had our different friends, so there were lots of people at the house always. My mother was a very hospitable person. . . Entertainment was very simple but a lot of fun.[10]

---

9 Confided to Iris Purnell by Sheila during their WRAN days (from a personal interview).

10 C Shervington, *Sheila Mary McClemans: Oral History Memoir*, by courtesy University of WA archives, p 1.

Her older sister, the late Dorothy Lucy Sanders, a school-teacher turned novelist who wrote in the Barbara Cartland genre, depicted the early years of that family in the first of her popular romantic novels, *Six For Heaven.*[11] Cosmetic treatment and literary licence aside, the sole survivor, Patricia ("Paddy") McFadyen (formerly Leschen) née McClemans, accepts the picture as reasonably accurate.[12] The authors of the official history of Christ Church feel justified in accepting it as one source for their brief history of the McClemans family.[13]

A visit to that limestone church and its attendant rectory will set the picture in reality except that a tower has since been added to the northwest corner of the church. Both buildings are reminiscent of many small English parish church precincts, although the walls lack the greyness of damp and age.

In Sheila's childhood years, Western Australia still had many of the characteristics of an English Crown Colony – *vide* the judicial references in *Haynes* to "the Mother Country". A recent historical survey in the *West Australian* described the community thus:

> Drawn from the English gentry, they were almost exclusively Church of England and sent their sons to be educated at the school which Bishop Blagden Hale opened in Perth in 1858. His pupils included a Chief Justice, the first Premier and most of the first Cabinet. With their wealth and influence the prominent families dominated nearly every aspect of colonial life. . .[14]

The Church of England was the establishment church and its clergy were very much part of the colonial aristocracy. The clergy and their families were accepted without question into the "First Family" society of the landed gentry. The western riverside suburbs were popular summer retreats for outback pastoralists who built many fine houses amidst spacious shady gardens along the river front. The yacht clubs of Claremont and Freshwater Bay were focal points of social life.

---

11 *Six For Heaven*, London: Hodder & Stoughton, 1952.

12 Mrs Paddy McFadyen, from a personal interview.

13 Patricia Sharp and Laurie O'Hara, *A Goodly Heritage: Christ Church Claremort 1892-1992*, Anglican Parish of Claremont and Edith Cowan University Publication Services, 1992, p 35.

14 *West Australian*, 16 March 1991, 6.

As Rector, the Canon was expected to join in this social life and, being a jovial fellow with all the ebullient characteristics of the Anglo-Irish gentry, he was happy to do so. Dorothy Lucy idolised her father and treats "Canon Lefroy", the father figure in *Six for Heaven*, with great sympathy. It is obvious, however, that under the facade of a happy united family, strains began to develop even before the outbreak of the Great War in 1914. Such strains were due both to the Canon's behaviour in drink and the drain on the household finances of keeping up with the Forrests and the Drake-Brockmans as well as subsidising his small private school.

It was the War, however, which undermined and shattered irretrievably the little family at Christ Church Rectory just as surely as it did the three great European Empires and the whole pre-War way of life. Sheila described her most vivid memory of that War in an Anzac Day talk to schools in the 1970s:

> One day when I was five my mother took me to the Claremont Station. When we got there the platform was filled with people. Presently a train came from Perth and as it passed through the station it went very slowly. The train was filled with soldiers. They waved and called goodbye and the people on the station all waved and called good bye and they cried. Then the train gathered speed and went on its way to Fremantle and we went sadly home.
>
> Those soldiers were the Anzacs.
>
> It did not seem very long before my mother called me and my sisters together and told us how, in a wonderful spirit of service, the Anzacs had been to fight a war so that we could all live safely at home. And now some of them had come back and they were sick and wounded and in the Base Hospital at Fremantle. My mother knew how to teach handcrafts and she wanted to go and teach the soldiers because they had done so much for us and it would help to pass the time for them. But she said she couldn't do it unless we children were prepared to help too. We would have to be very good and help a bit more with the washing up and the messages and making the beds and so on. We were willing to try and did try. And it was through those happenings that I first realised how people can serve one another.[15]

---

15 Manuscript of a speech in possession of Mr & Mrs Neil Kenworthy. The year of broadcast is not known.

As Sheila sets this scene at some time when she was five years old, the event must have taken place between the outbreak of War in August 1914 and her sixth birthday, 16 May 1915. Her father joined the ranks of the Anzacs in November 1915 and was posted overseas early in 1916.[16] He had turned 40 years of age in 1914 and his enlistment, therefore, was further indication of his strong sense of service. He could easily have stayed at home like his colleague, Canon Moore, whose contribution to the War effort was to make patriotic exhortations to the troops as they left and chide them for their dissolute behaviour on their return.[17]

The disastrous Gallipoli campaign having finished soon after his enlistment, the Canon served in France and Belgium where he was promoted to Chaplain General to the Australian Imperial Forces. He conducted church parades, visited the sick and gave what comfort and counselling he could to those whose faith sustained their belief that God could help them. His most exacting service, however, was to the dead. Over 50,000 Australians were killed in action, most of them on the Western Front, and it was the chaplains' duty to preside at their burials.

Canon McClemans had dedicated much of his life to the education of the young. The effect of those constant grisly rituals was quite overwhelming. Through almost 20 years of parish work in the small Western Australian community of that time, the Canon must have come to know personally many of the young men he buried. According to the School records, 14 of the lads he had enrolled into his small school at Queenslea Drive served in the War, and one, John Algernon Withnell, was killed in action on the Western Front at the age of 19. The School Honour Board still pays tribute to him.

According to his daughter Paddy, the Canon repeatedly recounted to his family the horror of burying over two hundred men a day for weeks on end. Dorothy painted much the same picture in *Six For Heaven.* Both agree that this agony, exacerbated by shell-shock

---

16 Patricia Sharp and Laurie O'Hara, *A Goodly Heritage: Christ Church Claremort 1892-1992*, Anglican Parish of Claremont and Edith Cowan University Publication Services, 1992, p 42.

17 Marian Aveling (ed), *Westralian Voices*, University of Western Australia Press, 1979, pp 324-325.

and a rheumatic heart, precipitated him into the alcohol addiction which destroyed his career, sundered his marriage and blighted the rest of his life.

A hint of what the family must have endured before the break up of the family is provided by a *Six For Heaven* passage in which Dorothy depicts Sheila (called Mary in the book) at the age of eight, intervening in a domestic argument and defending her mother with a tennis racquet. For the historian, *Six For Heaven* is something of a disappointment at this stage because Dorothy kills her fictional father off with a heart attack and the fictional "Montgomery" family is spared the conflict and humiliation of having to co-exist with a shell-shocked and frequently drunken father – the lot of the real-life McClemans.

The humiliation must have been particularly oppressive for Ada. A deeply religious woman, she placed great importance upon the concept of the family and, of course, upon the good standing of the Church. On the eve of the breakdown of her marriage, she addressed the Mothers' Union on the disastrous effects of alcohol upon the homes of its victims.[18]

Shortly after this address the Canon broke down during a service and, at his request, Ada tendered his resignation to the Archbishop.[19] Latter day gossip has created a defamatory legend that the Canon was formally defrocked.[20] This is untrue but the fate of the Canon and his family following his resignation may have given support to the rumour. The Church gave no financial support either to him or his family and seems to have expunged all record of this painful period.

This treatment is an indication of the lack of compassion meted out to persons with neurotic disorders at that time – particularly if

---

18 Patricia Sharp and Laurie O'Hara, *A Goodly Heritage: Christ Church Claremort 1892-1992*, Anglican Parish of Claremont and Edith Cowan University Publication Services, 1992, p.46.

19 Mrs P McFadyen. All parish records of the period covering the Canon's breakdown and resignation have disappeared and Mrs McFadyen's recollection has to be relied on to fill in these events. Dorothy Sanders covers the period in *Six for Heaven* but it is difficult to say how much of her detail is fact or fiction.

20 Patricia Sharp and Laurie O'Hara, *A Goodly Heritage: Christ Church Claremort 1892-1992*, Anglican Parish of Claremont and Edith Cowan University Publication Services, 1992, p 48.

associated with alcohol. The War service which precipitated his collapse and the years of devotion to the Church, the community and the schools by both the Canon and his wife were not acknowledged even by a vote of thanks. On 15 November 1922, Ada wrote to the Mothers' Union advising of her departure. It was accorded the mere wish of "every success in future" – for Ada alone, no mention was made of the Canon.[21] The nation had just emerged from a War in which men who succumbed to shell shock were court-martialled and shot for cowardice in the face of the enemy and was conditioned to spurn weakness. Those who gave way to stress by over-indulgence in alcohol were treated with disdain.

A little wisdom has come with time. Christ Church Grammar School has honoured the Canon by naming a house and a scholarship after him. There is also a scholarship named after Ada McClemans in recognition of her services to the school in its founding years. The centenary publication, *A Goodly Heritage*, published by the Anglican Parish of Claremont Parish, records with gratitude the valuable and devoted worth of both. Significantly it acknowledges that the Canon's disintegration was the direct result of his War service, reporting that he returned home a sick and broken man and quoting one parishioner's description of him as "shrunken, grey and bent".[22]

The McClemans family was treated more kindly at the time by the broader community. The Canon's many friends among the old landed families came to his aid. A succession of them took him in as a guest at their country properties. He was eventually allotted a "soldier settler" farm but never made enough from it ever to contribute to the support of his family.

One of Sheila's high-school mates recalls asking her in all innocence "What's it like now your father's a farmer instead of a minister?" and being nonplussed at the obvious embarrassment her question created.[23] The humiliation that her father's failure had caused the family was a life-long memory for Sheila who seems to have adopted the stern judgement of the community. She never

---

21 Ibid, p 47.

22 Ibid, p 47.

23 Mrs Pat De Castilla, from a personal interview.

forgave him.[24] It was otherwise with her younger sister Paddy, and her older sister Dorothy, both of whom, according to Paddy, regularly visited him during his last years in the Old Men's Home at Dalkeith with a little flask of whisky to cheer him up. Sheila refused to have any contact with him for the rest of his life.

When the Canon resigned from his duties and was taken to the country by kind friends there was no income and no home. The Rectory had to be surrendered to the Canon's successor, Brother Harper. As a consequence Ada was forced to find another home and some other means of subsistence – there being then no social security network to support abandoned wives and children.

A group of wealthy parishioners took up a collection for the maintenance of the family but this was mostly consumed in paying accounts that patient debtors had refrained from presenting. The indomitable Ada rented a large old home at 3 Havelock Street, West Perth, which, according to Dorothy's fictional description, was an architectural rabbit warren. She converted this into a lodging house, fitting her five children in as best she could on verandahs and balconies. Sheila in later years ascribed the origins of a chronic spinal complaint to bad posture incurred by doing her homework crouched on her verandah bed.

The Havelock Street property was not far from Edith Cowan's home in Mount Street and it may have been one reason why Ada chose it, although there were other advantages. In the 1920s, West Perth was a once fashionable suburb in decline and a number of private hospitals and nursing homes were established there in the former mansions of the wealthy. Ada took work as a part-time nursing sister in nearby institutions in order to supplement the income from her boarders. The work experience the girls had gained helping their mother to serve the Anzacs was now called upon as a matter of survival.

It is generally accepted by all who knew her that one of Sheila's great qualities was her energetic, good humoured practicality. It is reasonable to assume that those days of poverty and toil at Havelock Street did much to forge that quality. Household duties had to be

24 Mrs P McFadyen also Mr Loris Wood, Sheila's assistant on the Law Society executive, in personal interviews.

fitted in with school work. Ada McClemans shared the Canon's reverence for education and – unlike many of her generation – considered education was as essential for girls as for boys.

At the time of the move, Sheila and her younger sisters were attending the Claremont Practising School. This was reputed to be something of a model school because it was used as a training ground for the nearby Teachers' Training College. When they moved to West Perth all the girls went to an Anglican Girls' School, *Cowandilla* (Aboriginal for "happy place") which was two doors up the street on the corner block at 2 King's Park Road.

Ada realised in Sheila's early childhood that she was exceptionally talented intellectually. One day she consulted a fortune-teller who confirmed her in this assessment and predicted that Sheila would one day become "very famous".

More realistically, Ada then consulted Mr WJ Rooney, the Principal of the Claremont Teachers' College, for advice as to the best school for Sheila. Rooney advised that Perth Modern School was the best in the State but Sheila could only get there by attending a State school and winning a scholarship.[25]

Sheila was duly taken away from *Cowandilla* and enrolled at the Thomas Street State School in Subiaco where she vindicated the joint assessment of her mother and the soothsayer by winning a Modern School entry scholarship in 1921 at the age of 12. The academic standard she achieved at Thomas Street was so high that she was admitted straight into Year Two – a year ahead of her age group. The exceptional quality of this promotion may be assessed by Sir Paul Hasluck's comments upon Modern School's standards when describing his early days there:

> Instead of being the bright boy of the school I had to face the harder demands of the most exclusive secondary school in the State. Everyone there had been the bright boy or the bright girl of a primary school and most of them had been much more thoroughly taught than I had been.[26]

On this evidence it would be fair to say that, at the time of her entry, Sheila was classed as being the brightest of the bright. Sir Paul also

25 All the details relating to Sheila's early education were supplied by Mrs P McFadyen.

26 P Hasluck, *Mucking About*, University of Western Australia Press, 1994, p 75.

made some interesting observations upon standards of sexual conduct by Perth Modern School during Sheila's formative years there:

> Boys had to open doors for girls, stand aside to let them pass first and, at the end of a mixed class, allow them to leave the class before we did. There was also a code of not embarrassing them either by letting them see us go to a lavatory or by looking in their direction if they might be attending to any personal need. . . There were strict ideas about what subjects could be talked about and what words used in the presence of girls. Those were days of decorum. Boys and girls went swimming in separate enclosures. The girls could watch the boys' swimming and athletic sports but the girls had their swimming and athletics in private. Even when boys cheered on our team at a hockey match, nothing was ever revealed except knee-length voluminous black bloomers under a hockey girl's skirt.[27]

No official school records survive concerning Sheila's progress through four years at Modern School. It was contrary to school policy to award prizes or accolades of any kind for academic achievement. There is therefore nothing to demonstrate her scholastic brilliance except the fact that she achieved a creditable leaving certificate a year earlier than her age group.

Some history of Sheila's career at Perth Modern School is to be found in the school magazine, *Sphinx*. The magazine does not record her as having any role in any of the student cultural activities but features her prominently in sport. The first entry is in May 1922 when, at the age of 12 years and 8 months, she came third in the open 50 yards swimming race against girls four years her senior. In 1923 she came first in both the junior freestyle and breaststroke championships and was declared champion junior swimmer. In 1924 she was the champion senior swimmer and got a place in the girls' tennis team. In 1925 she was beaten by one point for open champion swimmer but won the junior swimming crown.

Sheila's proudest achievement for 1925 was probably her election as school prefect and captain of *Sphinx* faction for the coming year. At Modern School prefects were elected by their peers, so to achieve that rank one had to be well liked. A letter to the

---

27 Ibid, p 79.

author from Mrs Mollie Dickinson (née Gordon) of Nelson, New Zealand, enclosed a photograph of Sheila with her close friend, Edna Bottle, aged 15. Taken with a Box Brownie camera it shows a tall slender girl with a beautiful impish smile. In her letter Mrs Dickinson wrote:

> Sheila was one year ahead of me at school. A most successful student, good at school subjects and sport, especially swimming hockey and tennis. She was a heroine to us.

Many reports from contemporaries paint the same picture of a brilliant good-natured young woman, kind and helpful to her juniors and a fun-loving companion to her contemporaries yet at the same time notable for her serious dedication to study. Edith de Burgh (née Wedge) recalls that she befriended Sheila's sister, Dorothy, at Perth College and the whole McClemans family was frequently invited to stay at the Wedges' Gin-Gin farm during school vacations. Dorothy drew on these vacations for some romantic passages in *Six For Heaven* which feature a handsome, aloof, Heathcliffe type, squatter's son. Sheila was never able to enjoy these pastoral interludes, however, because she had to spend her holidays studying at home.[28]

In January 1926, Sheila had even more reason to be proud when the *West Australian* annual examination lists reported that she had passed her Leaving Examination and had matriculated for the University of Western Australia. Her results, kindly supplied by the University of Western Australia archives department, were: English (p), French (p+), Mathematics (p+), History (d). In the code employed in those days p+ meant "above average" and d meant "distinction". She was then sixteen-and-a-half, which meant that she could not enrol at the University because there was then a minimum age of 17. She, therefore, returned to school to repeat the year.

The May 1926 issue of *Sphinx* records her as a prefect, leader of "Sphinx" faction, captain of tennis and holder of top place on the tennis bumping board but regrets that she could not take part in the annual swimming sports because she had injured her arm on the eve of the competition. She appears in several photographs of various sporting teams which accord with Sir Paul's description of voluminous garb and demonstrate, in their stolidity, Dylan Thomas's

---

28 Mrs E De Burgh, from a personal interview.

ironic vision of "black-bloomered nymphs". A valedictory note in the August issue reports, again with regret:

> Miss McClemans left us early in the term to take up a position in the commercial world. Her departure necessitated the election of another "Pre", and the choice fell upon Miss Edna Bottle. We wish heartily to congratulate Miss Bottle upon her appointment and we also wish Miss McClemans the best of luck in her new position.

This is the first of many references in *Sphinx* to Sheila as an ex-student. The issue of May 1927 reported:

> Miss Sheila McClemans, who it will be remembered left school early in second term last year, has now taken up a full time Arts course at the University. She is to be congratulated upon winning the title of Champion Lady Swimmer at the recent University Swimming Carnival.

Another item in the same issue reported as follows:

> We also find Margaret Battye . . . doing full time Arts. Margaret is looking forward to seeing a chair of Law established by the end of the year. Otherwise she will be articled for five years.

Margaret Battye entered Modern School in the same year as Sheila but, because of Sheila's precocious promotion to Year Two, always trailed her by one year. Like Sheila, she had an early ambition to study Law. Her position following matriculation was identical to Sheila's. Because there was no Law School the achievement of an Arts degree did not assist their entry to the legal profession. To achieve this they would have to enter the five-year articles system supervised by the Barristers Board and pass its examinations.

At that time, however, many ambitious young men hoping to excel in the law entered upon Arts courses, either full time or part time, as well as entering into legal articles either contemporaneously with, or upon completion of, their Arts courses. It was thought that the holding of a degree would provide some extra status as well as bestowing a foundation for some alternative career if needed.

By 1927, entering upon an Arts course as a preliminary to entering the Law had become a smart tactical move because of the likelihood of a Law School being established at the campus. This had been a vision of the future ever since 1913 when the nucleus of the

University was founded in a collection of temporary timber buildings at Irwin Street, Perth – known to its students as "Tin Pot Alley".

Western Australia was the only State in the Commonwealth which did not have a Law School. Successive State governments had always promised to establish one but regretted that they did not have the funds at present. Fortunately, in 1927, the State was riding the crest of a boom and the government of the day promised the new Law School by the end of the year with a staff of one professor, supplemented by visiting lecturers provided by the Law Society.

This promise gave legal aspirants sufficient hope to enrol in the Faculty of Arts with a view to transferring to Law, the Arts subjects already passed being credited towards their Law degree. In fact Professor FR Beasley was appointed in September 1927 but enrolments for the Faculty of Law did not commence until the beginning of 1928.[29] It is fortunate that the funds were found and the appointment made before the 1929 stock market crash and the onset of the Great Depression.

Had Sheila been able to start at University in 1926, she would have enrolled in that year as an Arts student, but being under-age for enrolment, she began to repeat the school year in order to put up her pass rate. There is little doubt that had she done so she would have achieved straight distinctions in her Leaving results. Unfortunately, the strain on the family finances became too great and she was forced to take a job as a clerk in the Western Australian Savings Bank, a State Government institution which later failed in the 1929 crash. Sheila's task at the Bank was to look after the primary school children's accounts. This she found "very dull".[30]

An even more junior member of the staff, Bernard Jacques, who joined the bank at the same time, aged 15, remembers being very impressed by this beautiful, slender young woman with an "Eton crop" – a fashionable short hair style of that time. It was an era when trendy young women called themselves "flappers" and sang a song which went:

> Roll them girls! Roll them!
> Roll them down and show your pretty knees!

---

29 Fred Alexander, *Campus at Crawley*, University of Western Australia Press, 1963, p 19.

30 C Shervington, *Sheila Mary McClemans: Oral History Memoir*, by courtesy University of WA archives, p 1.

This was a reference to the "flapper" practice of dispensing with suspenders, rolling down stockings and exposing the knees, which the post-War shorter skirts made just possible. The stockings were kept from falling down altogether by decorative garters, worn just below the knee. Sheila caused much laughter among the staff one Monday morning by telling how she was standing at the edge of a river jetty during a weekend swimming carnival and heard two youths behind her arguing whether she was a boy or a girl. There was little difference in male and female swimming attire in those days, both wearing neck to knee costumes. The more observant of the two youths won the argument, exclaiming: "Of course she's a girl. Look at the garter marks".[31]

It is unlikely that Sheila wore garters and her "Eton crop" for any other than practical reasons. The actor, Nita Pannell, was a year ahead of Sheila at school and, as a young school teacher, stayed at a boarding house next-door to the McClemans' Havelock Street establishment where she frequently met the sisters coming and going. In later life she often encountered Sheila at various functions in and around the city. Her assessment of Sheila as a person was that she was very genuine and "down to earth", always dressing smartly but sensibly and could never be described as a "fashion-plate".[32]

After eight months at the bank, Sheila entered the University of Western Australia as a temporary Arts student pending the installation of Professor Beasley. Her course was made financially possible by a Hackett Bursary without which she would have had to remain at the bank and enrol in a part-time course. Her mother's position had improved by this time but only marginally. She had managed to find full-time employment by the help of an old Women's Service Guilds comrade, Dr Roberta Jull, and then only with some difficulty and much personal anguish.

Dr Jull was another remarkable woman of that time. Born Roberta Fergusson-Stewart, the daughter of a clergyman, she was educated at an English boarding school and took her degree in Medicine at Glasgow University. Migrating to Western Australia in 1896 she was the first woman to practise medicine in Perth. Two

31 B Jaques, from a personal interview.

32 Mrs N Pannell, from a personal interview.

years later she married ME Jull, the Under Secretary for Public Works. She was a foundation member of the Women's Service Guilds and of the University Senate.[33]

When her husband died in 1917, she joined the Department of Public Health as Medical Officer for Schools. As part of her work she created the post of visiting School Nurse and nominated her close friend, Sister Ada McClemans, to fill it. This was a welcome opportunity for Ada because it would relieve her of the uncertainty of casual nursing and the humiliating drudgery of keeping a boarding house.

There was, however, one obstacle. Public Service policy of those days prohibited the employment of married women even though they had been abandoned by their husbands. Despite Dr Jull's plea to make Ada an exception, the departmental head, Dr Everet Atkinson, would only agree to her employment upon the condition she petitioned for divorce.

It was a painful decision to make. Divorce was anathema to devout Anglicans in those days. Even innocent parties incurred disapproval and were regarded as pariahs. But the desperate poverty, the strain and sheer physical exhaustion both for her self and her children left her no option. Once more she was forced to sacrifice her religious principles to survive.[34] She filed her petition on 15 August 1927 on the ground of "Desertion". Her decree was made absolute on 9 July 1929. A nominal order of £5 per annum was made against the Canon.[35]

The archival file relating to Sheila's application for her bursary is eloquent of the privations of the McClemans family and Ada's fight for survival. On her application form, Sheila gave her age as 17 years 9 months and her address as 3 Havelock Street, West Perth. She answered the questions "Income and Occupation" as follows: "At present, owing to force of circumstances, junior clerk (first year) State Savings Bank. If successful in application no occupation. Nil if successful. . ."[36]

---

33 University of Western Australia archives.

34 Mrs P McFadyen.

35 Supreme Court Records, courtesy of the Battye Library.

36 University of Western Australia archives.

Her mother's occupation and income are given as "School Nurse, £192" and her father's as "Nil, Nil". One of her references was from Dr Roberta Jull:

> Mrs McClemans has been well known to me for some years, & I am aware that her financial circumstances make it impossible for her to support her daughter, Sheila, as a full time student at the University. Mrs McClemans has entirely supported herself and her family for four years. She has not received and does not receive any monetary or other assistance from her husband. I consider her daughter to be one of the students which the Hackett endowment was especially intended to help.[37]

Although Ada's job had improved the family finances, they were still in a parlous position as the following reference from Mr HM Jackman testifies.

> In furtherance of the application of Miss Sheila Mary McClemans for a Hackett Bursary, I desire to certify that the financial position of the applicant's parents render it impossible for them to meet the expense of their daughter's University education. On the retirement of Canon McClemans from the Rectorship of Christ Church, Claremont, in the year 1922, a loan fund was raised in Perth to enable Mrs McClemans to acquire a business and thus provide for herself and five daughters. The husband purchased a farming property under the SS Scheme on which he has since resided, and which has provided a living for himself only.
>
> As secretary of the Fund referred to (the Trustees being Messrs WM Padbury, WM Burges and myself) I have had charge of the financial affairs of Mrs McClemans during the past four years, and wish to state that the income of herself and those of her daughters who are earning is sufficient only to provide them with a bare living, and does not permit of their giving the applicant the University Course she aspires to.
>
> Of the amount loaned, only part had been refunded when the subscribers decided to release Mrs McClemans from any further repayments in view of the obvious difficulty of her making any reservations from her limited income. Having regard to the difficult position Mrs McClemans was placed in on her husband's retirement, I regard it a matter for commendation that she has succeeded in

37 Ibid.

> maintaining and educating her family during the past four years, and I sincerely trust that the means will be provided for giving her gifted daughter, Sheilah [sic], through the medium of a Hackett Bursary, that further opportunity of advancement which must otherwise be denied her.[38]

Her third referee was WJ Rooney, Principal of Claremont Teachers' College:

> Miss Sheilah [sic] McClemans has informed me that she has applied for one of the Hackett bequests and asks me to give her a reference. I have known her since childhood. At school she always distinguished herself in her class and at all times was held in high esteem by the Teachers and the Pupils. She is energetic and ambitious and possesses the characteristics of a student, in fact she is exceptionally gifted for University work. She has natural ability and with it possesses that power of application which means so much to the student. Possessed in addition of a fine, outstanding personality and a keen sense of responsibility, she is, in my opinion, exceptionally qualified as an Applicant for a Hackett bequest.[39]

A more personal account of the family's poverty is provided by Ada in her supporting letter:

> Dear Sir,
>
> In support of my daughter's application for a Hackett Bursary I desire to state
>
> (1) As my husband has not contributed to the support of myself or my five daughters for the past four years I have been the sole support of them except with respect to any salaries earned by them in the last four years.
>
> (2) My present means consist of salary £192 per annum obtained as School Nurse in the Public Health Dept. In addition I sublet portion of my rented house and the money so obtained partly pays my rent.
>
> (3) My eldest daughter as temporary clerk in the Teachers College receives 9/6 per day. My second daughter is entering the Training College for two years and receives a small grant of £30

38 Ibid.

39 Ibid.

> if non resident and no grant if resident. In either case I shall have to support her. My third daughter is the applicant.
>
> Two younger girls are still at school. My husband's address in [sic] Ballidu.
>
> I have the honour to be, Sir
>
> Yours truly
>
> (SGD) AL McClemans
>
> Mother & Guardian.[40]

The bursary was granted with a tenure of three years.

Sheila expressed her gratitude to her principal benefactors many years afterwards when, as former First Officer McClemans OBE, CMG, BA, LLB, she delivered her Anzac Day address to school children:

> I went on to school and when I was a senior student I met a most lovely woman. She was very beautiful. Her husband was very rich and he liked to see her wear beautiful clothes and beautiful jewels. He built a beautiful house for her at Cottesloe and filled it with treasures from all over the world.
>
> That woman could have, if she had wished, lived a life of idleness and pleasure. But she did not. She wanted to help other people, and for the whole of her very long life she worked unceasingly particularly for women and children. Her name was Bessie Rischbieth. . .
>
> At the same time there was another wonderful woman here. She wasn't rich and she wasn't beautiful, but she was just as dedicated to helping others. Her name was Edith Cowan and the tall monument you see at the entrance to this Park, with the clock on top of it, is a memorial to her. She was the first woman to become a member of Parliament and while she was in Parliament she had many Acts passed which particularly helped women and children. One of these Acts made it possible for women to be lawyers if they wished.
>
> By this time I knew that I wanted to be a lawyer. The only thing which would now prevent me was the fact that I was poor and could not afford to go to the University.

---

40 Ibid.

> But again I was helped by someone else who was imbued with the spirit of service. . . He was Sir Winthrop Hackett. He owned most of the *West Australian* newspaper which you see in your homes every morning. He believed he could best be of service by helping young people to become educated. So he left most of his money to help found a University and to grant scholarships for students who could not otherwise afford to go to the University. I had one of those scholarships, and so I was able to become a lawyer.[41]

The bursary was granted conditionally upon Sheila studying for an Arts degree. The archival file indicates that, even when the Law School opened in 1928, she had trouble in gaining entry because she had no Latin and the Law School required a Junior Latin pass as a condition precedent for matriculation to its LLB course. Sheila had to enrol for second year Arts whilst she did a crash course in Junior Latin. The Hackett Bursary file records much paper shuffling to cope with this problem. She tackled Junior Latin as well as her full year of Arts subjects ably enough to matriculate for Law at the end of 1928 and to qualify her to tutor others suddenly confronted with the Latin hurdle barring their chosen academic career.[42]

---

41 Anzac Day address: manuscript of a speech in possession of Mr and Mrs Neil Kenworthy. The year of broadcast is not known.

42 In a personal interview one of her pupils, Keir Wedd, advised that in his Leaving year he made a late decision to study Medicine but discovered Junior Latin was a prerequisite for that course. With Sheila's help as coach he was able to master Junior Latin in one year and matriculate.

3

LEARNING THE LAW

Sheila's first three years at University were served at the old "Tin Pot Alley" establishment in Irwin Street which she found "cramped and uncomfortable". The lecture rooms were small and draughty. The library was totally inadequate. The shortage of books was such that theft was common, as was the practice of excising passages from text books with razor-blades – photocopying being some 30 years in the future. In order to protect the more valuable works, a security section was instituted in which readers were kept under close scrutiny.

Student facilities were few. There was no joint common room where male and female students could socialise. The segregated common rooms were strictly "no go" areas for the opposite gender. Only the women's common room had tea-making facilities (a gas ring and a kettle), toast was made over an electric radiator. There being no playing grounds, public open space around the city was used for field sports. Swimmers used the ANA jetty at the foot of Barrack Street and the public baths in Crawley Bay for practice and carnivals.[1]

Crawley Baths was Perth's principal swimming venue until the building of an Olympic pool in the 1960s. It consisted of a fenced, shark-proof area of the Swan River with a kiosk and change-rooms on the shore side of the perimeter. Two tall cabbage palms, which flanked its entrance-jetty at the foreshore, still memorialise its site.

---

1 These aspects of Irwin Street and early days at Crawley have been drawn from C Shervington, *Sheila Mary McClemans: Oral History Memoir*, by courtesy University of WA archives, pp 1–7; and personal interviews with a number of Sheila's contemporaries: Ray Oldham, John Wheatley, Pat De Castilla, John O'Halloran and Grif Richards.

Despite the constant hazard of jelly-fish stings, throat and ear infections from its polluted waters and wind-whipped waves in rough weather, even international swimming carnivals were held there.

Crawley Baths was the scene of many of Sheila's aquatic triumphs, both at Modern School and at University where she won the titles of champion swimmer and diver and assumed the responsibility of organiser of women's swimming. In addition to swimming, Sheila also played tennis and hockey for University but not with the same degree of success.

Sport played an important part in university affairs in the Irwin Street days because of the lack of common-rooms and meeting areas in which to organise social activities. In her *Oral History Memoir*, Sheila recalled the social life:

> They were very unsophisticated activities. . . We would meet at the home of someone else, stand around a piano and sing. We had dances which took place on the verandah of somebody's house with very uneven floor boards . . . we would have things like sandwiches and cream puffs for supper. None of us had any money, none of us was very well dressed, so there was no competition about our social life. . . We had tennis parties, we went to the odd University dance.
>
> . . . we belonged to various societies in the University such as the Debating Society and the Dramatic Society . . . urged into it by Alexandra Darker as she then was, Alexandra Hasluck now, who was very keen on the Dramatic Society and she got me in, but I don't think I was ever meant to be a Sarah Bernhardt . . . I remember going to a debating society one night when "Nugget" Coombs, afterwards you know a very distinguished person, who I thought debated marvellously. The adjudicator at the end tore strips off him and said he had said in the course of his debate that he had ventured to suggest something and he said . . . "you do not venture to suggest, you either suggest or you don't".[2]

Grand occasions, such as the Graduation Ceremony and Graduation Ball, were held in Government House Ballroom, just across St George's Terrace from Irwin Street. The vice-regal venue was not always treated with appropriate respect. Student pranks so disrupted the dignity of ceremonial occasions that the Professorial Board

---

2 C Shervington, *Sheila Mary McClemans: Oral History Memoir*, by courtesy University of WA archives, p 2.

found it necessary to issue an edict to the effect that "the use of chemicals of any sort in the Government House Ballroom be prohibited".[3]

Lesser functions were held, after some shopping around by student organisers at cheaper venues such as the Young Australia League Hall and the Perth Literary Institute. Sheila apparently had little difficulty in finding escorts to these functions: "And we girls of course went to the various University dances. If you weren't invited to the Engineers' Ball you were obviously a failure socially".[4]

In those days the Law School was small enough for the Dean to extend personal hospitality to his students: "Professor Beasley was also very hospitable to us we used to go to his home often. . . We might play games or just talk or dance, anything".[5]

Whatever its architectural shortcomings the Irwin Street Campus engendered a great *esprit de corps* and there is a distinct note of nostalgia in Sheila's description of the move to the new campus at Crawley, which took place during her final year of Law – 1930:

> in my last year at the University we were moved to Crawley. Cramped and uncomfortable as the quarters were in Irwin Street, we were very close to each other and when we got down to the University we felt as though we had been dissipated in some way, it was too big.[6]

Ray Oldham, co-author with her husband, John, of several scholarly works on architecture, made the move to Crawley at the same time. In a personal interview, she made the following assessment of her student days at Irwin Street:

> I spent my first year at Tin Pot Alley and I'm glad I did. There is so much emphasis on grand buildings these days. People overlook the fact that buildings are not everything. The quality of university life at Irwin Street was outstanding.[7]

---

3 Fred Alexander, *Campus at Crawley*, University of Western Australia Press, 1963, p 476.

4 C Shervington, *Sheila Mary McClemans: Oral History Memoir*, by courtesy University of WA archives, p 6.

5 Ibid.

6 Ibid.

7 Mrs Ray Oldham, in a personal interview.

Ray praised the high calibre of the women students she mixed with, referring in particular to Alexandra Darker (later Lady Hasluck), Molly Kingston, Enid Russell, Margaret Battye, Sheila McClemans and her older sister Dorothy. During lunch hours she regularly played bridge with Sheila, Molly Kingston and Margaret Battye in the women's common room. Two other women writers, Connie Miller and Noel Stewart, make similar laudatory assessments of those final days at Irwin Street in their autobiographical works.[8]

The benefit of the grand buildings was not immediately apparent on arrival at Crawley because many of them were not completed. Sheila complained in her *Oral History Memoir* of the noise of the stone-masons disrupting her studies and the difficulty in negotiating "great limestone boulders" to get in and out of the lecture rooms.

The 1929 stock market crash and the ensuing Great Depression took something from the euphoria of the historic move. Although the refectory replaced the Irwin Street gas ring, Sheila and her friends could not afford to use it and took cut lunches to the University. She describes the Depression's effect upon the progress of the University construction as follows:

> Some time along there at the end, I don't remember when, the University ran out of money to complete it as far as they had hoped to go. This particularly left the pond, which is now in front of Winthrop Hall, unfinished and the Engineers and Law students agreed to finish it themselves and they did . . . I was living at Mount Lawley then and we used to go by tram from Mount Lawley into Perth and then from Perth around to the University, round Mount's Bay Road by tram.[9]

Shortly after Sheila's enrolment at University the family moved to 4 Glenroyd Street, Mount Lawley, presumably to be closer to Quinta's school, Perth College. They remained there until the late 1930s.

Law students seem to have played quite an active role in the Annual University Procession. *Black Swan*, the monthly student magazine, in its issue of June 1927 noted that Molly Kingston was a member of the committee organising the procession which contained much satirical comment upon the Royal Visit of that year.

---

8 Connie Miller, *Season of Learning*, Fremantle Arts Centre Press, 1983; Noel Stewart, *As I Remember Them*, Artlook Books, 1987.

9 C Shervington, *Sheila Mary McClemans: Oral History Memoir*, by courtesy University of WA archives, p 6.

Margaret Hicks (née Somerville), the daughter of Doctor Somerville, one of the University's founding fathers, has a clear memory of Sheila on a float with other women students holding banners protesting about discrimination against women lawyers.[10] This is interesting because in her own references to the subject over the years Sheila always played down the existence of discrimination against women in the legal profession. It may have been a reference to the difficulty Enid Russell encountered getting articles in her father's old firm described in the previous chapter. On the other hand, it may have expressed a foreboding that she and her fellow women students would have difficulty finding employment once they were qualified to practise. If so, their banners were prophetic indeed. Sheila makes no mention of this demonstration in her oral history.

There are numerous references to Sheila and her close associates in *Black Swan* from 1927 to 1929. Sheila's sister Dorothy, supported by her future husband, Colsell Sanders, is reported as opposing Margaret Battye and Roy (later Mr Justice) Neville in a debate on the subject of film censorship. A beautiful smiling photograph of Sheila in swimming cap appeared in the sporting notes under the caption of "Champion Woman Swimmer". The same photograph headed a full page in the issue of June 1929 depicting the champions of the annual swimming carnival. Sheila makes a second appearance mid-page, in full flight winning the Women's Neat Dive, framed by two muscular young male swimmers, one of whom is Paul Hasluck, giving no hint of the portly figure he would eventually present to the nation as Governor General of Australia.

Other issues report Molly Kingston as President, Sheila Vice-President and Margaret Battye on the Committee, of the Women's Club and make brief mention of Sheila's theatrical career. The anonymous drama critic in the June 1929 issue confirms Sheila's own assessment that she was "no Sarah Bernhardt" in his critique of the Dramatic Society's *The Whole Town's Talking*: "Miss Sheila McClemans is not worldly enough for a motion picture actress but is otherwise adequate. . ."

10 Margaret Hicks (née Somerville), in a personal interview.

Paul Hasluck (who at the time was the *West Australian's* drama critic) did not seem impressed with any part of the performance. He wrote a letter to the editor complaining that the Society's choice of plays was "too frivolous". Fellow law student John Dunphy was much kinder. In a piece of Pepysian pastiche entitled *Diary of a Law Student*, he recorded:

> I hie me to the sportive movements of the before-mentioned Uni. I see there certain fair damsels, namely one Sheila who playeth on the stage at the Playhouse and one Margot de Batt who is learned like unto a very sage.[11]

With the move to Crawley, sporting facilities began to move in-house. Tennis courts were established close to the river front and a women's hockey field on the then vacant land at the north-western corner of Thomas Street and Stirling Highway. The changing rooms for women's hockey were in a workshop belonging to the service station on the opposite side of Stirling Highway, then known as Alexander's Garage. Those changing rooms provided an early scoop for the student paper, *Pelican*, which exposed some unprincipled voyeurism on the part of the garage mechanics.

Pelican was probably the greatest initial bonus of the move to Crawley. Founded at the beginning of 1930 on the initiative of a future editor of the *West Australian*, Grif Richards, and published weekly, it did much to publicise student affairs and give cohesion to the student body, bemused by its geographic dispersal over the wider campus. It also did its best to voice student criticism of the paternalistic style of staff and Senate. An early issue was dissension over draconian measures proposed to prevent the stealing of books from the new library. This seems to indicate that at least one tradition had been carried over from Irwin Street.

Although Grif Richards went on to enjoy a distinguished career in journalism, his editorship of *Pelican* was brief. As a side line, he produced a humorous one-off broad sheet called *Sruss-Sruss* on the occasion of a student theatre night. This contained an article written by a contributor in light-hearted comment upon a member of the teaching staff. This the Senate considered to be "scurrilous", fined the Guild body £10, rusticated Richards and his co-editor for 12

---

11 *Black Swan*, June 1927, p 5.

months and declared them ineligible to hold Guild office for ever. Neither student was given an opportunity to speak in his own defence.[12] Richards' post as editor of *Pelican* was taken over by Ray Oldham (then Ray McClintock).

Once *Pelican* came into being, *Black Swan* became the literary organ of the University and was eventually succeeded by *Westerly*, an official publication of the English Department. In its graduation issue of 10 April 1931, *Pelican* carried a full report of the proud graduates of the class of 1930. The Law graduates were all female: Margaret Battye, Mary Kathleen Hartrey, Mary Connor Kingston and Sheila Mary McClemans.

According to John O'Halloran, who was a year behind Sheila at Law School, the absence of male graduates had much to do with the move to Crawley.[13] Before the founding of the Law School in 1928, the only path to admission to the legal profession was that attempted in vain by the ill-fated Edith Haynes – serving five years articles in a legal office and passing the Barrister's Board Examinations. If one wished to give more substance to one's qualifications one could take an Arts degree before, after or simultaneously with, service in articles. The value of such study of broader cultural subjects was recognised by the Law School which required law students to pass a number of Arts subjects (English I and Politics being mandatory) during the first two years of the Law course.

A number of articled-clerk law students was serving articles and studying Arts part-time when the Law School opened. Professor Beasley approached these students and offered them places in the Law School itself with a view to their graduating as a Bachelor of Laws (LLB) instead of a Bachelor of Arts (BA). Several of them, including Ken Hatfield (later Hatfield QC), accepted this offer. The offer was not as magnanimous as it might seem because the Professor was not overwhelmed with undergraduates when the Faculty opened, and was anxious to swell the numbers.

The Faculty only had the money to pay one full-time lecturer, Professor Beasley himself, who took the academic subjects such as

---

12 A guarded account of this incident appears in Fred Alexander, *Campus at Crawley*, University of Western Australia Press, 1963, pp 478-480.

13 John O'Halloran, in a personal interview.

Jurisprudence, Roman Law, Legal History, and Constitutional Law. The bread and butter subjects were allocated to practising lawyers – all very able and dedicated men – who came from the City at the end of their day's work to deliver late afternoon lectures, on their way home from the office, for a meagre fee. The clerk-students had to leave their offices promptly to attend these lectures which were usually scheduled for 5:15 pm.

While the Law School still operated at Irwin Street, the afternoon lectures were not a great problem for the clerk-students, because they could hurry along St George's Terrace ahead of the lecturers. The move to Crawley, however, entailed peak-hour tram journeys from the City for the clerk-students whereas the lecturers travelled in their own motor vehicles – a luxury which few students could afford. Another handicap was that, being articled clerks, they had to attend their masters' business which did not always end at 5:00 pm. Overtime commitments coupled with transport difficulties caused frequent missed lectures. Professor Beasley insisted upon a 90 percent attendance at lectures as a condition precedent for sitting the final examination – a quota many clerk students found impossible to fulfil.

The five-year students sought exemption from the 90 percent rule but Beasley was unyielding. Many of them, including Ken Hatfield, then reverted to the old system, achieving their ultimate admission to the profession by passing the Barristers' Board Final examinations and completing their articles. Those who had originally enrolled in Arts contented themselves with an Arts degree which they completed part-time. The Dean of Arts was much more tolerant of lecture-cutting than Professor Beasley.

The position of those who, like Sheila, had simply enrolled as Law students, without becoming articled, differed from the clerk-students. The tripartite negotiations between the State, the profession and the University which set up the Law School created an alternative method of entering the Profession. Graduates of the four-year LLB course at the University need serve only two years articles then pass the same final Bar Final examination as required of the five-year clerks. This meant that the degree course was a year longer than the five-year course. The recompense to students (and their parents) for assuming the burden of an extra year's study and lack of income was that the degree course was supposed to be a superior option and turn out better lawyers.

The superiority of the degree course was disputed by many in the profession who had been trained under the five-year scheme, as had their fathers and, in some cases, their grandfathers. Frank Ackland, who finished his legal career as a District Court judge, opted for the five-year system because his father was persuaded by a lawyer friend that the University course was inferior.[14]

The two schemes continued to co-exist for many years. In the poverty-stricken 1930s, financial reasons as well as professional conservatism often swayed parents and students in favour of the shorter non-academic course. Sheila's own assessment in her Anzac Day speech is that she could not have become a lawyer without the assistance of the Hackett bursary which would not have been available had she opted for the five-year non-academic course. Although Sheila did not say so, another compelling reason was that legal practitioners would not engage females as five-year clerks – Enid Russell is the only example of a female being engaged under that scheme at that time. The reality was that, for women, the University course was the only way to go.

It is thus no accident that the first group of school-leaver female admittees – Battye, Kingston McClemans and Hartrey, all of whom were admitted in 1933 – came from the Law School. Thereafter, the rate of female admittees dropped to less than one a year until 1943, whereafter there was a total cessation until 1954.[15] The falling-off of the female recruitment rate was probably due to the Depression and the World War, the latter causing the Law School to close down completely during 1942 and 1943.

According to her oral history interview, Sheila enjoyed a good rapport with Professor Beasley, in contrast to Ken Hatfield and his clerk-student colleagues. Beasley was most solicitous when an attack of encephalitis caused Sheila to miss a number of lectures in her final year.[16] He arranged for copies of the relevant lecture notes to be sent to her to enable her to complete her final year on schedule at the end

14 Frank Ackland, in a personal interview.

15 *Brief*, Law Society of WA, 1984, Vol 12, No 8, p 9.

16 Mrs McFadyen, in a personal interview.

of 1930. This rapport was a lasting one and was of much value to the profession in later years when Sheila became Secretary to the Law Society of Western Australia – particularly in the organisation of the Law Summer Schools which were the precursor to the Society's current Continuing Legal Education (CLE) programmes.

One of Sheila's fellow students at Law School was Frank Kenworthy whom she was to marry in 1949. Frank, then in his early thirties, was a graduate engineer employed by the Water Department with a wife and a young son. He had enrolled for a second degree because of intense competition for promotion amongst his peers in the Department. A superior officer advised him it would improve his prospects if he had a second degree. A law degree could be very useful in a bureaucracy faced with the need to enact multitudinous regulations. When he was confronted with the seemingly insurmountable 5 pm lecture problem, which had frustrated Ken Hatfield and his friends, Frank took long service leave from the Department and completed his fourth year full time. He graduated as a Bachelor of Laws in April 1934. According to John O'Halloran, Frank behaved as a very helpful, kindly "older brother" to his fellow students most of whom were ten years his junior. His relationship to Sheila was no different from the others, and there was no hint of the romantic involvement which developed almost 20 years later.[17]

Having passed her final law examinations at the end of 1930 and formally graduating at the April 1931 graduation ceremony, Sheila re-enrolled in the Faculty of Arts as a part-time external student to complete her Arts degree. She graduated as a Bachelor of Arts in April 1933. In 1931-32 she continued to take part in student affairs as appears from several references to her in *Pelican*.

The most significant of these references, for the legal historian, is a report of the foundation meeting of the law students' Blackstone Society on the evening of Tuesday, 21 April 1931, in which the aims of the Society were expressed as being "to foster a deeper appreciation of legal issues and to give a practical effect to legal knowledge".[18] The president was Joe Staricoff, the Rhodes scholar for 1931. Sheila and Margaret Battye were among the elected

---

17 John O'Halloran, in a personal interview.

18 *Pelican*, 24 April 1931, p 3.

officials. Joe Staricoff went to Oxford to further his studies and taught law there for some years. When he eventually returned to Australia, he practised at the New South Wales Bar and eventually became a QC. At some stage he anglicised his name to "Starke" and is better known to the profession as Joe Starke QC who was for many years the editor of the *Australian Law Journal.*

On completion of her Arts degree, Sheila withdrew from student activity to concentrate upon her work as an articled clerk and to prepare for her Barristers Board examinations. At the successful end of her final law year, 1930, Sheila's Hackett bursary ceased. She was granted articles with Mr Forman's firm, Stawell Hardwick and Forman, but was paid nothing for the first year and only ten shillings per week for her second.

The bursary records show that for her final University year, 1930, she had been granted £75 for the year. Her mother's income was £228 for the year – approximately the working man's basic wage at that time. The records also show that, besides Sheila, there was one other dependent child, the youngest daughter Quinta, who was in her sixteenth year and still at school. Although the other three girls were in employment, the female wage was fixed at two thirds of the male rate which in those Depression days was little above subsistence level. After paying board, there would be little to spare for any of them.

Sheila's only source of income during her first year articles was coaching. In *Six For Heaven,* her sister Dorothy describes how the Sheila character "Mary" had to keep herself by coaching "dullards", a somewhat unkind description, since most of her students were aspirants for tertiary education and had at least progressed to Junior standard. The likelihood would be that they, like Sheila herself and Keir Wedd (Chapter 2 n 42), had been suddenly confronted with a matriculation subject they had not previously studied or had an academic "blind spot" requiring special attention.

In her *Oral History Memoir*, Sheila describes her financial position as follows:

> Q. And you of course weren't being paid during this period?
>
> A. In my second year I was paid 10/-. I used to coach at night to give myself a few shillings for pocket money.

> Q. Coaching Law students?
>
> A. No, usually in mathematics for Leaving Students. Junior or Leaving students.[19]

Her coaching was in fact quite versatile, in addition to Keir Wedd's Junior Latin. Edna Longden (née Holland), who was admitted to practise in 1938 and who was a fresher in Sheila's final year, recalls that Sheila was enlisted to coach her in Logic, an Arts subject which she had opted to study as part of her law course. Sheila was very kind and helpful and successfully guided Edna through her exam.[20]

As a source of income, however, coaching was penurious, the hourly rate being a mere two shillings and sixpence. Erica Underwood, widow of a long-serving Professor of Agriculture at the University of Western Australia, had rueful memories of the period: "We were all poor in those days but the McClemans were the poorest of all us – they were dirt poor".[21]

Pat De Castilla, a close friend and constant visitor to the house, used to marvel how they kept going in those times.

> Of course, Sheila was always a wonderful manager with her money – and everything else. She always looked well dressed. Not fashion-plate of course, but smart. She made all her own clothes. There was a good cotton material on sale in those days called *Tobralco* which you watched for at the sales.[22]

It is unlikely Sheila would have made many calls upon her mother for help, eager though Ada would have been to give it. It is probable that she saved something from her bursary against the days when that would cease and burnt much midnight oil in coaching to survive. Many years afterwards, one of her sisters reminisced: "Mother always said Sheila was the one who was the least trouble. One always had the feeling that though she was not the eldest she was the key to the family".[23]

---

19 C Shervington, *Sheila Mary McClemans: Oral History Memoir*, by courtesy University of WA archives, p 8.

20 Edna Longden (née Holland), in a personal interview.

21 Erica Underwood, in a personal interview.

22 Pat De Castilla, in a personal interview.

23 Quoted in *Women in Profile* an article by Rodney Locke in the now defunct *Weekend News*, 8 December 1962, p 10. The sister is not named. This status is disputed by her niece, Judith Collett, who, in a personal interview, claims it was the eldest daughter Dorothy whose teaching salary greatly supplemented the family income at that time.

Sheila commenced her articles still branded by the attack of encephalitis that nearly wrecked her Fourth Year:

> I was a bit unfortunate, although it didn't really worry me very much at the time, but I didn't realise that as a woman I was such a strange object as an articled clerk . . . in my last year at the University I'd been very ill and had to have all my hair shaved, so I arrived not only as a woman but with hair all over my head about an inch long.[24]

In *Six For Heaven*, Dorothy Sanders describes the family's pride at "Mary's" graduation in Law but expresses grave misgivings at the discrimination she would inevitably face in the male world of the legal profession. This discrimination was not initially apparent. Although they were later to encounter the hard facts of economic discrimination and the rough-edged tongue of a sexist Chief Justice, the young women graduates were readily accepted by the rank and file of the profession. Leo Wood, who was to become one of Perth's leading practitioners of criminal law as well as one of the profession's great raconteurs, was serving a five-year articleship at the time Sheila and her friends began their two-year terms.

> We had a feeling – not of antipathy – but curiosity and wonder as to how they were going to go, as to how they'd get on. We all got on with Sheila. She was a very pleasant person and she was competent. Also she was articled to Arthur Hardwick and that gave her some status. He was the leading light in the Law Society and a real English gentleman.

The only instance of what might be considered sexist behaviour, Leo recalls, concerned Margaret Battye and that may well be considered an example of positive sexism:

> I remember one incident between Margaret Battye and old Jock Hambly. Margaret was a very big girl, and a bit of a tom boy. Jock was Clerk in Charge of the Supreme Court Central Office. You'd remember what an old larrikin he could be at times. Well Margaret was articled to Darbyshire Gillett and Jock had an antipathy towards them. Whenever he could knock their documents back he did. He got into trouble once when they sent poor Margaret down at the death-knock one Friday afternoon to file some documents. Old Jock started cursing and swearing then said:

24 C Shervington, *Sheila Mary McClemans: Oral History Memoir*, by courtesy University of WA archives, p 7.

> "Nothing personal Miss Battye. You're the only decent man in the firm".[25]

Sheila's own recollection – garnered from her *Oral History Memoir* – confirms Leo's impressions:

> you just did in your articles exactly the same things as the men did. There was no distinction made . . . I was never aware of any discrimination because I was a woman. If there was any it didn't come close enough to me for me to be aware of it. I was always treated by the men in the profession just as one of them.[26]

The social acceptance of the first women graduates by their peers in the legal profession is in contrast to the position in some other States at the time. In South Australia, according to Dame Roma Mitchell, women were excluded from membership of the Law Students' Society and were obliged to make their own arrangements to conduct moots – an essential part of legal education. In New South Wales, they were excluded from the law students' common room and the general feeling was "What are women doing here?". In Victoria, the Bar Council refused a pioneer woman lawyer, Joan Rosenove, permission to enter chambers on her first attempt to go to the Bar.[27]

The work Sheila did as an articled clerk is summarised in Shervington's *Oral History Memoir.* She began in the debt-collecting section which would have involved the drawing and filing of Local Court summonses, judgment summonses and warrants of execution. She mentions that, in the course of this, she learned about court procedures. One of the few court appearances actually permitted to articled clerks was the examination of judgment debtors as to their means to pay.

Probably the most valuable learning process about the Perth Local Court in those days was that one got to know many of the lower echelons of the court administration who, provided one was

25 Leo Wood: personal interview.

26 C Shervington, *Sheila Mary McClemans: Oral History Memoir*, by courtesy University of WA archives, p 7.

27 The experiences of Dame Roma Mitchell, and other women lawyers in the 1930s were recounted in interviews conducted by Jon Faine for the ABC's *The Law Report* programme. The transcripts have since been published in *Taken On Oath, A Generation of Lawyers*, Federation Press, 1992.

courteous to them, could become of great value in future years. Then, as in the early postwar years, the Perth Local Court was located in the old sandstone building at the corner of Roe and Beaufort Streets which now forms part of the Perth Cultural Centre complex. It was just over the road from the busy Perth Central Station, the focal point of all country, transcontinental and suburban trains. Nearly all rail locomotives at that time were steam engines which burnt low quality local coal and constantly polluted the station environs with thick clouds of sulphurous smoke. Beaufort Street Court House, in consequence, was a blackened, dingy pile giving no hint of the delicate colour of the stonework ultimately revealed in the 1970s when it was steam-cleaned for its new function of arts centre.

In operation, "Beaufort Street" was itself a bustling central station. It housed, in addition to the Local Court, the Bailiff's Office, the Married Women's Court, the Court of Petty Sessions, the Police Headquarters and the Central Lock-up. It was a very busy place. On Monday mornings when the week end drunks and the Saturday hauls of illegal street bookmakers had to be dealt with as well as the daily local court civil list, articled clerks would have to shoulder their way through crowds of unhappy people who thronged the corridors. Occasionally the throng was forced against the wall to make way for policemen shoving their manacled charges from cells to court and back again. The atmosphere was rank with a blend of body odour, stale alcohol and tobacco – the ban on smoking in public buildings was still many years in the future. There was a decidedly Dickensian air about the place, accentuated by the soot grimed exterior and the occasional whiff of coal smoke which eddied in through the windows.

An interminable queue along the Local Court counter spilled out into the corridor to compete with the crowd. The clerks, hunched over brief-cases full of typed blue forms (whose colour gave rise to the Australian vernacular expression "bluey" for any kind of summons or warrant), would wait their turn at the filing counter for the court staff to check their forms, grizzle at their mistakes, scribble alterations or reject any that were too bad. Those in the queue would shuffle on until they reached another bottleneck at the cashier's window.

The queues at the Local Court, repeated, on a lesser scale at the Supreme Court, the Titles Office and the Stamp Office, were great meeting places for the articled clerks and younger members of the profession. It is easy to visualise the youthful Leo Wood sidling up to Sheila or Margaret or any of the others with his early anecdotes of the doings of the profession and the bursts of their appreciative laughter bringing some relief to those gloomy corridors.

One aspect of Local Court work Sheila does not mention is process serving. It is reasonable to assume that she would have mentioned it if she had been given any to do because process serving was a much sought after source of extra income for articled clerks. Coping with enraged debtors brought an element of excitement into the task of process serving and was a test of agility – at times even of brawn. It is probable that the gentlemanly Arthur Hardwick would have thought it unseemly to expose a Canon's daughter or any other young lady to such hazards.

At Beaufort Street it was customary for clerks to spend a few moments on each visit in the public gallery of the various courts before a guilty conscience about work undone dragged them back to the office. If one had a principal who was concerned with his clerk's education and advancement, the clerk would carry the master's books to court and sit behind him taking notes during the course of any trials he was conducting. Local Court and Petty Sessions cases were valuable learning experiences and it is likely that Arthur Hardwick would have made certain that Sheila was given plenty of exposure to this.

Having served her time on debt collecting, Sheila progressed to drawing documents of all kinds and was even given opinion work to devil by the firm's in-house KC, Mr Stawell, from whom she learned one valuable lesson:

> First time he asked me to do that I did what I thought was a quite brilliant piece of work and he came up afterwards and thanked me for it, but said he had not asked me for a treatise on the Law of Torts. He had asked me to give an opinion as to whether A was liable in damages. That was my first recognition of the fact that you had all this theory behind you from your Law degree, but then you had to apply it to facts and actual circumstances.[28]

---

28 C Shervington, *Sheila Mary McClemans: Oral History Memoir*, by courtesy University of WA archives, p 8.

Being articled to Arthur Hardwick assured Sheila most congenial circumstances for the two years of her articles:

> He was a delightful person, very handsome, very well dressed. He had 42 suits of clothes, seven of which he kept in the office in case there should be a change of temperature during the day. . . There were two other articled clerks while I was there. Newton Mews who afterwards became the Chairman of the Workers' Compensation Board was one. John Moore was another, he did not practise, he went into the family business in Fremantle, WD Moore and Co. At the Fremantle office there was Clive Foreman, the son of one of the partners, who didn't like doing Law at all, another delightful person . . . [he] ultimately became the senior instructor pilot in TAA.
>
> Mr Hardwick loved to go into the Palace Hotel, which was nearby, to have a gin before lunch. . . He might sometimes come into me and say "Sheila do you think we could take a glass of wine for the stomach's sake?". And we would go to the Palace and have a gin and this was I thought very daring.
>
> . . . we were all very hard up, we used to have lunch in the drawing room of a firm of architects called Eales Cohen and Bennett. . . John Fitzhardinge was in the equivalent state of training with that firm as I was in Law, he was always hungry, so we used to try to take more sandwiches than we needed ourselves to fill John up.[29]

It was typical of Sheila's concern for others that, while she was articled to the firm, she used what influence she had to find a clerk's job for Ruby Bottle, the younger sister of her school friend, Edna. Ruby remembers Sheila as "a wonderful and loyal friend who referred to us as her second family". Ruby is the source of the schooldays photograph of Sheila and Edna, taken with an old Box Brownie camera in 1925.[30]

Sheila finished her articles and was admitted to practise on 16 May 1933 along with her friends and fellow students, Margaret Battye, Kathleen Hartrey, and Molly Kingston. Only two women had been admitted before them – Alice Cummins (20 May 1930) and Enid Russell (17 March 1931).

---

29 Ibid.

30 Ruby Jemyns (née Bottle): from a letter to the author in which she advises that the firm actually had three name changes during Sheila's stay there – Stawell Hardwick and Forman, Hardwick Forman and Slattery, Hardwick Slattery and Gibson.

4

KINGSTON AND McCLEMANS

Upon their admission to practise, the four women graduates encountered discrimination in its toughest and most overt form, and a form which still persists – economic discrimination.[1] The country was still in deep depression and not one of them could find employment in the Metropolitan Area.[2]

Kathleen Hartrey was fortunate that her brother Tom was in practice in Kalgoorlie and went to join him there. The other three were forced to resort to self-employment – a very risky enterprise for young, inexperienced practitioners. Sheila and Molly founded their own partnership. This brought them distinction, if not fortune, for theirs was the first all-female legal firm in Western Australia. Margaret Battye conducted a one-woman practice until her death in 1948.

The early days of practice can be quite perilous for the young practitioner. Even after four years of study and two years articles, there is so much of the law left unlearned. In the 1930s both the Law School and the Barristers Board courses completely ignored the fields of taxation, matrimonial, administrative and industrial law.

---

1 *West Australian*, 22 September 1997, reported High Court Justice Mary Gaudron complaining that "[women] were still under-represented at the partnership level of law firms, in the ranks of senior advocates and in the judiciary".

2 In C Shervington, *Sheila Mary McClemans: Oral History Memoir*, by courtesy University of WA archives, p 10, Sheila is quoted as recalling that the Crown Law Department would not employ women either as clerks or graduates until as late as 1970. In Jon Faine, *Taken On Oath, A Generation of Lawyers*, Federation Press, 1992, Victorian solicitor, Mary Whitehouse, recounts that in 1948 she applied for a job with the Victorian Crown Solicitor which was advertised at £8 a week. She was accepted but her salary reduced to £6 a week because she was a woman.

Young practitioners had to pick up their knowledge of these fields in the course of practice. Knowledge of the law is only one aspect of legal practice. Experience alone can teach one how to cope with the complexity of human problems and the perversity of human behaviour which daily confront the practising lawyer.

Opposing practitioners are quite merciless in exploiting the ignorance and inexperience of the young. As a matter of practice they are obliged to do so, their duty being to win for their client. A more experienced practitioner will, in kindness, often point out what the tyro should or should not have done after the case is over but never before. The process is referred to cynically as "learning the Law at the expense of one's client" and is one that is often very humiliating and sometimes quite costly.

More terrifying are those initial appearances in court. The legal mystique implants in young lawyers an awe of the Bench. Magistrates and judges have a frightening majesty for the inexperienced. There are so many mistakes one can make which one's opponent is always ready to seize upon – often with the collusion of an unkindly Bench. Many a youthful advocate has made one appearance in court and never returned, hiding defeat by pretending to enjoy the boredom of conveyancing in some labyrinthine back office. Many never have the desire even to attempt that first appearance.

Because of all these hazards it is usually wise for a young practitioner to commence practice as an employee so that there is always a senior person to fall back on for advice and reassurance. Likewise, it is preferable to learn advocacy as a junior counsel, sitting alongside a more experienced counsel, watching the master at work and examining the occasional peripheral witness to work oneself in. It must have been a daunting experience for those three young women to have entered the fray without such support.

Sir John Lavan, who was a year behind Sheila, remembers her as being very shy and nervous during her initial appearances. She was particularly intimidated by the ageing irascible Chief Justice of the day, Sir John Northmore, who did not approve of female practitioners and was pointedly rude and overbearing towards them. Jim Smythe, who spent his working life in the Crown Law Department, confirmed Sir John's recollections of Northmore CJ. Jim's impression was that he hated all women and was notorious for harassing female litigants and witnesses long before he was presented with young lady barristers to savage.[3]

Sheila's first Supreme Court case was that of *L v L*. It is numbered in the Supreme Court records as Matrimonial Causes Number 80 of 1933 and was commenced by the filing of a petition on 7 June 1933.[4] Mrs L, the petitioner, lived at Longroyd Street, Mount Lawley – two blocks away from Sheila's home in Glenroyd Street. It would seem probable that the back-fence network played a part in bringing solicitor and client together. Ada McClemans, Justice of the Peace, a qualified nursing sister and tireless worker for the Women's Service Guild, would have been well known in the district, as would the fame of her brilliant lawyer daughter.

Mrs L's petition was based on the ground that she had been separated from her husband for three years under an order of the Perth Court of Petty Sessions and that her husband had habitually failed to pay the weekly maintenance of £2 10s provided by the order. On this, her very first Supreme Court appearance, Sheila was listed before the dreaded Northmore CJ. One has to undergo a similar ordeal to appreciate the agonies of apprehension Sheila must have suffered on the eve of that appearance. On the day, her apprehension was fully justified – Jim Smythe recalled the occasion:

> I remember her first contact with me was when she was in a case in the Supreme Court. She got up to the part where the client was telling the Court about her order in the lower court, the Judge asked her for a copy and Sheila didn't have one. She came down to me in terrible stress. I told her I'd make her up a copy in no time. Sheila and I got very friendly after that. The judge was Northmore. He used to give Sheila a terrible time. And that other girl Molly Kingston. She had a pretty rough time with him too.[5]

Sheila must have persuaded the Chief Justice to adjourn the case until later in the day so that she could hurry over to Beaufort Street and use her good standing with the staff there because the record shows that the case was dealt with, and the decree granted, on the listed day and not adjourned to another hearing date. It was not the

---

3 Sir John Lavan and Mr J Smythe from personal interviews.

4 Supreme Court records, Battye Library, Perth.

5 Mr J Smythe, from a personal interview.

most auspicious case to record the first appearance ever of a woman barrister in the Supreme Court of Western Australia but Sheila was, perhaps, fortunate to escape the public mauling accorded her partner in the reported case of *O'Neil v O'Neil*.[6]

In this case Molly had proved a separation for three years and produced a separation order together with evidence from Mr Smythe in his capacity of Clerk of the Married Women's Relief Court to the effect that the husband was £315 in arrears of weekly maintenance payments of £2 15s. One would have thought that simple mathematics demanded the conclusion that this was an obvious case of habitual failure to comply with a maintenance order. Not so, according to Northmore CJ:

> When the case first came before me it was sought to establish that fact by showing that from the date of the inception of the order up to the filing of the petition the respondent was in arrears to the extent of £315. Obviously that falls short of the proof required under the section under which the suit was brought. What is required . . . is that throughout the whole period the respondent shall have repeatedly and habitually failed to make the payment required by the order, and that can only be done by producing and proving the details of payments actually made, giving, of course, the date of such payments. It is only then that it can be ascertained whether this failure had extended throughout the period of three years.[7]

The evidence to make good His Honour's requirements could not be obtained by a quick dash to Beaufort Street in the luncheon break. The matter was adjourned from 11 September until 26 October so that due search and enquiry could be made in the records of the Child Welfare Department and the Court of Petty Sessions to prove the habitual financial derelictions of the feckless Mr O'Neil who had not even bothered to defend the action.

The evidence was supplied on the adjourned date and the divorce granted. For an undefended divorce case to be written up in the Law Reports must mean that the judge himself requested it. One wonders why. Maybe it was to put his chastisement of Molly Kingston on permanent record. Maybe it was merely to demonstrate

6 (1934) 35 WALR 38.

7 Ibid, at 40.

the truth of Charles Dickens' assertion in *Bleak House*, "The one great principle of the English law is to make business for itself".

Other members of the Bench were kinder to the young women advocates. Margaret Battye was the first of them to appear in any court when she acted for a plaintiff in a defended assault case in the Perth Court of Petty Sessions. Her client was a man who charged an Italian woman with assaulting him. If there was any prejudice it was ethnic and not sexist, and Margaret was victorious. At the conclusion of the case, she was congratulated by both the Magistrate (Mr Henry Moseley SM) and opposing counsel (Mr Howard Bath) for the competent manner in which she had conducted her case.[8]

Jim Smythe saw a lot of Sheila at the Beaufort Street Court in the 1930s because she soon developed a busy practice amongst women seeking assistance in the Married Women's Summary Relief Court of which Jim was the Clerk. He watched her develop in a few months from a shy uncertain beginner to a confident and able counsel. It was plain that the magistrates respected her competence, integrity and pleasant manner as an advocate. The Chief Magistrate at the time, Henry Moseley, was an old family friend and Christ Church parishioner who had served in the 28th Battalion during the Great War.

Two of her surviving contemporaries, John O'Halloran and Leo Wood, also saw a lot of Sheila at that time and give a similar account of her progress through in the courts. In John's own words:

> She was a lovely person to talk to. So knowledgeable. She always fought for her clients to the finish and did a magnificent job for them. Yet she was never one for forcing clients into court. She was a good listener and always reasonable. You could tell her what your client's case was and trust her not to use it against you. You could always reach a reasonable settlement with Sheila.[9]

Leo Wood is also emphatic about her trustworthiness: "Always straight as a bloody die, was Sheila".[10]

The partners seem to have shared their superior court work fairly evenly. The Matrimonial Causes records of the Supreme Court

8 Noel Scott, *As I Remember Them,* Chapter 3, Artlook Books, 1987, p 98.

9 John O'Halloran, from a personal interview.

10 Leo Wood, from a personal interview.

show that, of the 16 undefended divorce actions in which the partnership was concerned, Sheila appeared in nine and Molly in seven. The partnership was involved in only two Supreme Court civil actions. In the first (*A No 7 of 1934*), they filed an appearance for a defendant mortgagor whose poultry farm was being foreclosed by the Agricultural Bank, no defence was subsequently filed and the matter concluded in judgment by default, the record does not show which of the partners acted for the client.[11]

In the second (*S No 8 of 1938*), Molly acted for a defendant in a claim for damages for negligence in a motor vehicle accident claim in which Mr Stan Tippett acted for the plaintiff.[12] Mr Tippett's client had walked on to Stirling Highway, Mosman Park, in front of the defendant's truck. It was a fairly audacious claim in the circumstances, particularly as it was before the days of apportionment of liability, and contributory negligence was an absolute defence to an action for negligence. Even though she seemed to be on a winner, Molly took the precaution of briefing senior counsel (Mr Len Seaton KC) to settle the defence and appear at the trial as her leader. Her defence was successful, the claim was dismissed with costs against the plaintiff after a two-day trial. It may be of historical interest to note the plaintiff's special damages:

Loss of wages @ £4.0.0 pw for 40 weeks	£160.0.0
Hospital	£7.5.6
Doctor	£2.12.6
Ambulance	£1.0.0
Trousers	£1.10.0
Shoes	£1.0.0

This comparatively trivial matter was argued in the Supreme Court because the District Court was not created until 1969 and the Local Court did not have the power to award the amount of damages the plaintiff hoped to receive.

In its issue of 16 February 1935, the *Mirror* reported a Supreme Court criminal trial which Sheila defended. Its patronising sexist style is typical of the time.

11 Supreme Court records, Battye Library, Perth.

12 Ibid.

A CHARMING YOUNG LADY BARRISTER FAILS TO WIN JURY'S VERDICT FOR MALE PRISONER

> Strange isn't it how most young ladies who wear wig and gown in our courts seem to have more male clients than those of their own sex!
>
> This week Miss Sheila McClemans, who in barrister's garb, fashionable street dress or beach shorts looks equally attractive, made history for her sex by appearing in a criminal trial. And it was a man she was defending.
>
> Those who would expect a female Arthur Haynes or Fred Curran to powder her dainty nose or rouge her lips before addressing a jury would be pleasantly disappointed. Miss McClemans, who is the daughter of a man who was once one of our leading clerics, displays none of these feminine foibles in court. Nor do her bewigged and begowned sisters.
>
> They all have a workmanlike style about them and, though there are times when the importance of the occasion may slightly overawe them they do their job well.
>
> But we're getting off the track.
>
> Miss McClemans in her first appearance in the criminal court was unlucky in her case. From the first it looked hopeless and the jury did not take long to say "Guilty".
>
> Her client was Charles Harold Kemp. His offence was a very cheeky one.
>
> Seeing a car for sale he bought it for £300 and paid for it by cheque which came back marked "no account".
>
> The day after, Kemp took the car to another dealer and sold it for £175, which he took in cash.

The last partnership Supreme Court case in which Sheila appeared was an undefended divorce, *N v N (No 312 of 1938)*, the decree nisi in which was granted on 9 March 1939.[13]

In her *Oral History Memoir* Sheila claims that she did not specialise in cases of matrimonial conflict. Her summation of her early years in practice was:

13 Ibid.

> one gradually moved into what I would call in broad terms "family law", but that was very different from what family law practice now is. You acted for a family, you perhaps bought a house for them, sold a house for them, bought a business for them, sold a business for them, drew their wills, proved those wills in due course, perhaps did a claim for damages for one of the children who perhaps had been injured in some way. You were really part of their life and that was very satisfying but enjoyable. You did of course have to do the occasional "break down in marriage" work, that was part of it too, but that was part of the life of that family.[14]

Undoubtedly, Sheila did a lot of general solicitor's work but the record of her Supreme Court cases and the recollection of such contemporaries as Sir John Lavan, Leo Wood, John O'Halloran, Jim Smythe and an early personal secretary, Constance Morgan, is that she was regarded as a specialist in contested matrimonial disputes and spent a lot of time in court arguing such matters and that her clients were mainly women.[15]

There would have been a number of factors which involved Sheila in this speciality. As mentioned previously, her mother was very much involved in the women's movement of the time, having also a professional connection with women and children in her capacity of school nurse as well as a judicial function as a justice of the peace. She would thus have been a personal channel for many women with matrimonial problems.

It is probable that most women prefer to discuss the intimacies of their personal life with female practitioners. It is the opinion both of John O'Halloran and Leo Wood that many clients came to Sheila for that reason alone. As she was one of a very small band of female practitioners, her specialisation in the field was almost inevitable. It has long been the complaint of women lawyers that they suffer the danger of being "type cast" as family lawyers simply because they are female.[16] The historical origin of this tendency is very likely the great

---

14 C Shervington, *Sheila Mary McClemans: Oral History Memoir*, by courtesy University of WA archives, p 9.

15 Sir John Lavan, Messrs Leo Wood, John O'Halloran and Mrs Constance Morgan in personal interviews.

16 In a news item in the *West Australian* of 2 October 1998, p 3, a group of female barristers jointly expressed their aversion to being so "type cast" and the difficulties encountered in resisting it.

demand for women lawyers to cope with women's problems and the initial shortage of supply.

Perhaps a basic underlying cause for Sheila's own involvement would be that she had a special empathy for deserted wives and children by reason of the breakdown of her own parents' marriage and her family's abandonment by their father. In her *Oral History Memoir*, Sheila revealed that she had strong personal views about the institution of marriage and the law relating to its dissolution:

> I don't like the *Family Law Act*, I don't like its philosophy. I think that it leads to very easy disruption of marriages. I think it leads to great problems with children and I just don't like it. We did have a Matrimonial Causes Code passed in 1948 . . . it was very good indeed, people accepted it in the main as being the right thing to do about marriages which were not very stable . . . the big thing was that the doctrine of fault applied. If you deserted your spouse or committed adultery and so on then the other party could get a divorce. This all took time whereas now under the *Family Law Act* you merely have to say "Well it's been very nice knowing you, goodbye". And stay away for twelve months and you can get a divorce, and I don't like it.[17]

Middle class women of Sheila's generation were very much opposed to the concept of "easy" divorce – particularly divorce by simple separation. They feared that it would open the flood gates for men to abandon their wives and children to live with new – and much younger – loves. Under the law, as it was then, the elderly husband's new love was obliged to live as a kept mistress not received in respectable society and snubbed at every possible occasion. To give such a person the status of a lawful wife and the faithless husband the comfort of a respectable establishment with the right to bring his woman to official functions – perhaps even to become the "Lady" to his politically or commercially manipulated knighthood – would be to spit in the eye of every dutiful, virtuous wife.

There was a lot more than mere middle class morality to support this hostility. Most women at that time were brought up to regard marriage as their career; having achieved marital status they worked hard to do well in that career. They kept house, bore and reared the

---

17 C Shervington, *Sheila Mary McClemans: Oral History Memoir*, by courtesy University of WA archives, p 15.

children, and accepted the necessity to support the husband in achieving his occupational objectives, often living quite frugally whilst he established himself in his business or profession. All this was compliantly performed under the social philosophy of the subservience of women.

Unless she was fortunate to have independent means, the wife's sole income was what her husband gave her for housekeeping. Estate and tax planners had not developed their expertise to the point where they were able to persuade the average husband to register the family home in joint names, to incorporate the family business to spread the tax burden amongst the family and to conceal other income-producing assets in family trusts. Few women equipped themselves for a career before they married. It was, therefore, much more unjust and oppressive than it is today for a husband to abandon his hard working and faithful wife because the wife had little capacity for economic survival on her own.

The Western Australian 1948 Matrimonial Causes Bill referred to by Sheila with such approval in the passage quoted above contained a provision that either party could sue for divorce in the event of a break down of marriage but only after a continuous separation of five years. This provision was the fore runner of the concept of "no fault divorce". The fault element still prevailed, however, because it was essential that during that period the petitioner had to abstain from sexual intercourse. Adultery by the petitioner during the five-year period was an absolute bar to a divorce on the ground of five years' separation.

This prohibition was modified by the enactment of the Commonwealth *Matrimonial Causes Act* in 1959, sponsored by the then Attorney-General, Sir Garfield Barwick. The passage of this Act faced considerable religious and moralistic opposition, as had a similar unsuccessful private member's Bill introduced by Percy Joske QC, MHR several years previously. The main reason for this opposition was the modified five years separation provision which gave the trial judge a discretion to grant a divorce notwithstanding adultery – a discretion which in practice was almost invariably exercised. The Barwick Act made "no fault" divorce a virtual reality albeit requiring a degree of patience on the part of the petitioner and his or her aspiring replacement spouse. Sheila was so concerned about this provision that she travelled to Canberra to express her personal opposition to Sir Garfield Barwick.[18]

Unconditional "no fault" divorce was finally achieved in 1975 with the passage of Lionel Murphy's *Family Law Act.* It was this last piece of legislation that attracted Sheila's particular ire in the passage cited above.

In taking her moral stand on the fault basis for matrimonial relief, Sheila was no doubt influenced by her Anglican background. But it is a reasonable assumption, that her personal involvement in a disintegrating marriage as a child, the family's struggle for bare existence during her adolescence and the final humiliation of her mother's divorce, provided the practical basis for her conservative opposition to the liberalisation of divorce law. Her mother, of course, faced no barrier to her divorce because her husband was at fault, having deserted and failed to maintain her and her children. Paradoxically Ada did not want a divorce but was forced into one by the requirements of the Public Service which would not employ married women.

In the day-to-day business of caring for her clients' interests, Sheila's personal background would have been invaluable. It frequently becomes the duty of a matrimonial advocate to say to a client "You have to think of yourself. You have to think of your children. You must protect yourself if only for their sake".

Matrimonial advocates are often accused of exacerbating the conflict between warring spouses – thus making any possibility of reconciliation impossible. No doubt there are some who are guilty of this. The truth of such situations is usually that, by the time parties seek out lawyers to solve their problems, an irreversible breakdown of marriage has already occurred. In such a situation, it is the duty of a legal adviser to give strength to the client's resolve and lend judicious support if the client shows signs of being emotionally overborne against his or her best interests or those of the unfortunate children of the marriage.

Sheila had a reputation in the profession for stubborn support for her female clients. One in particular, the late Mr WT Elphick, used to allege that she was "as hard as nails" in dealing with other

18 Mrs Paddy McFadyen (formerly Leschen née McClemans) in a personal interview.

peoples' clients and nicknamed her "Nails" McClemans as a consequence.[19] The majority, however, preferred the favourable assessment of Messrs Wood and O'Halloran quoted above. The opposing points of view were probably determined by the degree to which the critic tended to become subjectively identified with his own client.

Her mother's involvement with the women's movement was not regarded by Sheila simply as a useful source of clients. She became involved personally, joining the Business and Professional Women's Club of Perth and undertaking the secretaryship of the Infant Health Association, both off-shoots of the Women's Service Guild. As she lived in her mother's household throughout her early years in the law, this commitment is not surprising.

The most important case in which Sheila was involved in the 1930s was not argued in the Supreme Court but in the Court of Industrial Arbitration. She obtained this brief directly as a result of her mother's membership of the Australian Trained Nurses Association.

Ada McClemans always strongly supported her professional colleagues in their struggles to improve the wages and conditions of nurses. In the early 1930s nurses worked a 54-hour week for day duty and 60 for night duty. Other deficiencies are apparent in the following list of demands served on the Medical Department pursuant to a mass meeting of nurses held in June 1934:

- That nurses work eight hours a day for a six day week
- Lectures be given in duty time
- Salaries be increased to the following rates:
  - ⇒ Second year £36 per year
  - ⇒ Third year £52 per year
  - ⇒ Staff nurses £104 per year
  - ⇒ Sisters £120-£160 per year
- Overtime not to be allowed

To put these wage rates into perspective, it should be appreciated that the basic male annual wage was £208, for a 44-hour week (see the plaintiff's unsuccessful claim for lost wages in Molly Kingston's

19 Mrs Tyler, former personal Secretary to Sheila McClemans, in a personal interview. Mr Elphick declined a request for an interview.

negligence case above). On these figures it will be seen that qualified nursing sisters working 48 hours a week were seeking half the pay of an unskilled labourer working a 44-hour week. Even allowing for free board and working uniforms, the economic discrimination is obvious.[20]

Historically nurses had always been repressed by the medical establishment. This was reflected in the fact that their professional body, the Australian Trained Nurses' Association, included male doctors and nursing home owners amongst its membership and even on its executive body. The Florence Nightingale philosophy of self-sacrifice and hierarchical discipline was used as an ideological device to exorcise militancy. In these nuclear-conscious times it is startling to learn that, when radium treatment was introduced in 1928, no warning was given to nurses of its dangers and no protective clothing provided.

With the onset of the Depression, employers sought to reduce nurses' conditions even further. Private hospitals sacked professional staff and made do with unqualified aides. One country hospital imposed an 18 percent cut in nurses' salaries.

Radiography technicians and other health professionals banded together to resist attacks on their conditions, forming the Hospital Officers' Association which enrolled some of the nursing staff at Perth Public Hospital. The Nurses' Association council became alarmed at this, sensing a total body-snatch of its members. Ada McClemans was a member of the council which briefed Sheila to undertake the necessary legal procedures to save the Association from a take-over by the Hospital Officers. Sheila was present in an advisory role at a meeting of the Nurses' Association which took the decision to make an application to the Court of Industrial Arbitration to register the Association as an industrial union.

Sheila guided the nursing profession through the intricacies of registration and some unforeseen problems which arose. Because the Association included employers amongst its membership it could not legally become a union, nor could it cover trainee nurses and remain a body of qualified professionals. Another body, the Royal

---

20 Victoria Hobbs, *But Westward Look*, University of WA Press, 1988, pp 88-89. Sister Hobbs' work is the source for the description of nursing conditions in the 1930s.

Australian Nursing Federation (WA Branch) Industrial Union of Workers, had to be established and make application to the Court for registration.

Sheila prepared the necessary documents and filed them in the Court on 17 July 1934.[21] Objections to the registration were filed by the Mental Nurses Union and the Hospital Employees Federation. Such objections are common when a new union seeks registration because existing unions are always fearful that the new union may poach some of their members or move into fields of employment pegged out for future expansion of their own industrial empires.

Industrial law has always been particularly esoteric and the bulk of the legal profession then, as now, tended to leave it to a few specialists. The advocates were usually trade union officers with no formal legal education or qualifications but who picked up the procedure by constant confrontations with the Court in their official capacity. The reason for this was that, except in exceptional circumstances, legal practitioners were barred from appearing in the Court by s 65 of the *Industrial Arbitration Act* 1900.

The exceptions to exclusion of counsel were the prosecution or defence of penal actions and cases in which all parties consented to counsel appearing. Generally unions either employed their own executive members to appear or called upon experienced advocates from other unions to argue their cases.

The nurses' application was heard on 24 August 1934 before Industrial Registrar Frank Walsh. Sheila appeared for the nurses union, another solicitor, Mr TJ Hughes, represented the Mental Nurses Union and the union's own secretary, SG Severn, represented the Hospital Employees' Federation ("HEF"). Neither Sheila nor Hughes could have appeared in the matter without the consent of the Hospital Employees' Federation. There is no mention of the matter on the file relating to the initial application for registration or in the transcript of proceedings. It must be presumed that the HEF union did consent. Since Hughes was also opposing the registration of the nurses on behalf of his client union, the Hospital Employees probably regarded him as a useful potential ally and were only too

21 Application for Registration No 28 of 1934, Industrial Arbitration Court records Battye Library, Perth.

willing to have him there as a *quid pro quo* for consenting to Sheila's presence.

Hughes, who was notorious in the legal profession as something of a larrikin with a dubious strain of guile, was nicknamed "Diver". Whilst this was admirably expressive of one suspected of underhand tactics, it had originally nothing to do with that characteristic. It derived from the heroic deeds of a professional diver named Hughes who rescued a miner named Varischetti from a flooded underground working at Bonnie Vale near Coolgardie in 1907. For years afterwards, all boys with the name of "Hughes" were accorded the nickname "Diver" the first day they arrived at primary school. It was a title as inescapable as "Dusty" was to "Miller" or "Nobby" to "Clark". Whether the nickname followed them into their mature years probably depended upon whether it seemed appropriate to their peers.

Sheila was probably most apprehensive about what tactics the wily Hughes might use on her. All young practitioners were warned in their articled clerk days to "watch out for Diver" but the transcript shows she need not have been. Mr Hughes heaped praise upon the noble nursing profession and assured the Court that his union was simply concerned with the possibility of encroachment. This fear was allayed by adding a few words to the constitution of the applicant union excluding mental nurses.

Mr Severn was more of a problem, claiming that his organisation could conveniently cover all who worked in hospitals, thus the formation of a separate union for nurses was unnecessary and that the sort of work done by nurses outside hospitals (such as home nursing) would not come within the definition of "industry" and merit the industrial cover envisaged by an award. In any event, Mr Severn argued, trainee nurses should not come under the aegis of the professional body because they were, by definition, unskilled workers.

The last point was what the battle was all about. The HEF had offered a deal – a consent order for registration in exchange for HEF coverage of trainee nurses. Sheila advised the nurses to fight, because in her opinion they would probably win. There was no question that she would profit from the fight personally because she always acted as "honorary solicitor" and there is no record in the Nurses Association's minutes of her ever sending them a bill.

If Messrs Hughes and Severn thought they were in for an easy run being opposed by a young woman of 23 with barely one year's practice behind her and no experience at all in the Industrial Arbitration Court, they were greatly mistaken. Sheila unleashed a devastating argument, disposing of the "no industry" submission at the outset by citing decisions of the High Court of Australia and the Supreme Court of Western Australia as authorities for the proposition that the term "industry" at law encompasses "All forms of employment in which large numbers of workers are employed".[22]

Only the Arbitration Court in those days ran a full transcript of proceedings. We are thus fortunate that Sheila's address to the court is recorded in full. The following extracts provide a unique demonstration of the power of her pleading:

> The work of nurses is essentially different from that of the respondents' members. . . A nurse is a highly skilled professional worker. Skilled because she undergoes an educational course and passes an examination before commencing her training [trainee nurses were required to have attained a Public Examination Junior Certificate LLD]. She starts off more skilled than the ordinary member of the HEF. Every month of her training she becomes more skilled. Any attempt to regulate the employment of nurses can only be done by those trained in that profession and aware of its peculiar conditions. . . No award covering orderlies and domestic staff can apply to nurses. Nothing but inconvenience can result to them from being joined to persons with no knowledge of their conditions.[23]

She exposed the paucity of the argument that home nursing could not be included in an industrial award as follows:

> If I employ a plumber in my house I must pay him award wages. If I employ a nurse in my house – a highly skilled and technical worker – she does not become a domestic servant merely by changing the venue of her employment.[24]

---

22 *Australian Insurance Staffs v Accident Underwriters' Association* (1923) 33 CLR 527; *Faulding Co v Clerks Union of WA* (1914)16 WALR 32.

23 Court transcript, for *Registration No 28 of 1934*, Industrial Arbitration Court records, Battye Library, Perth.

24 Ibid.

Sheila's case was unanswerable. Subject to some minor amendments, registration was granted on 19 September 1934.

It was a great personal triumph for Sheila. It should be remembered that the University course of those times included no tuition in industrial law. The theory was that one was supposed to pick up the odd bits and pieces of non-mainstream law in the course of one's articles. It is doubtful that her old conveyancing/common law firm, Hardwick Forman and Slattery, provided Sheila with any experience of industrial law during her articles. The skill with which she handled that application and the courage with which she took on responsibility for the future livelihood of generations of nurses must be considered remarkable.

The medical establishment did not welcome the formation of the Union. Snobs in the nursing profession itself considered it demeaning to their professional status, and the employers were more concerned with economics. Owing to employer resistance the union found it impossible to negotiate an industrial agreement which could be registered by consent with the Court. It was forced into court once more, this time to mount two cases in the Court of Industrial Arbitration – one against the public hospitals and another against the private hospitals.[25]

Again Sheila assisted in the preparation of the documents. Her name appears as attesting witness, in the capacity of Commissioner for Affidavits, to the "Reference of Industrial Dispute", the initiating document by which the dispute was brought to court. The signatory to the document was the secretary of the union, Margaret Robertson. Unlike the Application for Registration, the documents do not bear the firm name of Kingston and McClemans, Solicitors, Perth. The prevailing philosophy of those days was that unions were supposed to fight their own forensic battles without the overt assistance of lawyers. The files relating to the dispute indicate that Sheila wrote a letter to the Industrial Registrar seeking an appointment to settle the issues in the dispute, but thereafter all correspondence is between the court and the union, correspondence for the union being signed by AH Panton.

---

25 *WANAIU v Perth Hospital* (*No 5 of 1935*); *WANAIU v Avro Hospital* (*No 7 of 1935*).

Mr AH Panton, later a minister in several Labor governments, was an experienced lay advocate who was briefed to argue the case for the Union in accordance with the philosophy outlined above. The case attracted much publicity in the daily press, particularly the use of "pedometers" to measure the amount of footwork expended by nurses from day to day in the course of their duties. A photograph of young women wearing this novel appliance appeared in the *West Australian* on 13 July 1935.

When they won, Mr Panton got all the publicity, which no doubt furthered his political career. Sheila contented herself with the gratitude of the nursing profession who, for the first time in the history of Western Australia, began to get something like reasonable conditions and appropriate pay for their service to the community.

Sheila's social life during the period of the partnership revolved largely around the household at Glenroyd Street. For most of the 1930s, the household numbered seven: Ada, her five daughters and the young Judith Leschen (later Judith Collett), daughter of the fourth daughter, Paddy. Paddy had eloped, somewhat to the family's disapproval, at an early age with a young man named Bill Leschen. Because of the economic strains inflicted by the Depression, Bill had to take work in the country and Paddy had to return home to mother with her baby daughter, born in 1930. It is interesting that this minor departure from middle class normality is, like the Canon's addiction to alcohol, glossed over by Dorothy in *Six For Heaven*. Using her favourite device she killed off Bill's unfortunate literary alter ego with a premature heart attack.

The early years of the McClemans family at Glenroyd Street, Mount Lawley, were very frugal because of the poverty level of the total family income, limited as it was by the legally endorsed discrimination against female wage earners. Erica Underwood remembers that, poor as they were, their morale was high.

> The McClemans always gave the impression that they were *someone*. They never forgot those years at the Rectory as members of the Canon's family and this seemed to carry them through.[26]

26 Erica Underwood, from a personal interview.

The writer, Paul Buddee, has fond memories of the household at Glenroyd Street.[27] Paul first came into contact with the McClemans family when he met Ada at Darlington Primary School. He was then a young school teacher and Ada the visiting school nurse. Paul was planning an overseas trip which caught Ada's interest as she also had ambitions to visit Britain and the Continent when her finances permitted.

When Paul returned he met Ada, by chance, in the City. She insisted he come to tea and tell the family about his travels. On arrival she mistakenly introduced him to the family as "Mr Len Harrop" – another teacher-writer who had gone overseas to earn fame and fortune. Sheila discerned the dismay in Paul's face and intervened: "Mother this is plainly a case of mistaken identity. You've obviously got the wrong man".

Despite this initial embarrassment, Paul become a frequent guest at the McClemans for Sunday night high teas. He recalls that these were very stimulating occasions at which he met many of the bright young people of the time, some of whom would eventually achieve considerable fame. These included Paul Hasluck, then a journalist and drama critic with the *West Australian*, Hasluck's future wife, Alexandra Darker, and Colsell Sanders, then a lecturer at Teachers' Training College who later married Sheila's sister Dorothy and from whom she took part of her nom de plum "Dorothy Lucie Sanders". Another frequent visitor was a young business-man, Peter Wright, who would soon marry the eldest sister, Pauline, eventually amass a great fortune from mining iron ore in association with Lang Hancock and fundamentally transform the State of Western Australia. Paul's impression of Peter Wright was that he was "an exceptionally charming man".

The sister who stood out most at the gatherings for Paul Buddee was not Sheila, but Dorothy. She was the jolliest and wittiest and she was a fellow teacher. She paid Paul the compliment of using some of his early books in her classes. He has never forgotten her prophetic words: "Paul you've inspired me. If you can write books so can I".

Paul likes to think that his works were the original catalyst for Dorothy's impressive output of popular novels. A particularly memorable occasion at Glenroyd Street was a family party to

---

27 Buddee's reminiscences of the McClemans household at Glenroyd Street were obtained in a lengthy personal interview.

celebrate the conferring of a Master of Arts degree upon Colsell Sanders, who was by then engaged to marry Dorothy.

Looking back over 60 years, Paul recalled that Sheila was the most practical member of the gatherings, tending to bring the discussions back to more serious subjects. In her capacity as secretary to the Infant Health Association, she was then working on a charter of children's rights. Above all he recalls the kindness and good-humoured hospitality of Ada McClemans and her great managing capacity. The McClemans high teas came to an end for Paul when he joined the 2nd AIF at the outbreak of war in September 1939 and left for the Middle East, by which time most of the girls had gone their separate ways and Sheila and Ada had moved to a flat at 70 Victoria Avenue, Claremont.

Whilst Colsell Sanders and Peter Wright were courting their future wives, Sheila was involved in a more pedestrian relationship of her own. Dorothy's friends, the Wedges, had befriended a young British migrant named Monty Mouatt who was struggling to make a living growing grapes on a block near their farm at Gin Gin. Monty had served briefly with the Gordon Highlanders at the end of the Great War and was persuaded to leave a job in a London Bank by the spate of dubious propaganda the State of Western Australia put about overseas in order to attract migrants.

The Wedges used to invite Monty to Sunday tea and provide him with the only good meal he had for the week. Monty met Mrs McClemans on one of her visits to the Wedges and she invited him to call if ever he came to town. Monty soon realised the folly of trying to farm virgin land with no previous agricultural experience or capital and obtained a sales job with an oil company. Although he was a travelling country salesman, this job at least brought him to the city with some frequency. Whenever he did, he called at the McClemans home and became particularly attached to Sheila.

Although he was ten years her senior, Monty and Sheila kept company for nine years, and friends and family generally expected they would eventually marry.[28] They were close enough to spend out-of-town weekends with married friends, such as the Haslucks, but on a strictly separate room basis. In those respectable upper-

28 Paddy McFadyen, from a personal interview.

middle class circles, it would be unheard of for married couples to extend hospitality to an unmarried couple on any other basis. The married couple friends were expected to act as chaperones and guarantors of the respectability of the weekend. As for the unmarried couples themselves, it was normal for conventional morality and propriety to be observed, sexual relations before marriage were eschewed and engagements to marry were usually platonic, albeit frustrating, relationships.[29]

Sheila has left no written memoir of her association with Monty Mouatt but one of her close Navy friends, Mary Howard, recalls that in about 1944 in Melbourne she made some rather unemotional remark that she had broken off a long-standing friendship with a man without much regret.[30] When interviewed by the author at the age of 93, Monty Mouatt had only a dim recollection. He remembered being very fond of Sheila and taking her out to theatres, restaurants and the trotting races whenever he visited town but never contemplating marrying her, his explanation being: "I could never have afforded to. I didn't have a good enough job".[31]

It is more likely that the nature of the relationship and not economic circumstances was the explanation for its not ending in marriage. Monty's economic status did not prevent him marrying a young war widow, Patricia Moseley, in 1945 and he still held the same job as he did when Sheila left Perth to join the Women's Royal Australian Naval Service (WRANS) in 1943. At the time of her enlistment Sheila was a senior solicitor in Hardwick Slattery and Gibson and earning a good salary. It is reasonable to assume that, before her enlistment, Sheila was intent on establishing her career and deliberately deferred all thoughts of marriage until she had done so.

Monty's bride, Patricia Moseley (née Monger), was the widow of Doyle Moseley, son of Henry Moseley SM an old McClemans family friend. Doyle was killed in 1943 whilst on active service with the RAAF. Ada McClemans was very caring towards his grief-stricken

---

29 Particulars of Sheila's social life at this period and the prevailing mores of the time were obtained from personal interviews with Sir Paul Hasluck and Mr John Lefroy, a fellow lawyer who was about four years senior to Sheila. Both were close personal friends of Sheila.

30 Mary Howard, from a personal interview.

31 Monty Mouatt, from a personal interview.

Above: Canon William McClemans in chaplain's uniform, 1916
(Photo: Christ Church Grammar School archives)

Left: Ada Lucy McClemans on her 21st birthday
(Photo: Mrs Judith Collett)

Pauline, Dorothy and Sheila McClemans, *circa* 1910
(Photo: Mrs Judith Collett)

Sheila aged 15 with school friend Edna Bottle
(Photo: Mrs Mollie Dickinson)

UNIVERSITY SWIMMING CARNIVAL.

The Most Prominent Swimmers.

P. Verscheur. S. McClemans, H. Wilson.

F. Hosking (on right) and P. Hasluck (left) were second and third respectively in the 440 Yards Championship. Verscheur was first. In the middle is Miss McClemans winning the Women's Neat Dive.

The Start of the 100 Yards Championship.

Sheet from *The Black Swan*, Vol XIII, No 1, June 1929, depicting University of Western Australia swimming carnival in which Sheila features prominently. (Photo: WA Guild of Undergraduates)

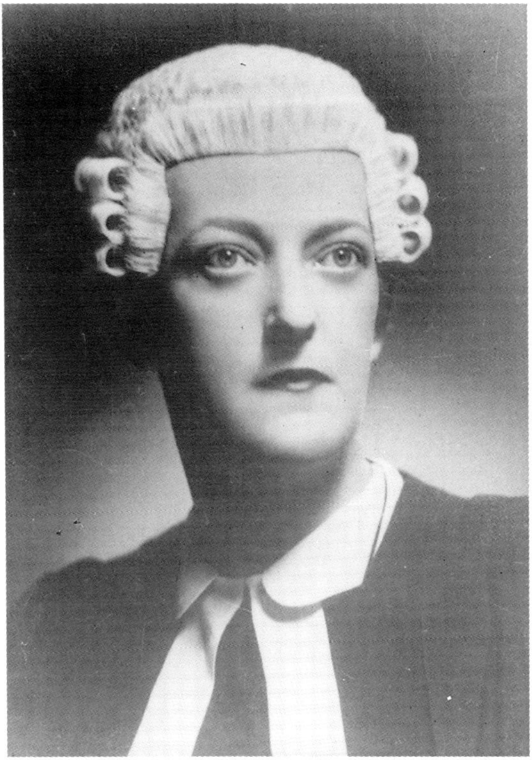

Studio portrait, 1933
(Photo: Law Society of WA)

Sheila and partner, Mollie Kingston, 1933
(Photo: Law Society of WA)

Chief Officer Sheila McClemans, OBE, 1945
(Photo: Mr Neil Kenworthy)

Major Frank Kenworthy, 1945
(Photo: Mr Neil Kenworthy)

Marching in the third rank (sixth from right) behind the colours at the Victory March, 1946
(Photo: Mr Arthur Cooper)

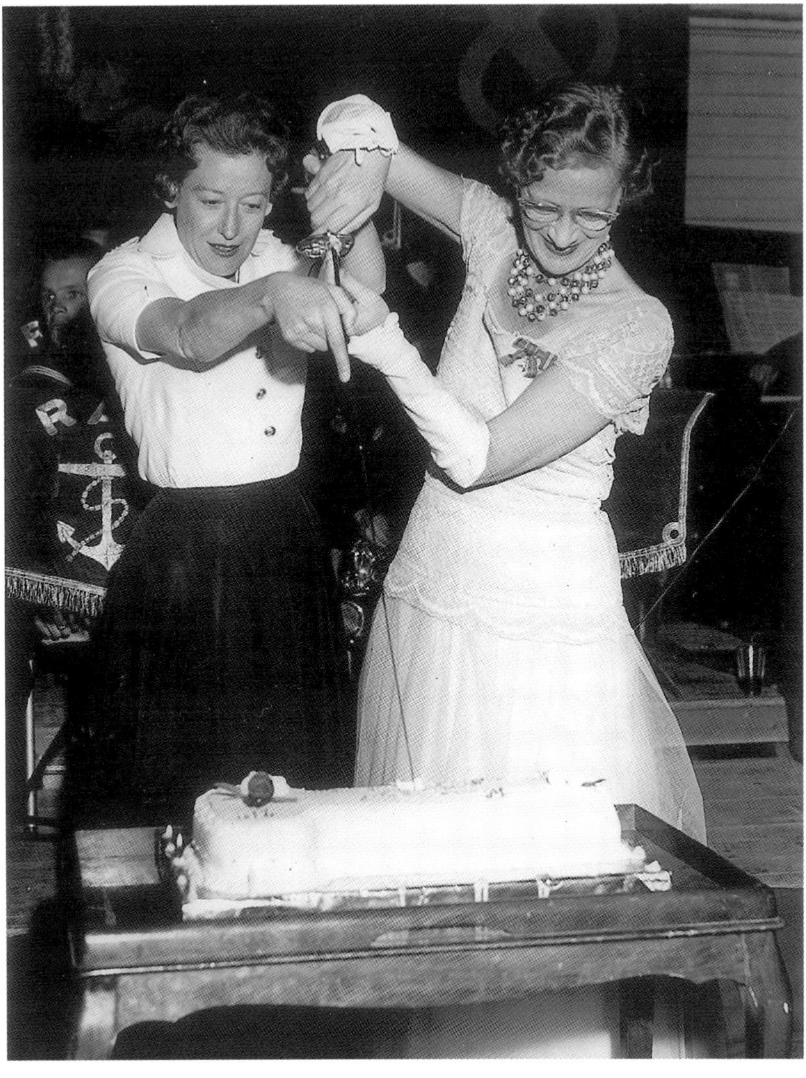

With WRANS Chief Officer Streeter, cutting birthday cake
at WRANS 21st Anniversary Ball, Flinders Naval Depot, 1963
(Photo: Mrs R Patterson)

As Secretary of the Law Society of WA, 1963
(Photo: Law Society of WA)

Frank and Sheila Kenworthy attending Royal Ball, Perth, 1954
(Photo: Mr Neil Kenworthy)

Celebrating her 50th year of practice, 1983
(Photo: Law Society of WA)

widow and gave her an open invitation to visit her Victoria Avenue flat. It was there that Patricia's romance with Monty developed, with Ada's encouragement. Patricia was grateful for this encouragement because her own mother opposed the marriage, claiming Monty to be too old for her. The wedding reception was held at the McClemans' flat and Sheila sent a message of congratulations from Melbourne.[32]

The quality of Sheila's relationship with Monty can be judged by the fact that Sheila went out socially with a number of other men during the period of their association. One affair was quite serious and greatly concerned both the family and Sheila's partner, Molly Kingston. The man involved, a member of one of the leading pastoral families, was married, but temporarily estranged from his wife. No one living knows how intimate that affair became but Paddy is certain that Sheila felt much more passion for her anonymous pastoralist than she did for Monty Mouatt.[33] She is also certain that Sheila's religious principles, which forbade ex-marital sex, would have prevented her from actually committing an act of adultery. The danger, however, was that others may draw an inference of guilt from indiscreet conduct.

According to a close personal friend, Erica Underwood,[34] Sheila finally broke off the affair at Molly's entreaties in fear of a scandal which would ruin the partnership.[35] This would not have been an exaggerated fear on Molly's part. In those days it was common for estranged husbands and wives to have each other followed by private detectives in the hope of catching the other in adultery, thus achieving a ground for a quick divorce. All that was needed was to produce evidence of circumstances from which adultery could be inferred. To catch a husband or wife in a parked car in a secluded spot at night with someone of the opposite sex would often be enough. Once the trap had been sprung divorce proceedings would follow and all the embarrassing details would eventually be published under raunchy headlines in the *Mirror*, a scurrilous weekend news-

32 Patricia Mouatt, from a personal interview.

33 Mrs Paddy McFadyen in a personal interview.

34 Mrs Erica Underwood, from a personal interview.

35 Neither Erica Underwood nor Paddy McFadyen would reveal the identity of the gentleman concerned.

paper of the time.[36] The *Mirror* focused upon a plebeian readership and took particular delight in exposing the decadent behaviour of the upper classes. One can imagine Molly, a devout Roman Catholic, awakening from nightmares of headlines like: "LADY BARRISTER IN SEX TRYST WITH SOUATTER".

Whilst it was not an activity for which a male practitioner could be disciplined, a very definite double standard operated in public life at that time and the all-male Barristers' Board may well have felt it appropriate to censure a female practitioner who was caught in adultery. There being no precedent for such an occurrence, it was certainly not worth risking. In any event, many of their more genteel clients would have been outraged by such conduct and taken their business away.

According to her sister, Paddy, Sheila did at that time have one very genuine romance with a young man named Alan Roe which could well have ended in marriage. Unfortunately, Alan joined the Air Force at the outbreak of war and was killed in action.[37]

Throughout the six years of its existence, the firm of Kingston and McClemans was carried on in the Royal Insurance Building at 133 Saint George's Terrace, one of a group of old sandstone fronted buildings the facades of which yet survive under the aegis of the National Trust. The practice never employed a permanent typist or any other full-time staff. Each partner did her own typing. It is not known how Molly learned to type but family sources report that Sheila learnt from a Pitman's teach-yourself book, practising on a second-hand portable Remington which she bought with her coaching money and which she used until the end of her days. In 1939 Sheila retired from the partnership to accept an offer of more lucrative employment. Looking back upon Kingston and McClemans after almost 50 years, Sheila's comments were:

> By that time the depression had deepened and there was nothing to do but start in practice and hope. . . We were, I suppose, fools rushing in where angels fear to tread. Anyway we survived. . .[38]

---

36 For an entertaining history of the *Mirror*, see Ron Davidson, *High Jinks At The Hot Pool*, Fremantle Arts Centre Press, 1994.

37 Mrs Paddy McFadyen in a personal interview.

38 C Shervington, *Sheila Mary McClemans: Oral History Memoir*, by courtesy University of WA archives, p 8.

In 1985 Molly Kingston was also called upon to say a few words about that historic partnership:

> Sheila McClemans and I qualified in the depth of the great depression and decided to practise in partnership as there seemed to be little if any prospect of employment. While not exactly a smashing success we continued into the early years of the war and were probably as well off financially as we would have been in employment. Sheila then went to Hardwick Slattery and Gibson and I went to Stone James and Co for a few years".[39]

By early 1939 it was obvious, even in isolated Perth, that war was inevitable. Travelling to work in public transport young men buried their noses in military training manuals and wore service uniforms on parade days. Uniformed teenage cadets cluttered the aisles lugging heavy Lee Enfield rifles along with their school bags, dangling side-arms slapping against the seats to the annoyance of their fellow passengers. At night searchlights followed slow droning *Wirraway* aircraft across the sky in practice runs.

The McClemans family gained some first-hand experience of the developing fascist threat. In 1938 Ada travelled to England to holiday with Dorothy and her husband, Col Sanders, who was then completing his PhD in London. Whilst overseas Ada toured Europe. In Italy she listened to Mussolini blustering one of his war-mongering harangues to a sycophantic mob in the Piazza di Venezia.

In Germany she came even closer to another of the dogs of war. In a Berlin street there was a sudden blare of martial music and much guttural shouting. People lined the kerb excitedly. Ada squeezed through to confront a procession of black Mercedes be-flagged with swastikas. Servile right arms shot up all along both sides of the road accompanied by cries of "Heil Hitler". A family friend asked for her reaction, Ada replied: "I put my arm up and called out 'Heil Hitler'. I was too scared to do anything else!".[40]

General re-armament and the demand for raw materials revived the Australian economy. This flowed on to the legal profession. Sheila's old firm offered her a place in its Fremantle office. Sheila

---

39 Fred M Robinson, "Mary (Molly) Connor Kingston", *Brief*, Law Society of Western Australia, 1985 Pt 12, pp 6, 11.

40 Mrs Paddy McFadyen in a personal interview.

accepted and retired from Kingston and McClemans. Molly carried on the firm into 1940, then wound it up when she accepted a position in the prestigious old firm of Stone James whose ranks had been depleted by enlistments into the armed forces.

Hardwick and Slattery had by now become Hardwick Slattery and Gibson with the entry of a former Crown Prosecutor and criminal law expert, Cliff Gibson, to the partnership. The kindly Mr Forman had died in 1934 and Sheila's new position probably would have been filled by John Forman's son, Clive, in accordance with the profession's traditional nepotism. Clive, however, abandoned the firm to become a professional air pilot soon after his father's death.

It was at the Fremantle office that Sheila first met one of her life-long friends, Constance Morgan, then a junior typist, aged 19. One incident recalled by Constance is typical of Sheila's kindness and consideration as an employer. Constance mentioned in conversation that she was taking the train to Bunbury for a long weekend. Coincidentally, the McClemans were also spending the weekend there. "You must come with us in my mother's car", Sheila insisted.

Readers of Dorothy Lucy's books would know that journeys in the mother-character's car are depicted as perilous ordeals because Mother talked incessantly to those in the back seat, looking over her shoulder as she did so and leaving the small Austin 10 to keep its own course along the road. Constance testifies that Ada McClemans drove exactly as depicted in the pages of her daughter's works. Constance, however, was too grateful for her hospitality to criticise and, in any event, she recalls that Ada never drove fast enough to put her in real fear. Sheila ultimately inherited that ancient vehicle, the only car she ever owned. She seldom drove it, however, as she had an aversion to driving, probably because she suffered chronic travel sickness all her life as well as a spinal disability incurred during her war service.[41]

According to Constance, Sheila took on the matrimonial law work of the office and was very heavily engaged in the Fremantle Married Persons' Relief Court for all of her time in the Port. This is not surprising, as the maritime work force contained many heavy

41 Mrs Constance Morgan, from a personal interview.

drinkers whose attitude towards their women left much to be desired. The young unmarried men of the town tended to adopt an irresponsible attitude to the young women they seduced – particularly if they were able to escape to sea before they could be compelled to recognise their illegitimate offspring. "Hillcrest", the Salvation Army hospital at North Fremantle, was one of the principal laying-in centres for unmarried mothers in Australia – many girls being sent thither from other States to "hide their shame" from the world during their confinements. A veritable adoption industry, centred around "Hillcrest", was a steady source of income for Fremantle's family lawyers.[42]

Family law at Petty Sessions level was both dreary and harrowing. It was dreary because it was repetitious, one case being so like the next. It was harrowing because the drunken abuse, the betrayals, the beatings, the failure to maintain, happened to real people – poor sad-eyed women and children. It must have been something of a relief to Sheila when occasionally a matter like *Garnaut v Rowse*[43] took her from the lower depths of the Married Women's Relief Court to the forensic heights of the Supreme Court.

The defendant, Rowse, was patently what in those days would have been called a cad and a bounder. He had married the plaintiff, Mrs Garnaut, who was at that time a widow, assuring her that he was a divorcee. He was, in fact, still married to another woman. The lawful wife died and, somehow, Mrs Garnaut learnt the truth of his deceit. She demanded that he go through a second marriage with her to legalise their union. Not only did he refuse but he left her and married another woman – but not before he had extracted a loan of £102 3s 4d from Mrs Garnaut.

It seems Rowse made a habit of such deception and extortion. The trial judge (Northmore CJ) was quite scathing in his judgment:

> From all points of view the plaintiff was fortunate that her marriage to the defendant was not a valid one, because judging from the life history of the defendant, so far as we know it, legally married or not,

42 Sheila would not at that time have called herself a "family lawyer". The expression is a comparatively recent euphemism, not in common use in Western Australia before the 1970s. Those who specialised in the field before that time were referred to as "divorce" or "matrimonial" lawyers.

43 *Garnaut v Rowse* (1941) 42 WALR 29.

> he would not have hesitated to desert her as soon as he got all he could out of her and had some other confiding female with money at her command. It is in evidence that he deserted his wife in New South Wales, and cleared out with another woman to New Zealand. Whether he went through the form of marriage with her we do not know. He says he did not, so it is probable that he did, but in any event he lived with her as man and wife for some time. In the meantime he had succeeded in obtaining £700 from her for which, after he had deserted her, she sued and recovered judgment.[44]

Garnaut v Rowse was reported in the WALR because it involved some important legal principles. The plaintiff sued for breach of promise of marriage – a cause of action widely publicised by Gilbert and Sullivan in *Trial By Jury* but now abolished in Australia by the *Family Law Act* 1975. In the alternative, the plaintiff claimed damages for an implied breach of warranty that he was free to marry and further, in the alternative for deceit, there was also an additional claim for money lent, Mr Rowse having run true to form and borrowed over £100 from Mrs Garnaut during the course of the "marriage".

It was as well that these alternative claims were included in the writ because the Chief Justice held, with some logic, that one cannot get damages for breach of a contract which was impossible to perform at the time of its making. However, he was clearly on the plaintiff's side and awarded her £200 damages for deceit – which would have been more than a year's wages for a working woman at that time. Rowse was also ordered to repay the money lent by Mrs Garnaut.

History does not record whether the plaintiff ever recovered any part of her judgment. The Chief Justice plainly had his doubts about her chances, observing that a heavier verdict "would probably prove a barren one".[45] Perhaps the other woman paid Rowse's debts for him. If so the victory could have been just as sweet for the jilted Mrs Garnaut.

Any residual fears Sheila might have held appearing before her old ogre, Northmore CJ, would have been allayed in *Rowse* because she acted as junior counsel to Cliff Gibson who did all the major counsel work for the firm. According to Leo Wood, Sheila often

44 Ibid, at 33.

45 Ibid, at 33.

juniored Cliff in Supreme Court trials. She would have found this experience both instructive and enjoyable.

Cliff Gibson, who was about ten years her senior, was a very able advocate; he was also a witty and attractive personality. He looked at his best when he was robed and bewigged because he was totally bald, his bullet shaped skull deeply suntanned from weekends spent boating and fishing. When he rose to address a jury, tugging his robes about his squat but powerful frame, there was always an air of expectancy in the court both because of his reputation as a wit and the sense of character his movements and his mischievous smile exuded even in the tensest of trials.

Cliff rejected all legal pomposity. His speech was forthright and direct. He was always approachable by younger practitioners and encouraged them to call him by his Christian name. Sheila, however, always addressed him as "Sir" and continued to do so throughout her legal career, even on social occasions. This was probably due to the senior partner, Mr Hardwick, who, although a most charming man, conducted himself as an English gentleman should and presumably expected such standards of others – especially his staff. As an articled clerk Sheila would have been expected to call her superiors "Sir" and she would have continued to observe the protocol when she rejoined the firm as an employed practitioner. The influence of both these men could be discerned in Sheila's own professional conduct and demeanour. She was always a stickler for the rules of professional ethics and etiquette, good manners and proper deference to those in authority. Yet in her dealings with others, fellow practitioners, staff or general public, she was direct, casual – except when the occasion demanded a sterner edge – and markedly preferred colloquial speech to polysyllabic legal jargon. She spoke as an educated Australian with no trace of the artificial upper class "English" accent affected by many middle class women of her time.

Both Sheila and Cliff shared a strong sense of humour. They must have had great fun conducting *Garnaut v Rowse* which, judging from his comments on Rowse's character, even provided some amusement for the irascible Sir John Northmore. Sheila demonstrated her gratitude to Cliff by making a gift of her old academic gown to his son, Athol, when he started at Law School in 1940.

At the beginning of 1942, Sheila accepted an offer of a part-time lectureship at the Law School. The war situation became so ominous, however, that all potential students were drafted for national service, forcing the temporary closure of the Law School, as a result of which the position lapsed.[46]

Hardwick Slattery and Gibson continued to employ Sheila until the end of 1942 when she resigned to join the Women's Royal Australian Naval Service (WRANS) which was then in the process of formation. According to Mrs McFadyen, the firm did not react with patriotic generosity when she gave notice. One of the partners told her she need not expect to get her job back after the war if she persisted with her resignation.[47] The reluctance of the firm to agree to Sheila's enlistment seems to have been a matter of some notoriety at the time because the Vice-Chancellor of the University, Professor Currie, recalled in a reference dated 26 October 1945, "Her work was of such great value that I can assure you the firm concerned was most loath to lose her services when she decided to go into the Navy".[48]

Mrs McFadyen was not told which partner threatened Sheila with future ostracism. It was certainly not Cliff Gibson because he had already taken leave from the firm to join the forces. In March 1942 he achieved some fame as Town Major of Broome when it was raided by the Japanese air force and he became temporary custodian of many thousands of pounds worth of diamonds salvaged from a downed Dutch aircraft.

Molly Kingston followed Sheila's lead and enlisted. She took a commission in the Women's Australian Auxiliary Air Force (WAAF) in 1943 and left Western Australia for Sydney. Upon her discharge she served as General Secretary of the Australian Institute of International Affairs for three years. She then took up residence in Victoria and practised as a solicitor until 1962 when she joined Joan Rosanove at the Victorian Bar and thereafter enjoyed a distinguished career until she retired in 1978. In 1975 she became a consultant to

46 Application to Women's College within the University of Sydney for appointment as Principal, dated 1 December 1945: archives call Series 8/4.

47 Mrs Paddy McFadyen in a personal interview.

48 Reference supplied with Application to Women's College within the University of Sydney for appointment as Principal, dated 1 December 1945: archives call Series 8/4.

the Commonwealth Government to advise upon the establishment of the Family Court of Australia.[49] According to her close friend, Erica Underwood, she was approached to become its first Chief Justice but declined on account of her age.[50] She died in 1991.

49 Fred M Robinson, "Mary (Molly) Connor Kingston", *Brief*, Law Society of Western Australia, 1985 Pt 12.

50 Mrs Erica Underwood, in a personal interview.

5

"I WAS A WRAN"

Historically, the Australian attitude to military service for women was even more patriarchal than that to women in the professions. It has been estimated that there were about a dozen women practising law in Western Australia at the beginning of 1941.[1] There were then no women in the defence forces, other than nurses, even though by this time Australia had been at war for 16 months and Australian troops were locked in battle with Mussolini's forces in North Africa.[2]

Also, at this time, the Japanese were overtly mustering their forces to conquer South-East Asia, having already occupied a substantial part of China. Until the Japanese began their wide-spread offensive on 8 December 1941, the attitude of Australian officialdom towards the female defence role was still that expressed by the Minister for Defence on the 27 February 1938:

> It is considered that the general manpower available for the Armed Forces is sufficient to obviate any great demand for the utilisation of women's services in the way of substitution for men in the early stages of war.[3]

As a result of this policy, women eager to serve their country had no role other than as members of part-time amateur service groups. At the outbreak of war in September 1939, many lawyers of military age

---

1 Jon Faine, Australian Broadcasting Commission's *Law Report*, broadcast 16 January 1991.

2 For the history of the enrolment of women in the Australian Defence Forces, see Patsy Adam-Smith, *Australian Women at War*, Thomas Nelson, 1980.

3 Ibid, p 139.

enlisted in the Services with the consequence that those who stayed behind had plenty of work and opportunity to advance their careers. Women lawyers, with no option but to remain civilians, were initially presented with ideal conditions in which to thrive and were even told they were "doing more good by staying at home and minding the fort".[4]

The Japanese attack forced Australia onto a full war-footing and all but essential civilian commercial activity was phased out. This eased the demand for legal services and Sheila was glad she need no longer prosper at the expense of her male contemporaries.[5] She described how she resolved this dilemma to historian Patsy Adam-Smith some 40 years afterwards:

> Men were going to the war, and I suppose I was getting more opportunities at the Bar than perhaps I would have done otherwise. But it was no use I, too, wanted to go to war, or at least to serve.
>
> In 1942, I saw an advertisement in the morning paper for women to train as officers – if suitable – in the WRANS. I thought they were looking for someone here in Perth for *HMAS Leeuwin*. When I arrived for interview I found they were looking for a Director for the whole Service! There were three terrifying naval officers doing the interview. They gave no indication that I was of any value or that they could tolerate any woman at all getting into their Service.[6]

Sheila's assessment of her interrogators was probably quite accurate. The Navy was the most resistant of the three services to the induction of women. Although a small group of female telegraphists had been enrolled in March 1941, the Women's Royal Australian Naval Service (WRANS) was not formally constituted until 24 July 1942 as compared with the Women's Australian Auxiliary Air Force (WAAAF) (9 June 1941) and the Australian Women's Army Service (AWAS) (13 August 1941). It had no commissioned officers of its own – except a very temporary First Officer – until the completion of its first Training Course in February 1943.

---

4 C Shervington, *Sheila Mary McClemans: Oral History Memoir*, by courtesy University of WA archives, p 10.

5 Ibid.

6 Adam-Smith, *Australian Women at War*, Thomas Nelson, 1980, p 213.

The extraordinary circumstances of the appointment and forced retirement of its initial First Officer may have reinforced the Naval bureaucracy's initial suspicion of the reliability of women. There were actually two advertisements seeking WRANS officers in 1942. The first, which appeared in all daily newspapers from 20-21 October, specifically sought applicants for the post of First Officer; it stipulated the following requirements:

- A Leaving [Matriculation] Certificate
- University Study [sic]
- Proved organising capacity
- Business experience and training

Sheila responded to this advertisement enclosing two excellent references, one from Ross McDonald KC, MLA, who had taught her in Law School, and the other from her old family friend, Lieutenant Colonel Henry Moseley, who took leave from the Bench to assume the post of Deputy Director of Military Security.[7] The following extract from Ross McDonald's letter contains a fascinating example of totally unconscious sexism, typical of the time:

> She is possessed of really good abilities and a temperament which I am sure would enable her to secure the best results from those working with and under her. I know that for some years she has been Secretary of the Infant Health Association and more latterly Vice President of that Association. She has had an exceptional business experience *for a woman* [emphasis added] and knowledge of business and administrative matters, and should be well fitted for an executive position in which organising ability is required.

Lt Colonel Moseley's reference is a testimony to the value of her services to Hardwick Slattery and Gibson and underlines their reluctance to release her:

> She holds the Degrees of BA and LLB. She practised her profession successfully in Perth for some six years and then joined the firm of Messers Hardwick Slattery and Gibson, in which firm she has held and still holds a very senior position... She possesses a wide knowledge and, in my opinion, is eminently fitted for an administrative post in the Navy...

7 Lt Colonel Moseley served on the Western Front in the Great War as a subaltern in the 28th Infantry Battalion AIF.

Notwithstanding Sheila's imposing references and outstanding academic qualifications, she was not even placed on the short list of 12 potential First Officers. From that list, to its ultimate public embarrassment, the Navy selected one, Annette Oldfield, who seemed to have the most desirable qualities.

Miss Oldfield had attended the University of Western Australia without, however, completing a degree, and had completed a non-graduate course in salesmanship at the University of Pittsburg in the United States. The Pittsburg course enabled her to get a position as staff training officer in Myer's Emporium, Melbourne. In addition to her university studies and her business experience, Miss Oldfield was President of the YWCA Business Girls Group and had achieved notable success in organising a war charity known as the Lady Gowrie Drive which had raised a large amount of money.

Annette Oldfield was duly installed as First Officer to considerable acclaim in the daily press and began with great energy to tour the country recruiting personnel to enlist as "WRANS", as they came to be known in popular speech. She appointed as her assistant a young WRAN, Driver Mary Butler, who experienced at first hand the disastrous days of Oldfield's brief command.

Mary Butler had interrupted an Arts course at the University of Adelaide and a brilliant amateur tennis career to join the WRANS at its first intake in July 1942. She had progressed through a number of crash courses to become senior WRAN at the Adelaide depot, *HMAS Torrens*, but had been accorded no rank other than that of Driver. She answered the October advertisement and applied for the position of First Officer only to be advised in due course that she was not successful. Unknown to her, she was in fact ranked third on the short list.

Annette Oldfield must have been told of the Selection Board's high opinion of Mary's potential because she had her transferred to Melbourne and introduced her to the Second Naval Officer and other high ranking naval personnel. Mary assumed that this was in recognition of her good conduct and course marks since her enlistment, not being aware of her ranking on the short list.[8]

---

8 She remained ignorant of this distinction until 1992 when the author found the short list on the Oldfield archival file.

Oldfield also arranged to have Mary measured for a uniform to replace the "RAANS" arm band which, worn over civilian clothing, was the only official item of service dress for WRANS at that stage. It seems obvious that Oldfield had a significant role planned for Mary in her recruiting campaign.

One can imagine Mary Butler's dismay when she reported for duty at Naval Headquarters, Melbourne, on the morning of 13 December 1942 to be met with the puzzled query from the Lieutenant Commander in charge of recruiting, "What have you done with your boss?". The *Melbourne Age* had reported that morning that Oldfield had been asked to resign and that she was currently in hospital suffering a nervous breakdown.[9] It concluded that the Minister for the Navy advised that her resignation had been accepted and that he was not prepared to discuss reasons at that stage. Nor at any stage it seems. No further official public statement was ever made and the whole pathetic affair was privately interred in the Commonwealth archives.[10]

The archival file on the matter indicates that, in her application, Oldfield had claimed that she had studied Science at the University of Western Australia and had followed this with postgraduate study in the United States. This was duly reported in the national press including the Perth *Daily News* in its issue of 16 November 1942.[11] On 18 November 1942 Dr Colsell Sanders, in his capacity of Registrar of the University of Western Australia, wrote a letter to the Secretary for the Department of the Navy as follows:

> The attached photograph and letter press appeared in the Daily News on Monday the 16th of November. I do not know whether the details regarding Miss Oldfield have been incorrectly reported but after discussing the matter with the Vice Chancellor I desire to inform you that we have no record of any such person graduating in this University.[12]

---

9 *The Age*, Melbourne, 13 December 1942.

10 The Oldfield File is held in the Melbourne repository of the Australian Archives. The involvement of the late Mrs Mary Howard (née Butler) in the Oldfield matter has been recounted in a number of personal interviews which Mrs Howard kindly granted the author before her death on 14 September 1993. Her invaluable assistance with many other aspects of Sheila's naval career is gratefully acknowledged.

11 *The Daily News*, Perth, 16 November 1942.

12 Oldfield file, held in the Melbourne repository of the Australian Archives.

The letter enclosed a press cutting which ran a photograph of First Officer Oldfield, reported her appointment and added that she had studied Science at the University of Western Australia with postgraduate study in the USA. The next item on the file is a letter from Oldfield addressed to Commodore GD Moore, 2nd Naval Member, Navy Office, Melbourne:

> In view of the fact which is to my discredit and known to you Sir, I hereby tender my resignation as First Officer WRANS. May I be permitted to express, Sir, to you and to the Naval Board my most sincere and very humble apologies for such a dishonourable action. Will you please state the time I am to be released of my duties Sir?[13]

In fairness to Oldfield it should be noted that the requirements of the official advertisement only stipulated a "university education" and not a university degree. This may have been bad drafting on the part of the Navy Office but, literally, Oldfield's uncompleted Science course at the University of Western Australia certainly qualified her to claim that she had a university education. Had she merely stated that she had attended the University of Western Australia and later the University of Pittsburg there would have been no deception and, one would think, no letter from Dr Sanders to the Secretary to the Navy.

It was Oldfield's reference to having done a postgraduate course in the United States which led to her undoing. A postgraduate course implies that one has graduated, which Oldfield had not, and the Navy Office took the view that this was a deliberate deception. As the holding of a degree was not expressed as a necessary qualification, it was hardly a deception that went to the essence of the appointment. At the most it was a false exaggeration of her qualifications and well within commercial ethics at least. It was not good enough for the Navy, however, and Oldfield obviously realised there was no point in arguing. Her last written comment upon the subject appears to have been a letter she sent Mary Howard from her hospital bed in which she thanked her for a bunch of flowers Mary had sent her and urged her to "give the Service the best you've got".[14]

13 Ibid.

14 Letter in possession of the estate of the Late Mrs Mary Howard.

A rumour current at the time in Western Australia suggested that Colsell Sanders blew the whistle on Oldfield because he was miffed that she had won the post his sister-in-law had set her heart on. There is no evidence to support this and it is an unworthy allegation. The appointment was to a very important post involving national security and much public prominence was given to it. Oldfield was a contemporary of Sanders and her short attendance at the University of Western Australia must have coincided with his own student days, either as an undergraduate or during his postgraduate studies. In the small pre-war campus community he would have known her, at least by name, and known that she had dropped-out.

According to solicitor Geoffrey White, a contemporary of Oldfield, she was quite well known in Perth in the 1930s, being the manager of the Perth Radiological Clinic, the city's only private x-ray practice and active in the party-going social scene.[15] Sanders would have been well aware, without even having to check his records, that Oldfield was not a graduate and that the press item was incorrect. Had he not noticed the news item personally, others would have brought it to his notice. It should be remembered that one of Sheila's referees was the Deputy Director of Military Security whose staff was obliged to scan the daily press with microscopic care and, if necessary, censor it in the national interest.

It was simply not possible for a glaring misstatement of that sort to be made in a Perth newspaper of those days and pass unnoticed. Immediately that item was brought to the notice of the Registrar of the University he had a public duty to take the action he did. That this action had a decisive effect upon his sister-in-law's future was simply a historic co-incidence made slightly more probable, perhaps, by the compact nature of the Western Australian academic community.

The resignation of First Officer Oldfield left the WRANS with no officers at all. Instead of selecting one of the short-listed earlier applicants, the Department of the Navy decided to subject its potential First Officer and all others of commissioned rank to an intense scrutiny under field conditions. A second press advertisement appeared on Boxing Day 1942. Under a banner headline,

15 In a personal interview.

"WRANS URGENTLY REQUIRED", it called upon all Australian women, married or single, between the ages of 18 and 40, to volunteer for "The Senior Service".

The advertisement listed a whole range of categories from cooks to telegraphists, the majority of whom would undergo initial training at the Victorian shore-based establishment, *HMAS Cerberus.* This establishment, also known as Flinders Naval Depot and commonly shortened to "Flinders", was situated on Western Port Bay on the eastern shore of Mornington Peninsula, some 80 kilometres south east of Melbourne.

It is easy to detect the spectre of the Oldfield debacle in the provisions regarding promotion to commissioned rank: "All recruits will be eligible for selection for officer training courses. WRANS officers will be appointed only from the ranks".[16]

According to an article published in the extinct commercial throw-away, *Living Today*, dated 23 February 1978, Sheila recalled volunteering in response to this advertisement. She was prepared to serve in any capacity, not necessarily as an officer.[17] She never referred to the October advertisement nor its unhappy *sequelae* in any of her naval reminiscences, nor is the subject mentioned by either Margaret Curtis-Offer or Patsy Adam-Smith in their histories of the WRANS. Sheila was intensely proud of the WRANS and may have thought that the incident was best forgotten. She described her own feelings about her enlistment in her *Oral History Memoir*:

> We were very strongly imbued with the idea that we fought this war you know with man, woman and child helping or we wouldn't have a place to live in. We didn't feel at any time that we were hardly done by, although sometimes we had very rigorous conditions. We thought that was the least we could do.[18]

After a four-day rail trip across the Continent, Sheila joined the rest of the training course at Flinders Street Station in Melbourne on 16 January 1943. Mary Butler was also selected for the course and met

---

16 National Department of the Navy advertisement inserted in all Australian dailies, 26 December 1942 (*West Australian*, p 4).

17 *Living Today,* Perth, p 21.

18 C Shervington, *Sheila Mary McClemans: Oral History Memoir*, by courtesy University of WA archives, p 11.

Sheila at the station. She remembered her as a tall athletic figure wearing a purple dress with a wide-brimmed white hat and looking decidedly travel weary. The *Oral History* tells Sheila's recollection of the encounter:

> The first part was absolutely harrowing. I'd never even been to a boarding school. I got on a train here with two other girls, who were recruits, travelled second class in the most cramped and dreadful conditions to Melbourne, from there down to Flinders Naval Depot . . . we were met at the little Crib Point railway station by a gunner's mate and he said "Fall in, tallest on the right, shortest on the left". And automatically I and a girl called Margaret Curtis-Offer went to the top of the rank, we were used to being the tallest in any crocodile.
>
> We went through a terribly rigorous officers' training course. Later they carved it down a bit. At that stage of course no one really knew how much women could take and they really did make it a bit strong. . .[19]

Although Sheila had kept up her swimming and tennis on a social basis and was reasonably fit, she had no experience at all in marching or parade ground manoeuvres. A number of women on the course, like Mary Butler, had served in the WRANS since October and had drilled with its predecessor, the part-time Women's Auxiliary Naval Service (WANS), before that. It is a recognised service technique to gear the tempo of training courses to the standard of its most able members to ensure that a ruthless weeding out process will operate. It is no wonder that Sheila found the going tough and was pessimistic about her chances. She told a Melbourne newspaper on the eve of her discharge from the Service in 1947: "At the training school I felt out of my depth. I was amazed at the Navy's staggering efficiency and never thought I would be able to reach the required standards".[20]

In the event Sheila came third in the course results. Top of the class was Frances Provan, whose service number was WRAN 1, she having enlisted as a naval telegraphist in 1941 before the WRANS was officially formed. Mary Butler came second. When the course

---

19 Ibid, p 10.

20 *Melbourne Sun*, 24 January 1947.

finished Sheila and Mary, now close friends, were kept at *Cerberus* to train the next intake. After several months together at *Cerberus*, Mary began to appreciate Sheila's leadership potential and could see that the senior officers did also. She expected that Sheila would eventually become Director of the Service.[21]

Whatever its initial assessment of Sheila's qualities, the Department of the Navy was slow in according recognition. Sheila was awarded the low commissioned rank of probationary Third Officer and kept at *Cerberus* for three months on training duties when, in May 1943, she was appointed to the Navy Office as Staff Officer WRANS, and then only with the rank of Second Officer. She was not made Director with the rank of First Officer until August 1944. In contrast, the Directors of the WAAAF and the AWAS had been appointed to their posts in June 1941 and September 1941 respectively and in each case with a higher comparative rank.[22]

Because of her low rank, Sheila was not provided with a staff car to attend formal functions. On the frequent occasions that she visited *Cerberus* from Navy Office in Melbourne, she was expected to catch a train to the halfway point at Frankston where a car would come from the Depot to meet her. As senior female officer in charge of the WRANS training programme at *Cerberus*, Mary Butler always met Sheila at Frankston. On those journeys to and from Frankston they would combine the business of discussing Service affairs with the pleasure of friendly re-union.

Despite the inconvenience of the journey, Sheila visited *Cerberus* whenever she could. She had formed an attachment to the place during her initial three months stay there and referred to it as her "Navy home". She had more than sentimental reasons for visiting *Cerberus*, however. All WRANS from Victoria had to pass through their initial training period at Flinders and Sheila appreciated the importance to the quality of the Service of that training. However busy her official programme, she never missed a *Cerberus* passing-out parade.

Sheila had a passion to serve the Navy. A significant group of her rank and file and the constant flow of new recruits, the future

---

21 Mary Howard, personal interview.

22 Adam-Smith, *Australian Women at War*, above, pp 229, 250.

potential of the Service which it was her duty to create and lead, were at *Cerberus*. Here she could observe their activities and their environment at first hand. Always solicitous of her staff Sheila knew that, for the Service to work efficiently, its living and working conditions had to be congenial. The Navy had been an all male organisation and had no idea of the special needs of women, particularly as regards food, clothing and accommodation. One example was the Navy's practice of serving stew for breakfast. It seems that the WRANS found this totally unpalatable and Sheila prevailed upon the catering authorities to change it.

Although the Navy did not appoint Sheila to be a social worker she took personal responsibility to ensure that the Navy adapted its ways to ensure the reasonable comfort of her troops – including changes in the menu. At least two of her senior officers believe that her failure to achieve higher rank was due to the fact that she devoted her time to serving others and gave no thought to promoting herself. If that was so, she was simply doing what a good lawyer is supposed to do – concentrating on the job in hand and putting the interests of the client first.

Once the WRANS was established, *Cerberus* was its place of greatest concentration in Victoria, about five hundred being stationed there at any time, including trainee officers. It supplied Sheila with an important public relations unit, a detachment of young women who could put on a display of precision marching at a moment's notice. This detachment marched on every official parade through wartime Melbourne.

Cerberus also produced its problems. In addition to the five hundred young women, there was also a shifting population of three thousand men, many of whom were imbued with the traditional sailor's philosophy of loving and leaving. In that part of *Australian Women at War*, indexed under the heading "Sex: Attitudes To", Patsy Adam-Smith quotes Sheila as follows:

> All women were unsophisticated by today's standards. A naval officer took a shine to one of our girls and swept her off her feet. This man was ill with psychological problems and had been put ashore for this reason but no one spoke of it. That girl should have been taken aside and told. No one could expect a girl of that period to recognise what this man could be capable of.

> There was no social security. Churches would hide girls. There is no other word for it. The Salvos had a hard wooden table with oil cloth on it and hard wooden chairs. "They have to be taught their lesson", I was told. The Church of England had a shabby house in Melbourne. A few were well ahead of their time, even encouraged girls to wash themselves and put make-up on. It doesn't sound much today but that was really forward thinking then. Clare Stevenson (Director WAAAF) and I had decided to do something about it. We saw a chance when they were having trouble with women in munitions. The Social Service Director extended assistance to girls who had been scorned previously. At least it was the beginning to the end of a sorry period that had scarred numberless young girls.[23]

Other senior officers in the Women's Services found Sheila's legal experience – particularly in the family law field – of great value. Seducers were brought to boot by the issue of paternity summonses and not just for pregnant WRANS. The AWAS alone suffered 500 unmarried wartime pregnancies and both the AWAS and WAAAF directors obtained occasional legal advice and guidance from Sheila.[24]

Sheila's care for WRANS in trouble was often personal as well as administrative. One WRAN, embarrassed because her unwanted pregnancy was becoming obvious, was brought into the privacy of Sheila's office and found work there until her confinement. One of her office staff returned somewhat distressed from a session with an unsympathetic naval dentist. Sheila sent her off to bed and shortly after brought in a hot water bottle to comfort her. There are many similar anecdotes of such instances of Sheila's personal kindness which became a legend among the WRANS. The feeling of the ratings was summed up by a WRAN driver in a news report on Sheila's retirement in 1947:

> Chief Officer McClemans is rated one hundred percent by all of us. If she orders a car she always sits in front, offers you a cigarette and is not a bit stand-offish. She is the most approachable person I know.[25]

---

23 Ibid, pp 288-289.

24 Mary Howard, personal interview.

25 Interview in Melbourne Sun 24 January 1947.

Sheila's involvement in the personal life of her WRANS was not always in a trouble-shooting capacity. It must have been a pleasant interlude for her when she attended the wedding of Lieutenant Commander WE Howard RANR(S) to her friend, Second Officer Mary Butler, on 8 September 1944 in the Wesley Church, Melbourne. Coincidentally Lieutenant Commander Howard, as Officer of the Day, had received that first WRANS Officers' Training Course (including Sheila and Mary) when it entered *Cerberus* on 16 January 1943.

What is remarkable about Sheila's care and attention to personal detail is that it was expended over and above her official duties. What the Navy expected her to do was to direct the enrolment, training, discipline and provision of some 3000 young women in a wide range of specialties including signallers, radio-operators, telegraphists, coders, cooks, stewards, de-gaussers, gunnery markers, drivers, coast watchers, sick-bay attendants, clerks, map makers, boarding officers and even motor cyclists.

These women had to be placed in depots and out posts from Townsville to Geraldton. Towards the end of the war some were even stationed in Darwin. It was a tremendous responsibility, not simply because of the organisational task involved, but because the plans of the Naval Staff had constantly to be transposed to adjust to the fact that the personnel being organised were women – a fact which the all-male higher echelons frequently overlooked.

WRANS were not sent to operational areas such as Darwin until after hostilities ceased. Only one WRAN served overseas during the war, Third Officer Ruby Boye, a coast-watcher, who was already in a war zone when the war overtook her, and who was given official status in the hope her life would be spared should she be captured. The ban on overseas service was particularly galling for those who were working in close liaison with the Americans because, when the Pacific war moved victoriously northwards, American service women took their places and embarked with the units Australian WRANS had previously supported loyally and with affection.

The WRANS was eager to serve overseas and Sheila pleaded the case for it to do so. She was met by the traditionally archaic attitude of the Australian male establishment and her plea was rejected:

"Mr Makin, Minister for the Navy, thought we would be raped if we were to do so. So we were banned".[26]

The many scattered establishments meant constant travel, a great deal of it by air. Monty Mouatt recalls Sheila waving farewell from a Catalina flying boat at the wartime base on the banks of the Swan River near the University.

According to one apocryphal anecdote, Sheila was flying from Darwin to Perth with a group of officers when the pilot reported that he had to shut down one engine. He explained that he was near the point of no return and wanted to know whether to go on or turn back. Sheila suggested they all consult their palms for the length of their collective "life-lines". She then made a quick assessment. "They all look pretty long. Let's go on", she counselled.

A problem about all these journeys was that Sheila suffered congenital travel sickness whatever the form of transport. Only her close friends knew of this and she never held back or complained. Margaret Curtis-Offer paid this tribute to her dedication:

> The amount of travelling done by the Director would in peace-time have seemed excessive even to one smitten with the wanderlust. In war-time, under service conditions, long journeys became tests of endurance; the thousands of miles travelled by train and plane were tiring to the point of exhaustion, . . . [she] placed service before self to the detriment, ultimately, of her health.[27]

That Sheila did the job the Navy entrusted her and did it magnificently was acknowledged by Rear-Admiral Moore in his introduction to Curtis-Offer's book *WRANS*:

> I know the great worth of the 3000 WRANS who took over so many and varied tasks, and thereby released the equivalent number of men who were used to man ships and bases abroad, and thus helped very materially in the ultimate defeat of our enemies . . . in my opinion the success of the WRANS was largely due to Sheila McClemans. Her untiring interest in the health of every WRAN, her kindness, and perhaps above all her sound common sense made her the ideal Director.

---

26 Adam-Smith, *Australian Women At War*, p 215.

27 Margaret Curtis-Offer, *WRANS*, Naval Historical Society of Sydney, 1975, p 26.

> The RAN was very proud of its Sister Service and very grateful for its assistance.[28]

When the Japanese surrendered on 15 August 1945, the question of peace-time re-employment in civilian life became the major concern of almost a million service personnel, Sheila among them. On 1 December 1945, in response to a call for applicants for the position of Principal of the Women's College in the University of Sydney, she wrote the following letter of application from the WRANS Directorate, Navy Office Melbourne:

> Dear Madam,
>
> I wish to apply for the position of Principal of the Women's College within the University of Sydney.
>
> I am thirty-six years of age and unmarried.
>
> I received my education at Perth Modern School and the University of Western Australia where I obtained the degree of Bachelor of Laws in 1931 and Bachelor of Arts in 1933. The following subjects were taken with the respective passes shown:
>
> English I (Pass)
>
> French I (Pass)
>
> Mathematics I (Distinction)
>
> Physics I (Distinction)
>
> History A (Major Pass)
>
> History B (Major Pass)
>
> Modern Political Institutions (Major Pass)
>
> English II (Major Pass)
>
> Mathematics II (Distinction)
>
> Roman Law (Major Pass)
>
> Contracts and Personal Property (Distinction)
>
> Real Property and Conveyancing (Pass)
>
> Criminal Law & Torts (Distinction)
>
> Sources and History of Law (Distinction)

28 Ibid, Introduction.

Practice & Procedure (Pass)

Equity & Company Law (Pass)

Private International Law (Distinction)

Evidence & Legal Interpretation (Distinction)

Constitutional Law (Distinction)

I was admitted to the Bar in 1933 and practised law for approximately nine years in Western Australia.

I joined the Navy in January 1943 and became the Director of the Women's Royal Australian Naval Service with the ultimate rank of Chief Officer. In that capacity I have been responsible for the organisation of the Service, for the morale and well-being of its personnel, and for advising the Naval Board on all matters affecting this responsibility, as, for example, pay and conditions of service, accommodation, messing, recruiting, and the selection, appointments and promotions of officers. I still hold this office.

If I were appointed to this position I would like the opportunity to lecture and to do tutorial work in Law. I was asked by the University of Western Australia after the outbreak of war to lecture in the Law School but a subsequent decision to close the Law School temporarily prevented my doing so.

It is not clear to me from the particulars given concerning the appointment whether you are seeking someone with greater academic qualifications than I have, or whether you are seeking someone with administrative experience. My reason for applying is that, in the practice of my profession, in the experience gained in a number of philanthropic organisations during my civilian life, and particularly during my service life, I have felt an increasing desire to assist, as far as I am able to do so, in the guidance of young people, and through them in the development of this country I enclose six copies of reference from the following:

1. Lt Colonel HD Moseley – Chief Magistrate and, during the War, Director of Security Services in WA

2. Mr Ross McDonald KC

3. Professor RG Currie

> I enclose also six copies of the report received by me from Rear-Admiral GD Moore when he relinquished his appointment as Second Naval Member.
>
> I hold the originals.
>
> Yours faithfully,
>
> Sheila McClemans.[29]

The references from McDonald QC and Lt Colonel Moseley were copies of those provided in 1942 on Sheila's initial application to enlist. Rear Admiral Moore's report was dated 14 October 1944 – more than a year before the application – and appears to be a routine Service document not directed to any projected move by Sheila, notwithstanding which it concludes in glowing terms: "The success of WRANS is due almost entirely to the great keenness ability, wisdom and judgment of this officer, in whom I have complete confidence".[30]

Professor Currie's reference was written in his capacity of Vice-Chancellor of the University of Western Australia. It is dated 26 October 1945 – five weeks earlier than Sheila's letter of application – and is not on the face of it directed specifically to the Women's College application. It is equally laudatory:

> TO WHOM IT MAY CONCERN
>
> This is to certify to the academic distinction and personal excellence of Miss Sheila McClemans an Honours graduate of this University.
>
> Miss McClemans had a highly distinguished academic record while studying for her degree in Law, which she obtained in 1931, and she further obtained a degree in Arts which was conferred in 1933. Thereafter she went into practice both on her own in partnership with another lawyer and later in the office of one of the better known firms in Perth. Her work was of such great value that I can assure you the firm concerned was most loath to lose her services when she decided to go into the Navy.
>
> By the people here she was known for her energy, efficiency and drive. She did not by any means restrict her interest and activities to the Law but was a prominent member of the women graduates, and

29 Application to Women's College, above Ch 4 n 46.

30 Ibid.

> in fact took part not only in social affairs but in the activities of a number of organisations concerned with social betterment. She appeals to people not only for her academic brilliance and her energetic temperament, but also for her attractive personality which has made her many good friends in Perth.
>
> It is difficult to speak of one who has already made her mark so capably in many fields of endeavour and all I can say is she has not failed in anything I know of so far and does not appear likely to do so in the future. She has my best wishes.[31]

An additional document is deposited in the College archives with those relating to Sheila's application. It is not referred to in her letter and, in view of its contents, is hardly likely to have been submitted by her. It is unsigned, undated and not addressed "To whom it may concern" or to anyone else. It appears to be an independent assessment by some anonymous person of Sheila's character and antecedents. It reads as follows:

> Sheila McClemans LLB, BA, aged about 35, is of good appearance and address, nicely mannered and able to adapt herself to all occasions. She has a bright personality with good reserve and is well respected. Her position as Chief Officer WRANS is a testimony to her administrative ability.
>
> She is the third of a family of five daughters – all full of character and possessing brains above the average. Her father – a former C of E Canon – had to resign from the Church when the family was very young, owing to his persistent drinking habits. His wife was of a very forceful and masterful character and was interested in outside affairs, and the family ran wild, which did not help the Father in his position. The Mother (a nurse before her marriage) now does part-time nursing. Some years ago she obtained a divorce. The father has recently married again – one of the old Forrest family – an elderly well-respected woman.
>
> All the McClemans girls went to good schools – mostly to Perth College (C of E), but Sheila won an entrance to Modern School (probably comparable with Sydney Girls High School). She was for a time in partnership with Molly Kingston (a well respected and clever woman, recently appointed to the Australasian Institute of International Affairs, Sydney and Melbourne), but they found clients

31 Ibid.

> difficult to obtain and the partnership was dissolved, each girl joining a different well established legal firm in Perth.[32]

Some elements of this document are outrageous. What relevance to his daughter's application was the Canon's drunkenness and marriage break-up some 25 years previous? Or the fact her mother was a forceful and masterful character whose implied neglect of her children caused them to "run wild"? Or the fact that the father had re-married a respectable elderly woman of good family? What motive did this person have for supplying this scandalous and misleading information?

The College archives do not reveal the identity of this informant. Nor can they provide any answers to the questions posed. One can only comment that the document provides yet another example of the relentless gender bias of the time. Whoever fabricated this family background material was obviously taking advantage of an opportunity gratuitously to deprecate Ada McClemans and her work with the Women's Service Guilds.

When I first began to gather material for this work I asked a fellow writer and Anglican historian, Jean Lang, whether she knew anything about Canon McClemans. She replied that her only knowledge was general church gossip to the effect that the Canon had been de-frocked for drunkenness and that his wife had driven him to it by her nagging and her total pre-occupation with the affairs of the Women's Service Guilds. That the Canon was driven to drink by the neglect of his do-gooding wife is, therefore, obviously a well established myth within the Anglican community. It is difficult to understand the motives behind making an Eve of Ada to explain the Canon's fall from grace. The most probable explanation seems to be that it was a sexist device employed by conservative elements in that community to belittle the socially challenging work of the Women's Service Guilds. It would also be a means of obscuring the basic cause of the Canon's breakdown, namely his ghastly experiences on the Western Front during the Great War.

In fairness to Jean Lang I should emphasise that she stressed that her information was merely gossip and insisted I go to reputable sources to establish the facts. As a start she recommended

32 Ibid.

Alexander's *Two Bishops and Their See* which described the Canon's important contributions to the church – particularly in education.[33] My research has, of course, revealed an entirely different picture of the circumstances of his retirement. It is heartening to see that the McClemans saga has been dealt with sympathetically by Sharp and O'Hara in *A Goodly Heritage*[34] and the malicious gossip authoritatively refuted.

Sheila's application for the Women's College post did not succeed. The successful applicant was Miss Betty Archdale who was the war-time commander in Australia of the British Women's Royal Naval Service. Miss Archdale later became headmistress of the prestigious Sydney Anglican girls' school, Abbotsleigh, as well as a well-known media personality and authority on cultural affairs.

It must have been a great disappointment for Sheila to have failed in her application. As mentioned in Professor Currie's testimonial, she always held a strong interest in the affairs of university women and eventually became the National President of the Australian Federation of University Women. It is probable also that, like Molly Kingston and many other Western Australian service men and women given their first taste of life in a big city by wartime Sydney and Melbourne, she wished to break free of the deadening provincialism of the Perth scene. The Women's College post would have provided her a great opportunity to do this. Perhaps this was why she kept the application secret from her family and confided it only to her close naval friends.[35]

Sheila's expressed desire to help young people was not altogether frustrated by the rejection of her application. There was an important role for her in the rehabilitation of her own young women facing the uncertainties of civilian life. Although she could have resigned from the Service at any time to resume her professional career, Sheila remained at her post until 27 February 1947 to prepare and conduct personally a programme of rehabilitation lectures, travelling throughout the country to ensure that the message was taken to all hands. Margaret Curtis-Offer recorded an

33 Alexander, *Four Bishops and Their See*, above, Chapter 2 n 5.

34 Sharp and O'Hara, *A Goodly Heritage*, above Chapter 2 n 8.

35 Mrs Iris Purnell, personal interview.

occasion when Sheila had given her lecture at an establishment then discovered that one WRAN had not been able to attend. She sought her out and repeated the lecture to her one-to-one.[36]

A bonus of her late discharge (and surely some compensation for missing out on the Women's College post) was that Sheila was available to accept the Navy's invitation to attend the Commonwealth Victory March in London in the summer of 1946. The Australian contingent, representing all services, travelled to the United Kingdom on *HMAS Shropshire*, the heavy cruiser donated by the Royal Navy to the Royal Australian Navy to replace *HMAS Canberra*, lost in the Battle of the Solomons in 1942.

Shropshire left Melbourne on 18 April and returned on 28 June. The departure was delayed by a strike, not by waterside workers, but by the Army contingent who objected to two of their mates being culled out at the last minute. "We all go or none of us go", was their demand. Faced with the prospect of a Victory Parade minus any bronzed Anzacs in slouch hats, the authorities capitulated.

Sheila and Sister Cherry Wilson from the Royal Australian Naval Nursing Service, were the only two naval women aboard. Commander JC Morrow frequently invited them to his cabin for drinks. Another guest at these small gatherings was Chief Petty Officer Arthur Cooper DSM who had joined the Navy in the 1930s and served in *HMAS Voyager* through the Greek campaign, and in *Shropshire* during the Philippines re-conquest, winning the Greek DSM in the first and the British DSM in the second. In fact Arthur had been sent to wartime London in 1943 to join *Shropshire* for her voyage to Australia. He and Sheila became close friends.[37]

Having no other ranks to command, Sheila had no duties to perform and occupied her time helping with the ship's social programme to amuse the troops on the long journey via the Cape of Good Hope. The programme included the traditional tourist sequence of concerts, quizzes, spelling bees, "crossing the Line"

---

36 Margaret Curtis-Offer, *WRANS*, Naval Historical Society of Sydney, 1975, p 28.

37 Arthur Cooper kept a diary of the entire victory march journey which is the source of most of the material relating to that journey not directly attributed to Sheila's own reminiscences. Sheila maintained her friendship with Arthur Cooper for the rest of her life, both personally and as his family solicitor. On Anzac Day, in latter years, no longer fit to march, they would sit together at the saluting dais.

ceremony and a fancy dress ball. Unique, and by far the most popular, was a mock radio show, broadcast over the ship's PA system, called "Sheila's Show" in which Sheila ran a shipboard agony column giving advice to the love-lorn under the pseudonym of "Dorothy McClemans".

The journey was described by Sheila in a series of letters which she posted home en route to the WRANS journal *Dit* so that she could share the experience with her WRANS in Australia These letters are still preserved in the museum at *HMAS Cerberus.* The following extracts are published with the kind consent of the curator, Mr Dennis Berry.

> 22 April 1946
>
> Dear WRANS,
>
> I thought that by this time I would be able to write and tell you of the joys of life at sea, but I can't as yet. I'll start from the beginning.
>
> After we left Melbourne we were really very tired and sank gratefully into the Wardroom chairs and fell on a cup of tea and large slices of bread and butter – from which you may gather that afternoon tea in the Navy at sea bears a marked resemblance to the Navy ashore. . .
>
> By 1900 we started going through the Rip and really got through it very well – so they say – but my stomach took a very dismal view of the whole thing. Because the Wardroom is very crowded, Matron Sage and I dine with the Captain, General Eather and Brigadier Moten in the Captain's cabin. It sounds very attractive but his cabin is as aft as it is possible to be without popping into the ocean and it vibrates and jumps up and down from side to side with reckless abandon. Once again the stomach took a dismal view. . .
>
> By Saturday night we were beginning to feel a little better and were so encouraged that we would be near the end of our tribulations. Then a signal came in which said there was a storm approaching so we thought we'd get into our bunks before it happened, but it hit us before we even got there and we spent the most incredible night. Those of us who were lying fore and aft spent the night being thrown out of our bunks – those lying athwart ships had their heads and feet bashed regularly. The din was terrific. I personally didn't sleep at all and every now and then when a particularly loud crash came I'd fly out of bed and expect to see all the women mangled on the floor; but, amazingly, they all escaped injury. We couldn't get

from cabin to cabin so we just made signs at each other to indicate that we were still alive.

All sorts of things came adrift in the ship and did a lot of damage. . . The Captain's table came adrift and crashed madly round his dining cabin and the crockery which bit the dust simply tore my housewifely soul to shreds. I thought the night would never end. It gave an interesting side light on the sailors though – they simply shrieked with laughter every time something tore to bits and shot across the deck and that even though it was obvious they would have to clean it all up.

Morning eventually came and the storm had abated very little. I got up and slowly staggered into my overalls. You would be sorry for me if you knew of the terrific nausea you get when bending down. . . However, I eventually stumbled out of the cabin and was hurled towards the Wardroom – most of the way on my seat! Everyone said how brave I was to be up at all to which I replied – "I was not brave – I'm only up because my bunk is full of water" (which had leaked through the scuttle).

The Wardroom presented a scene of indescribable confusion – broken furniture and crockery everywhere. All the other girls just lay in their bunks all day and prayed for death. Every now and then I would stagger forth with biscuits or soda water for them and wish that I were dead too instead of "near-dead". . .

With the afternoon the storm abated a bit, but supper in the evening was a repetition of lunch, and the food and the people just crashed madly about. The crockery would hurtle and crash with a terrific din and stewards would shriek with laughter. We had to laugh too, in spite of the sea-sickness. One of the lieutenants told me that I could truthfully say that it was incredibly rough and the worst spasm in the Bight for fifty years. . . I like to think that what he said was true. . .

Sister Wilson has been very sick but she is up today and Lt Commander Peek (the leader of the Victory Contingent) has made us do an hour's vigorous marching up and down the deck to fit us for the march through Perth. We arrive there tomorrow morning and march through the city at mid-day. Then we have shore leave – over night for the natives – and sail again at 11:00 on Wednesday.

The sailors have all been incredibly kind to us. We thought when the storm came that they would blame us for being on board, but we find instead that they are blaming it on the fact that there are three padres in the ship!. . .

16th May 1946

Ever so much has happened since I wrote last. First of all Capetown. We all manned ship and the band played us into harbour. The two favourite numbers were Gundagai and Waltzing Matilda of course. . . We were given shore leave at about 1100 and Sister Wilson and I raced ashore. We had a perfectly lovely orgy of shopping. Clothing is not rationed there, but the styles are reminiscent of a country town. This was most apparent in the women who had anything to do with us – we did not see a smartly dressed one among them, though most had the most marvellous good looks. We had our really best fun in the jewellery shops. Every one in the ship bought at least one watch, as they are both cheap and good. . . They also had lots of semi-precious stones and rough silver and gold jewellery. We both bought a silver charm bracelet. . .

The next day we were supposed to march through the city at noon but it rained and blew so hard that the march was cancelled. The Lord Mayor had arranged a reception for the marchers so he carried on with those arrangements and we had a lovely time at it. Before I go any further I must tell you that throughout the whole of our visit to Capetown the whole of the Contingent and the ship's company behaved with the utmost propriety and you would have been very proud of your folk. The people were most terribly kind to us and just overwhelmed us with hospitality. . .

And now I must tell you about the Swans. Except for the WRANS I have never seen more attractive and smart service girls. If it had not been for the WRANS I'd have said they were the best anyway. . . They wear the same uniform as the Wrens except that they have SANF and an anchor on their cap ribbons. They were terribly thrilled about seeing a WRAN and arranged a party on the second evening for the women members of the Contingent. Unfortunately I was unable to attend as the Shropshire was giving a party to return hospitality and I had to be there, but I asked their senior officer in Capetown to come to that. You would have liked her. Very striking in appearance, tall and well made, with grey hair wound in plaits round her head and a very well-groomed appearance. We had lots and lots to talk about as you may imagine. She has a son of twenty-one – who for a time was a POW in Germany – and a daughter of sixteen. . .

> It was still raining and cold the day we left but we had all made so many friends in Capetown that the wharves were thronged with people to see us off. We manned ship again and just as we were leaving the wharf the clouds lifted and we saw the top of Table Mountain. We thought that was a lovely gesture on the part of this terribly attractive place and its charming people. . .
>
> Monday 20th
>
> Since I wrote last a good deal has happened to fill our days. . . First we had gun trials on Wednesday last. They fire off everything but the four inch and the eight inch guns, and you can have no idea of the din. . . It brought home to me very strongly the real purpose of this ship and its armament – its deadly destructive quality. . . The trials took an hour or so, and at the end of them I felt that my nerves could not have stood any more.
>
> The Crossing the line ceremony has come and gone. It started on Friday evening at 2000 when there was a profound bump, a flash of light, and Neptune's Emissary came on board in the fo'c'sle. With much pomp and ceremony he served summonses on those who were to appear before the Court next day and paraded the ship with the band leading on in the most weird and wonderful garbs. . . I was given a decoration – the Order of The Sea She Dog.
>
> Everyone in the ship is terribly busy making felt toys. They are to be given to the orphanages in Shropshire which is the county which paid for this cruiser. . . The deck presents a most comical sight. Brave fighting men all squatting down and stitching with the utmost gravity. . .

On 27 May 1946, the contingent landed in Portsmouth where it was given a civic reception before entraining for London. The London accommodation was in four-person tents which the troops thought to be a let-down, particularly as it rained most of the time they were there. The situation was not improved by a week spent rehearsing marching line abreast and saluting.

The Royal Family visited them in camp before the march and the troops lined the drive as they passed. Sheila was conspicuous because of her tall stature and the Queen singled her out for a one-to-one chat. When she moved away she said to Sheila "Thank you for coming all this way to see us".[38] Sheila described the Victory march itself in her *Oral History*:

> to start the march we had been assembled in a park nearby the beginning of the route and we were given over the loud speaker only three orders:
>
> "The Australian contingent will move off in five minutes' time."
>
> "The Australian contingent will move off in one minute's time."
>
> "The Australian contingent by the right quick march!"
>
> And off we went for fourteen miles. It was quite magnificent.[39]

In the official photograph Sheila stands out clearly in the second rank of the Australian contingent as it sweeps past the saluting dais with the band playing *Waltzing Matilda*. It was a grand moment and a well deserved reward for all those whose service to Australia had earned them their place in the Victory Parade. Another highlight was a Royal party at Hampton Court where Sheila was formally presented to King George VI and Queen Elizabeth. The dowager Queen Mary (widow of King George V) was also there. Sheila's description of her is not very flattering:

> very frightening, very regal . . . still wearing Louis XIV heels on her shoes and toque and long black parasol, and I felt myself if she said black was white I'd say "Yes Ma'am". I wouldn't have dared to do anything else. On the other hand King George . . . had a lovely personality. At that stage the Duke of Gloucester was Governor General in Australia and when I was presented he said to me "Have you seen my brother out there?". It was all on a very natural note.[40]

Arthur Cooper was a very useful man to have in the company because he was familiar with Great Britain and the Mediterranean through his past years of service. He took Sheila and Cherry pub-crawling to the *Elephant and Castle* and other famous taverns whilst in London and guided them around Gibraltar and the Red Sea ports on the way home.

---

38 C Shervington, *Sheila Mary McClemans: Oral History Memoir*, by courtesy University of WA archives, p 11.

39 Ibid, p 12.

40 Ibid, p 12.

When *Shropshire* tied up at Melbourne, Sheila resumed the hectic task of winding-up the WRANS and preparing her young women for civilian life. In doing so she over-taxed her health. In a passage quoted above, Margaret Curtis-Offer has been quoted as saying of Sheila that she "placed Service before self to the detriment, ultimately of her health".[41] Throughout her life Sheila suffered recurrent bouts of illness apparently connected with a hyper-thyroid condition. Those close to her in the WRANS were aware of this condition. Both Mary Howard and her other close Navy friend, Iris Purnell, recalled that she had episodes of it whilst in the WRANS but carried on in spite of them.[42] Her prowess as a sports woman and her patience and good humour at all times masked this quite distressing condition from all but those closest to her.

The long period of stress and responsibility which her post imposed upon her and her ceaseless worry over the problems of others had a cumulative effect. Sadly, another disability was superimposed on this congenital condition. During the course of her journeys from depot to depot around Australia, she suffered a severe jarring of her back from which she never recovered. In November 1946, her repatriation work almost completed, she was admitted to the military hospital at Heidelberg where she remained under treatment until January 1947.

On discharge from hospital she was interviewed by a reporter from *The Sun* and lightly referred to her treatment as "being renovated".[43] Navy medical records are still regarded as confidential so there is no official account to draw on. Her close friend, Mary Howard, who visited her frequently in hospital is an authority for the fact that she was under treatment for both conditions.[44] Applying basic principles of medico-legal jurisprudence, it is reasonable to assume that the hectic five months which followed her return from the Victory March exacerbated her pre-existing complaints and precipitated the eventual breakdown of her health.

---

41 Margaret Curtis-Offer, *WRANS*, Naval Historical Society of Sydney, 1975, p 11.

42 Mary Howard and Iris Purnell, personal interviews.

43 *Melbourne Sun*, 24 January 1947.

44 Mary Howard, personal interview.

Sheila entered the Service a champion swimmer and an excellent tennis player. She left it with a back injury which gave her constant pain. This pain troubled her for the rest of her life, particularly during long days in court.

Upon her discharge from hospital, the WRANS and the Royal Australian Nursing Service gave Sheila a grand farewell party which took pride of place in the Melbourne social notes. She was described as wearing "a small cocktail hat trimmed with red roses and a black dress finished with a duck-egg blue collar to which she pinned a spray of gardenias presented by her admiring hosts".[45]

She left Melbourne on 27 January 1947 to return to Perth. Her official discharge (dated 27 February 1947) followed her home to *King's Lynn,* 70 Victoria Avenue, Claremont, a riverside flat not far from the old Rectory which she shared with her mother until her marriage to Frank Kenworthy in 1949.

All WRANS closely associated with Sheila during the war received personal letters of thanks from her. The letters thanked them for their assistance in the "many difficulties" which she had overcome during her time as Director. Close WRANS associates interpret many difficulties as a reference to the battles she had with the naval bureaucracy in her constant struggle for a fair deal for her WRANS.[46]

Nora Heysen, an official war artist, painted portraits of Sheila and the leaders of the other wartime women's services. These hang in the Australian War Museum in Canberra. A place which would be closer to Sheila's spiritual heart is the little naval museum at *HMAS Cerberus* to which she bequeathed her decorations and second official portrait, painted in London during her visit for the Victory celebrations. This portrait hangs in a special WRANS section above the "Sheila Mary McClemans Trophy", donated by the Ex-WRANS Association and awarded annually to the most efficient WRANS unit until the WRANS ceased to exist as a separate service in 1985. The decorations repose in a glass case in the museum's "Honours Room" opposite the battle-torn flag of the *HMAS Arunta.* They are accompanied by an inscription which begins:

---

45 *Melbourne Sun*, 24 January 1947.

46 Iris Purnell, personal interview.

> Sheila Mary McClemans, daughter of a clergyman, BA, LLB a practitioner of the Supreme Court of Western Australia, joined the WRANS in 1943 as a writer. She had been prepared to see the war out in this capacity had she failed to qualify as an officer. Sheila McClemans (Kenworthy) was a remarkable woman and we all owe an enormous debt to her memory. She made a magnificent contribution to the WRANS and the WRANS who served during the war owed a lot to Chief Officer McClemans' leadership.

The citation to her Order of the British Empire which she was awarded on the 7 June 1951 states that the wartime success of the WRANS was almost entirely due to her "great knowledge, wisdom and judgment".

A more personal tribute is paid by Margaret Curtis-Offer in *WRANS:*

> As one of a family of five girls she cultivated at an early age the art of getting along with her contemporaries, but her academic qualifications tended to blind all save those who knew her well to the deeply sympathetic side of her character: in newspaper interviews she was usually presented as a being descended from Olympian heights, and few who met her casually saw beyond this facade to the woman whose fondness for home life and sport was carried into her Service career. It was noticeable always that WRANS Quarters were made as comfortable and attractive as could be and that facilities for sport were made available on as wide a scale as possible.[47]

The affection and admiration the WRANS held for Sheila was reciprocated. In a general demobilisation message promulgated in October 1945, Sheila wrote:

> The farewells have begun and there is a gradual movement of WRANS to their dispersal depots . . . new homes, new careers and new contacts lie ahead, but it is safe to assume that the experiences of the past few years will not soon be forgotten . . . and if, in the future, small children should paraphrase the 1914-18 catchline "What did you do in the Second World War, Grandma?" there are worse replies than the simple statement, "I was a WRAN".[48]

47 Margaret Curtis-Offer, *WRANS*, Naval Historical Society of Sydney, 1975, p 27.

48 *Living Today*, Perth, 23 February 1978, p 21.

Postwar Sheila was a member of the Ex-WRANS Association and attended re-unions and Anzac Day parades almost to the end of her days. Her pride in the Service shines through the following extract from an interview she gave to *West Australian* reporter, Derryn Thorpe, in 1984:

> We had a former WRAN who is now a South Perth Mother Superior marching in the RSL Anzac Day parade. She was dressed in her habit but was stepping it out and marching with the best of them. I felt so proud.[49]

Iris Purnell epitomised the lasting value of Sheila's years in the WRANS with the following tribute:

> I know her years in the WRANS were but a short period in Sheila's life, but, without a doubt, in those few years she had an influence on the character and ambitions of a greater number of people than at any other time in her life. The ripples from that influence would still be spreading even though so many years have passed.

49 *West Australian*, 21 June 1985, p 26.

6

POSTWAR PRACTICE

Upon her return to Western Australia in January 1947, Sheila resumed practice with her old firm, Hardwick Slattery and Gibson, despite the unpatriotic threat which overshadowed her enlistment. That unpleasantry appears to have been forgotten in the intervening years, although there is a brief reference to her enlistment and re-employment in Sheila's *Oral History* which leaves the question of her employers' attitude open. It certainly suggests that she did not enlist with their enthusiastic permission. It also makes it plain that they had little option but to re-employ her on her discharge from the Navy:

> And had you taken leave without pay or had you resigned from Hardwick? Was it an understanding that you would return?
>
> You just went and you didn't think beyond that, but during the war some legislation had been passed which said that people who had been employed in any particular occupation and then returned from active service would have to have their jobs back. So I suppose we just settled down to the fact that that was going to happen. We were going there.[1]

Although Commonwealth repatriation legislation made it obligatory for employers to re-employ and to give preference to ex-service personnel, it is unlikely that Sheila resorted to its provisions.[2] It would have been wholly contrary to Sheila's sense of propriety to force herself upon her employers by invoking the legislation, nor

1 C Shervington, *Sheila Mary McClemans: Oral History Memoir*, by courtesy University of WA archives, p 11.

2 *Re-Establishment and Employment Act* 1945 (Cth).

would it have been necessary. She was a highly valued practitioner when she left in January 1943 and the national prestige she had earned as Director WRANS and participant in the Victory March would have greatly enhanced her value to any potential employer. There is not even anecdotal evidence from family members to suggest that resistance to Sheila's re-employment was ever raised again.

Her impending resumption of practice was the subject of a lengthy article in the *West Australian* headed "A CIVILIAN AGAIN", which predicted that her "vital personality and keen alert mind will be a contribution to women's interests in Perth". Describing her as an advocate for equality of the sexes, the article quoted her as saying that Australia made too much of an issue of sex and wasted its woman power. She suggested that one way of taking advantage of women power was for men to "take their daughters into business as they did their sons".

The article continued:

> Miss McClemans practises as well as preaches sexual equality. During a recent gas strike in Melbourne she volunteered to shift coal and was one of 200 women who staged a protest on the steps of Parliament House in Melbourne.[3]

According to the article Sheila intended to complete a legal refresher course before commencing practice. Another benefit accorded ex-service personnel was free refresher tuition for anyone who practised a trade or profession before enlistment.

The firm allocated Sheila a junior typist, Miss Jo Buckeridge, as her personal secretary. Miss Buckeridge eventually married and, years later, as Mrs Jo Hawkins, commenced mature-age studies at the University of Western Australia, majoring in history and eventually attaining a Doctorate of Philosophy. Dr Hawkins has a very clear recollection of Sheila's return to practise. Advance publicity in the press had created an awesome impression and she expected the former Director WRANS to be a most exacting and critical employer.[4]

Sheila soon put her at ease. She recalls that Sheila would always thank and compliment her for her work before indicating any errors

3 *West Australian*, 2 February 1947.

4 Dr Jo Hawkins, from a personal interview.

she might want corrected. If it was close to a lunch break or knock-off time and Sheila wanted some typing done urgently she would bustle Jo out of her chair and release her saying "You go along now dear. I'll just borrow your machine". She would then settle down behind the typewriter and do it herself. She never asked any employee to work into a lunch hour or stay back late to finish work, preferring to finish it herself if it was urgent. It was typical also for her to address younger people – male or female – as "dear". I had personal experience of this the first time I ever spoke to Sheila It was during my first year in practice in 1950, when she telephoned in response to a letter I had written on behalf of an Italian client who wanted access to his 13-year-old daughter.

The only background the father gave me was that he had been divorced by his wife and that her solicitor, Miss McClemans, wouldn't let him see the child. I knew only of Sheila's fame as a scholar, lawyer and prominent former naval person and anticipated a fairly haughty response to my letter. Instead, I got a disarming telephone call in a voice which could have belonged to anyone's affectionate older sister:

> "My dear has your client told you that he's just got out of gaol for committing incest on this little girl?"
>
> "That does put a different complexion on things", I responded and silently cursed my client for hiding this vital information. "I suppose, there's no possibility of a bit of forgiving and forgetting now that he's done his time?".
>
> "I'm afraid not dear. The poor child's absolutely terrified of him".
>
> "Well I suppose I'd better tell him he's got no case." Thinking aloud I added "I hope he doesn't do what my last client did when I said that to him".
>
> "And what was that dear?"
>
> "He took a rifle and shot dead both the people on the other side".
>
> "I hope you don't mention that to your man. We're a bit afraid he might do that any way."

Fortunately father accepted the situation and refrained from any drastic action. Dr Hawkins also has a clear recollection of the case, it being her first vicarious experience of the horrible realities of family law. According to her, the girl's mother and brothers had sought Sheila out because the girl could not be persuaded to tell her story to a male solicitor.[5]

In their histories, both Patsy Adam-Smith and Margaret Curtis-Offer state that Sheila claimed her first duty on her return to the law was to arrest a ship.[6] The story made great copy for both of them but it seems to fall into the category of being a good story rather than historical fact. The Admiralty records of the Supreme Court of Western Australia have no record of Sheila or her firm ever having been involved in the arrest of a ship. Furthermore, no ship was arrested by anyone in the State of Western Australia in 1947, the year Sheila returned to practise. Dr Hawkins has no recollection of any such incident, which would have been an unusual event for her had it occurred in the humdrum course of daily practice. Like the Marie Celeste, the fate of that ill-fated barque remains a mystery.[7]

The bulk of Sheila's legal work was matrimonial – a great deal of it pursuant to the *Married Women's Protection Act* before magistrates in the Courts of Petty Session. In these proceedings, women sought orders for separation and maintenance for themselves and their children against brutal, drunken, neglectful and adulterous husbands. There were also parallel proceedings in the Children's Court for unmarried mothers seeking confinement expenses, custody and future maintenance for their illegitimate children.

These were people in desperate need and to Sheila this work was a matter of dedication. For many, she acted without fee. She explained to Dr Hawkins that she did this because she was in a position to help people who could not help themselves. She had been privileged to have an education and she felt obliged to assist people less fortunate than herself.[8]

---

5 Ibid.

6 Adam-Smith, Patsy, *Australian Women at War,* Thomas Nelson, 1980, p 216. Margaret Curtis-Offer, *WRANS*, Naval Historical Society of Sydney, 1975, p 28.

7 In a personal interview Mrs McFadyen recalled Sheila discussed arresting a ship at about that time but gave no details. A possible explanation is that Sheila may have instructed solicitors in another State to arrest a ship on behalf of a local client in which case the action would have taken place elsewhere.

8 Dr Jo Hawkins, from a personal interview.

Before the creation of the Law Society's Legal Aid Scheme it was fairly common for caring lawyers to act without fee for people in distress and hope to get paid by winning and getting an order for costs. In matrimonial proceedings in the Courts of Petty Sessions, the magistrates would order an unsuccessful husband to pay costs or go to gaol in default – the husbands usually preferred to pay up. The amount of costs was meagre, however, and barely worth the effort. The work was done because someone had to do it and the burden fell upon those lawyers who had a conscience. In legal jargon it was called *pro bono* work – short for *pro bono publico* – "for the public good".

There was some profitable potential in work of this kind, because it built up a clientele. An occasional reward occurred when people one had helped brought in more profitable work, like a motor vehicle claim or a family probate application. In matrimonial work, there was the possibility that a divorce would eventually follow successful Petty Sessions proceedings.

Divorce work in the Supreme Court was qualitatively different from summary proceedings in the Petty Sessions. A woman seeking relief in the Petty Sessions was forced to do so to prevent herself and her children being beaten or starved to death. People usually only need a divorce if they wish to remarry. Marriage is never a necessity, however desirable it may seem to people in love wishing to set up house together.

In the days when what Bernard Shaw called "middle class respectability" permeated down even to the working class, many clients were motivated to pay for the privilege of freedom to re-marry. It was, therefore, the practice, even with the most caring solicitors, to be quite firm about requiring adequate payment from the client – usually in advance – before they would commence divorce proceedings. Because divorce was Supreme Court work, the fees were high and a busy divorce practice could be quite profitable. In building up the firm's divorce practice, Sheila would certainly have earned her salary despite her unpaid work for indigent clients.

There was little kudos in this work. Sheila took no cases to the High Court of Australia, in fact her name never appeared as counsel in the Commonwealth Law Reports and appears only once in the Western Australian Law Reports, as junior to Cliff Gibson in the quaint case of *Garnaut v Rowse*.[9] Dr Hawkins can only recall two cases which stood out during the three years she worked for Sheila and those for their intriguing facts and not their forensic importance. The first was the Italian incest case described above and the second a divorce in which, to Sheila's embarrassment, the offending husband lived in her next-door flat. This gentleman, a high local government dignitary prominent in amateur sport, had a number of mistresses on the side all of whom bore him children. Imprudently he kept a written record of all these misalliances in a diary reminiscent, it seems, of Leporello's famous catalogue aria in *Don Giovanni*. This document fell into his wife's hands and was passed on to Sheila who gave them to her secretary to transcribe. The frank confessions of this civic dignitary's sexual misdemeanours were a startling revelation to a young unmarried woman from a respectable professional family.

Dr Hawkins recalls that the most tedious work for Sheila was prosecuting for the Shire of Mundaring at least once a month in the Midland Court of Petty Sessions. Sheila never actually complained about the work but she always looked very jaded and exasperated when she returned to the office from these excursions.

This, at first sight, seems surprising. The walk across the city to Perth Railway Station is not even as far as the journey Sheila would have taken almost daily to the old Beaufort Street Court of Petty Sessions. The train journey to Midland would have been, if anything, restful. One can only assume that Sheila's ennui at her local government prosecutions arose from the total soul-lessness of the work. A day listening to health inspectors describing the finding of "solids" in septic tanks before certification, or cockroaches in cafe kitchens, or excess sulphur dioxide in mince-meat, would be pretty dreary stuff for one who once commanded three thousand women, sailed two mighty oceans to march to the cheers of ten million Londoners and shake hands with the King and Queen of England.

In contrast to her low profile work in the courts, Sheila took a leading role in public affairs through two women's organisations, the Women's Service Guilds and the Federation of University Women. In April 1947, the State Executive of the Guilds established a special

9 *Garnaut v Rowse* (1941) 42 WALR 29 at 109-111. See Chapter 4.

Night Guild to draw in young working women who could not attend meetings during the day and enlisted Sheila to become its first President.[10] In 1949, Margaret Battye died and Sheila replaced her as the Guilds' honorary solicitor. She was also an active member of the Law Society (the lawyers' professional organisation), the Ex-WRANS Association and the committee administering the Canteens Trust Fund, a body created by the Commonwealth to apply the profits made by the war-time service canteens to assist needy ex-service personnel and their families.

One aspect of Sheila's work with the Guilds was to act in a liaison capacity with a Law Society sub-committee to amend some unsatisfactory provisions of the *Married Women's Protection Act*.[11] The Law Society, like the Guilds, had always concerned itself with law reform from its inception in 1927. Its main concern was not the wide sweep of social welfare which motivated the Guilds but the correction of unjust anomalies in the law revealed in the operation of day-to-day practice. Lawyers call this kind of reform "lawyers law reform" to distinguish it from social law reform which often has a partisan political flavour. As a member of both organisations, Sheila was able to bring the two strands together when considering the reform of matrimonial law.

Between 1947 and 1951 Sheila contributed so much to the work of the Guilds that President Bessie Rischbieth accorded her a special acknowledgement at the front of her book, *March of Australian Women*.[12] In 1948, Sheila was a delegate from the Guilds to the Eighth Triennial Conference of the Australian Federation of Women Voters held in Melbourne. Mrs Rischbieth described her contribution as follows:

> Miss McClemans, LLB (Western Australia) spoke on the Rights of Married Women, emphasising in particular the legal status and property rights of married women. She pointed out that the wife was entirely dependent upon the generosity or otherwise of the husband and referred to desperate conditions which came under her notice

---

10 Dianne Davidson, *Women on the Warpath*, University of Western Australia Press, 1997, p 213.

11 Dr Jo Hawkins, from a personal interview.

12 Bessie M Rischbieth, *March of Australian Women*, Paterson, Brokensha Pty Ltd, 1964, p 21.

> from time to time. She advocated that married men's earnings should be the joint property of the man and his wife who should jointly provide for the home and the children out of their respective incomes.[13]

In 1949 Sheila played quite a decisive role in the direction of the policy of the Guilds in a political struggle which had developed between Mrs Rischbieth and Lady Jessie Street, wife of the Chief Justice of New South Wales and left-wing Labor stalwart. Lady Street led a national organisation called the Australian Women's Charter Committee which promoted the Australian Women's Charter, a document of general feminist principals, originally drafted by Lady Street in 1942. It is set out in detail by Lady Street in her work *Truth or Repose*.[14] Davidson summarises its provisions as follows:

> The contents basically summarised the goals for which most of the feminist organisations in Australia had been striving, and the Charter certainly reflected fairly accurately the principles and aims of the Guilds.[15]

Initially, the Guilds supported the Charter but eventually withdrew their support following a warning from Mrs Rischbieth in 1944 that the Charter Committee was encroaching upon and duplicating the work of the Guilds and its associate body, the Australian Federation of Women Voters. Mrs Rischbieth was not alone in this. In 1945 and 1946 a number of organisations in New South Wales, including the National Council of Women, dissociated themselves from the Charter, not because they disagreed with its terms but because they objected to Lady Street's modus operandi. According to Davidson, there appears to have been a general suspicion that Lady Street's objective was to "build an Australia-wide power base" for herself and would use "high-handed tactics" to do so.[16]

By 1948 the opponents of the Charter were given a bigger stick with which to beat it. In 1942 Lady Street had formed the Australia-

---

13 Ibid, p 92.

14 Jessie Street, *Truth or Repose*, Australasian Book Society, 1966, p 252.

15 Dianne Davidson, *Women on the Warpath*, above n 10, 1997, p 199.

16 Ibid, p 203.

Russia Society, mainly to conduct a fund-raising "Sheep skins for Russia" campaign. Initially, this was popularly acclaimed as patriotic war work in view of the fact that the Russians were bearing the main brunt of the war against Germany. By 1948, however, with the development of the Cold War, attitudes had changed. Russia was no longer regarded as a gallant ally but as a potential enemy. The Australian Labor Party condemned the Australia-Russia Society as a Communist front organisation and asked Lady Street to resign. Dorothy Tagney, the only female Labor senator, attacked the Charter Committee in the Senate and branded it as a Communist organisation although she did not produce any evidence to support this allegation.[17]

In 1949 the Charter Committee announced that it would hold a national conference in April with Lady Street as the main speaker and invited the Guilds to send a delegation. The State Executive of the Guilds met in Perth on 18 March 1949 to consider the invitation. At the meeting, Sheila moved that the Guilds reject the invitation. In support of her motion, she cited Senator Tagney's Senate speech branding the Charter as Communist inspired and pointed out that Lady Street had been asked to resign from the Labor Party because of her association with the Australia-Russia Society. The meeting voted unanimously to boycott the conference.[18]

Davidson makes the following comment upon this decision:

> This prelude was to lead to a well documented public clash between Bessie Rischbieth and Jessie Street, which has been described by some commentators as heralding the dissolution of the women's movement and the end of the first wave of feminism in Australia.[19]

She attributes this assessment to feminist historian Kate White.[20] She does not, however, accept the validity of this proposition in her own text. Her history of the Guilds depicts them as continuing to be active in many fields of social activity – including the successful

---

17 Ibid, p 218.

18 Ibid, p 219.

19 Ibid, p 219.

20 K White, "Bessie Rischbieth, Jessie Street and the End of First wave Feminism in Australia", in Bevege, James and Shute, *Worth Her Salt*, Hale & Iremonger, 1982, pp 319-329.

campaign for female jury service – for more than 20 years before the first clear signs of the arrival of the second wave feminists in 1972.[21]

In opposing Lady Street and the Australian Women's Charter Committee, Sheila clearly identified herself as a political conservative. In 1950 she made a bid to move into a higher level of political activity by seeking Liberal Party endorsement for election to the State Parliament as member for the blue ribbon seat of Cottesloe. According to her sister, Paddy McFadyen, she was persuaded to do this by a number of Liberal Party acquaintances who assured her that, in view of her status and fame, she would be certain of preselection. She was bitterly disappointed when she was defeated for pre-selection by school teacher and popular league footballer, Ross Hutchinson DFC. Sheila regarded her defeat as a gross example of sexual discrimination and never forgave the Liberal Party for this humiliation nor did she ever seek political pre-selection again.[22]

Sheila's role in the rebuff to Lady Street by the Guilds is not mentioned in Mrs Rischbieth's book which entirely ignores the Australian Women's Charter Committee and the underlying political division in the women's movement of which it was a symptom.[23] Ironically, she gives Sheila further prominence for her part in the promulgation, in 1951, of another proclamation of women's rights – the Declaration of Equality, an ornate formal document, very similar in content to Lady Street's Charter.

Headed "Declaration October 22nd 1951", this document reads:

> We The Australian Federation of Women Voters. . . The Federation of University Women. . . The Business and Professional Women's Clubs. . . The Soroptomists Clubs unanimously declare ourselves in favour of the complete equality of men and women in all social, economical, political and legal spheres, and pledge ourselves to work

---

21 Davidson lists three 1972 events as indicators of the advent of the second wave: the formation of the Women's Electoral Lobby in Melbourne in February; the formation of Women's Liberation at a public meeting in the Perth Trades Hall in May and a call for the legal advertising of contraceptives by Harvest Guild President Wendy Fatin on ABC television in October. The last event was followed in May 1973 by a debate on the legalisation of abortion organised by the Harvest Guild and chaired by a prominent woman lawyer, Liza Newby.

22 Mrs P McFadyen, from a personal interview.

23 Reciprocally Lady Street makes no mention of Bessie Rischbieth in her book.

> for the unprejudiced acceptance by all authorities of the principle of equality which postulates equal opportunity, responsibility and reward.[24]

The Declaration was signed by a representative of each of the subscribing organisations. Sheila signed on behalf of the Australian Federation of University Women.

The occasion on which the Declaration was promulgated was the Ninth Triennial Conference of the Australian Federation of Women Voters – an affiliate of the Women's Service Guilds – held in Perth on 22 October 1951. At this conference, Sheila represented the Australian Federation of University Women of which she was national President from 1950-1952. In addition to participating in the execution and presentation of the Charter of Equality, Sheila presented a forum of professional speakers which Mrs Rischbieth describes in her book:

> An unusual and interesting public session, arranged by Miss Sheila McClemans, LLB, on Thursday evening, October 25, was entitled "Pioneers of the Future". This proved a most lively and stimulating session. Miss McClemans introduced, with a brief biography, each of the four members of the younger generation. . .[25]

The claim for economic equality in the joint declaration had a special significance for the Federation of University Women. In 1947 the Federation began a campaign for equal pay for University professional staff at the instigation of Enid Russell, who was then lecturing in Private International Law as well as acting as Professor Beasley's managing secretary. It appears that there had been an overall increase in salaries for University staff but the increase granted to female lecturers was markedly less than that granted to males even though they were of equal qualification and doing the same work. Despite vigorous agitation by the Federation, equal pay was denied female academics until 1967.[26]

---

24 Bessie M Rischbieth, *March of Australian Women*, Paterson, Brokensha Pty Ltd, 1964, p 99.

25 Ibid, p 106.

26 Mary V Woods and Winifred W Bisset, *The History of the Western Australian Association of University Women 1923-1973*, Self published, 1973, pp 16-17.

The 1951 Conference of the Australian Federation of Women Voters appears to have been the high point in Sheila's involvement in the feminist movement. Although she remained the Guilds' honorary solicitor for many years and a member of the Australian Federation of University Women all her life, there is no record of her taking a prominent part in any public activity of the Guilds or any of their affiliates after the 1951 conference. This apparent withdrawal from Guilds activities was due to the demands of her personal and professional life and not to any differences with the policy of the guilds which she continued to support for the rest of her life.

In her *Oral History* she makes a reference to the increase in her work-load in the immediate postwar years: "It was beginning to get busy. The law work was the same type still, there was no great change in it, but of course there was an upsurge as the wheels of commerce began to grind again".[27]

In addition to her increased work-load, Sheila assumed a very onerous personal responsibility when she married Frank Kenworthy on 4 August 1949, taking on the management of his household and the care of his two orphaned children, Neil 19 and Lesley 13 years of age.

Although the ceremony was private, the marriage was accorded a two-column heading and a photograph in the social page of the *West Australian* of 6 August 1949. The item was headlined "MARRIAGE OF FORMER WRANS LEADER" and the photograph was captioned "Surprise Wedding". The text did not explain to whom the wedding was a surprise and readers were left in mystery about that. They were informed, however, that the bride wore "two silver fox furs and a matching hat of light weight felt with her simply-cut long-sleeved frock of pale blue angora".

As mentioned in Chapter 3, Frank Kenworthy, an engineer by profession, had met Sheila at the University while completing a law degree to enhance his position in the Water Supply Department. Because they lived in neighbouring suburbs and had mutual friends, they made casual contact from time to time in later years. Both

27 C Shervington, *Sheila Mary McClemans: Oral History Memoir*, by courtesy University of WA archives, p 12.

Judith Collett (née Leschen) and Neil Kenworthy recall holidaying together as children at Caves House, Yallingup, in 1940. Judith was accompanied by her aunt Sheila, Neil was with his parents and younger sister Lesley.[28]

Frank had graduated in Law in 1934 but did not take up articles to qualify as a practising lawyer because he always regarded engineering as his profession. He made good use of his legal training within the department by drafting its by-laws and regulations. According to Brian Fleay, a senior career engineer with the department for many years, many of the Kenworthy by-laws were still in use in 1990.[29]

When war broke out in 1939 Frank was in an essential occupation and precluded from enlisting until the whole scene changed in 1941. The Japanese invasion necessitated the hasty construction of defence works in Western Australia and the 22nd Army Field Company was formed to do this. Frank was commissioned as a senior officer in this unit. Among the works he supervised was the underground command post at Rottnest – now a tourist museum. He later served overseas with the 8th Army Field Division Engineers at Morotai and Balikpapan during the Allied counter-offensive in South East Asia. He rejoined his department as Deputy Chief Engineer on his discharge in February 1946.

It was a sad homecoming. Frank's wife, Muriel, was terminally ill with cancer of the liver and died soon after. At the time of their mother's death, Neil was in his first year at University and Lesley still at primary school. His elderly mother kept house for him for a while after Muriel's death but soon realised she was too old to cope. According to Neil, Sheila came to the rescue by introducing Frank to a recently widowed client who was seeking a housekeeping job. The arrangement proved very satisfactory and the housekeeper carried on until Sheila married Frank and took over the management of the household.

The romance between Sheila and Frank apparently developed quietly over quite a period of time. The staff at Hardwick Slattery and Gibson began to observe Sheila coming to work once or twice a

28 Judith Collett and Neil Kenworthy, from personal interviews.

29 Brian Fleay, from a personal interview.

week in a black evening dress and carrying a silver fox fur which was locked in the strong room for the rest of the day for safe keeping. Towards five o'clock, Sheila would put on fresh make-up and, as the staff were leaving, they would notice the arrival of a tall handsome middle-aged gentleman whom they got to know as Frank Kenworthy. The first they knew of the wedding was when they read it in the morning paper on Monday, 6 August.[30]

Although the wedding attracted headlines this was not intended. Sheila always tried to keep her private life to herself. At her wish the wedding was a very private affair. It was celebrated on a Saturday morning in her father's old church, Christ Church, Claremont, the congregation consisting only of her mother, her niece Judith and her old friends, Paul and Alexandra Hasluck. The Haslucks held a small reception at their home in Dalkeith later in the morning for close relatives and friends. After her marriage, Sheila continued to practise under her maiden name and many in the profession were not aware she was a married woman.

At the time of the marriage, Neil Kenworthy was a fourth year engineering student still living at home. He recalls that Sheila was very precise and business like in her household management, of necessity as well as habit. She was extremely busy professionally and usually brought files home to work on at night, doing her own typing on the little portable she had bought many years ago. In Neil's own words, "Sheila ran a pretty tight ship".

Neil adjusted very well to the advent of his step-mother. This does not appear to be the case with his sister with whom, on several accounts, there was a high level of inter-familial conflict. During this period Sheila frequently agonised over the problems of her relationship with Lesley to her old navy friend Iris Purnell, both in correspondence and during occasional visits to Melbourne.[31] Elizabeth Davies (née Jensen), now of Sydney, was a class mate of Lesley through all her high-school years and recalls that the situation was very unhappy, so much so that Elizabeth and her friends, siding with their class-mate, would refer to Sheila as "that old witch".[32]

---

30 Dr Jo Hawkins, from a personal interview.

31 Iris Purnell, from a personal interview.

32 Elizabeth Davies, from a personal interview.

Sheila's niece Judith Collett (then Leschen), who was a frequent visitor to the household at the time and empathised with both parties, was greatly saddened by the situation.[33] Lesley herself has firmly declined to be interviewed for her recollections of the relationship, which is, perhaps, some confirmation of what the other sources have reported.

It was a situation in which problems were bound to arise. Conflicts between adolescent daughters and their natural mothers are a common phenomenon. They are even more likely to occur when a step-mother arrives on the scene to take over a household, impose her own regime and divert the father's attention from a grieving step-daughter. In those days, professional grief-counselling was unknown, orphans were expected to "get over" their grief and carry on. The treatment accorded to the orphans of the poor in the now notorious British Commonwealth child migration schemes of the day is indicative of the prevailing philosophy.

No doubt Sheila would have done her best to take the part of a loving and responsible mother. Family Court judge, Justice David Anderson, particularly recalls the care she took to arrange Lesley's coming-out as a debutante. According to him, Lesley was squired by his younger brother Peter. David claims that in his days as a young family lawyer, many years her junior, Sheila treated him with special consideration and he has always felt that he was bathing in his brother's reflected glory.[34]

In running the household and carrying out her quasi-parental duties, Sheila would have applied the experience and skills she had developed as Chief Officer WRANS during the war. This may not have been entirely appropriate to that particular household and it may well not have been appreciated by her step-daughter. As in all things Sheila would have done what she thought was best and her anguish at her unhappy relationship with Lesley would have been very real.

The fact that Sheila was taking work home confirms the intensity of her work-load at the time of her marriage. It would have been very rare for a salaried employee, as distinct from a principal, to take work home at that time. A demanding domestic situation added

33 Judith Collett, from a personal interview.

34 Justice David Anderson, from a personal interview.

to her work-load would have subjected her to considerable pressure. The pressure increased as Sheila's reputation both for professional excellence and personal empathy became widely known.

One section of the community which benefited particularly from Sheila's skills were the migrant women, many of them refugees from postwar Europe. Again, the extra-mural activities of the McClemans family complemented Sheila's professional work. In 1949 Veronica Kviesis, a Latvian lawyer who had come to Western Australia as a refugee with her family, made contact with the Women's Service Guilds. In pre-war Latvia she had belonged to an international pacifist organisation, the Women's League of Peace and Friendship which was affiliated to the Guilds. She was referred to Ada McClemans who had special responsibility for migrant women through her membership of the Good Neighbour Council, a body dedicated to assisting migrants. Ada in turn referred her to Sheila in her capacity as a member of the Association of University Women which had a policy of assistance to professional migrant women. Sheila immediately recognised the potential of a woman with a legal education who could speak several European languages – a potential totally wasted in her current job as a cleaner.[35]

Migrant women with family problems were coming to Sheila's office in increasing numbers. They were being referred to her by her old friend Jim Smythe in his position as Clerk of the Perth Married Women's Summary Relief Court. Sheila persuaded her principals to employ Mrs Kviesis as a law clerk specialising in matrimonial work, a move which greatly boosted her clientele.

In 1949 the staff of the firm was enhanced by the arrival of two very bright articled clerks, close friends Athol Gibson and Geoff Hammond. Athol was Cliff Gibson's son and Geoff the son of Les Hammond, the firm's managing law clerk of many years' standing. Both had interrupted their University courses to join the RAAF, in which both had served with distinction. Geoff being awarded a Distinguished Flying Cross and Athol a Mention in Dispatches. Both received helpful guidance and instruction from Sheila which they were to remember with gratitude throughout their years in practice.[36]

35 Veronica Kviesis, from a personal interview.

36 Athol Gibson and Geoff Hammond, from personal interviews.

On their admission to practise, the two parted company. Athol remained with the firm and eventually became a partner. Geoff left with his father to set up in practice on his own accord in the same building, Victoria House at 98 St George's Terrace, Perth, now demolished.

Athol and Geoff were succeeded by an articled clerk whose relations with Sheila were not so cordial, Billie Mackie Snedden. His service in the firm was so unsatisfactory that Sheila refused to sign his certificate of fitness to practise which he needed for admission to the profession. Although he eventually persuaded someone to certify him fit and practised for a short while, Billie did not see much future in the Law. He joined the Liberal Party and entered federal politics. To the surprise of all his contemporaries, he rose to serve as Commonwealth Attorney-General under Sir Robert Menzies. Later, he was Leader of the Opposition during the Whitlam Government until ousted by Malcolm Fraser in a leadership spill in 1975. In 1964, as Secretary of the Law Society, Sheila found it ironically amusing having to welcome visiting Attorney-General Snedden to a Law Society function held in his honour.

The firm of Hardwick and Slattery dissolved in 1953. Cliff and Athol continued to practise at the former Perth office in Victoria House under the name of Hardwick Gibson and Gibson. Bill Slattery retained the Fremantle office at the corner of High and Packenham Streets, practising under the name of Hardwick and Slattery. Sheila was not offered a partnership and left the firm to set up in practice on her own under the name of Sheila McClemans in a suite of offices adjoining Geoff Hammond's on a lower floor of Victoria House. She took with her her highly valued secretary, Veronica Kviesis, with whose help Sheila quickly built up one of the biggest divorce practices in Perth.[37]

Victoria House was also the home of another prestigious law firm of the time, Joseph Muir and Williams. Two of its partners, Francis Burt (universally known by his boyhood nick-name "Red") and John Wickham, were generally regarded as the most brilliant young lawyers of their time. Both retired from the firm in 1961 to establish the Independent Bar of Western Australia and within ten

37 Veronica Kviesis, from a personal interview.

years both were elevated to the Supreme Court Bench. "Red" Burt was appointed Chief Justice and knighted in 1979 – the last judicial knighthood awarded in Western Australia. After his retirement, he served as State Governor for several years.

Another Joseph Muir and Williams partner was Bill Elphick who, as mentioned above, accorded Sheila the nickname "Nails" because of her alleged toughness to opposing husbands.[38] Bill and Sheila were often on opposing sides because he did most of the divorce work for his firm. He acted, in the main, for husbands, being a former AIF veteran with active service in both the Middle East and New Guinea and having a general reputation for being a man's man and a tough fighter.

One man who learned how tough Sheila could be was a money lender named Morgan, husband of Constance Morgan, Sheila's secretary in her early Fremantle days with Hardwick Slattery and Gibson. Morgan was a very ruthless businessman who specialised in making loans to desperate people at high rates of interest on most inequitable terms. He was notorious in legal circles for foreclosing on the goods and chattels of his debtors. In 1953 he was imprisoned for five years for perverting the course of justice in a scandalous *cause celebre* involving the disgrace and ruin of a magistrate and a medical practitioner.

Constance nobly stood by Morgan through his troubles but, after his release from gaol, he became mentally disturbed and so maltreated her and her children that she was forced to leave him and the Peppermint Grove house he had bought with the profits of his dubious enterprises. Morgan would not let her take anything from the house and refused to maintain her or her children. Having no private means, Constance was destitute. Sheila heard of this and volunteered to act without fee to ensure that Constance received justice.

Early in the proceedings against Morgan, Sheila discovered that he had vested most of his property in Constance's name in order avoid potential creditors – the Commissioner of taxation in particular. Holding the whip hand, Sheila meted out to Morgan some

38 See Chapter 4, p 71.

of his own treatment and extracted from him a very generous settlement for Constance and her children.[39]

Although the Morgan case was a typical example of much of her work, Sheila was not a professional man-hater. Her principal matrimonial clientele was female because social and economic circumstances continually drove women into the courts as a matter of survival for themselves and their children. They came to Sheila because of her reputation for competence, empathy and generosity.

Sheila also had many male clients and fought for them as fairly and firmly as for her female clients. Beryl Bruce, a former WRAN at Sheila's Melbourne headquarters, worked for a while as a typist in her postwar practice. She was present when Sheila staggered back from court one day, badly bruised and slightly concussed. Dazedly Sheila kept repeating, "She clocked me! She clocked me!". She had just won a case for a husband in the Summary Relief Court and as she was gathering up her papers at the Bar table the defeated wife charged at her, striking her on the face repeatedly with a wildly swinging hand-bag. The bruising was so severe that Sheila was obliged to take several days off work to recover.[40]

A less traumatic incident of Sheila's matrimonial practice was the occasional visit from a mildly paranoid female client – a member of the Un-identified Flying Objects Society – who had a fixation that the Duke of Edinburgh was secretly in love with her. She repeatedly demanded that Sheila issue a divorce petition on behalf of the Duke against Queen Elizabeth so that he would be free to marry her. Beryl had strict instructions to keep this lady at bay whenever she came to the office demanding an appointment.

That court room attack was characteristic of the bitterness engendered in matrimonial disputes which the comfortable classification "Family Law" serves to conceal. It is unlikely that Sheila's assailant had any lawful justification for her actions. In the assessment of her contemporaries, Sheila was always scrupulously fair and reasonable in her conduct towards the opposing side.[41] Alan Barblett, who later became President of the Family Court, was one

---

39 Constance Morgan, from a personal interview.

40 Beryl Bruce, from a personal interview.

41 Leo Wood and John O'Halloran, personal interviews.

of the younger generation of practitioners moving up through the profession in the 1950s. In his opinion, Sheila's conduct in child-custody cases was outstanding in that she always put the interest of the child first. Where children were concerned, it was never a question of "my client right or wrong" with Sheila. He also recalls with gratitude Sheila's consideration for younger practitioners who often got a hard time from some of their senior win-at-all-costs opponents.[42]

1955 was a year of mixed fortunes for Sheila. She suffered great sadness from the death of her mother with whom she had always remained close. In the same year, however, Frank was promoted to the post of Principal Engineer for the Water Department and the couple moved to the grand Departmental residence overlooking the city of Perth in the idyllic surroundings of King's Park.

In 1958 Sheila enjoyed some relief from the demands of her practice when she and Frank embarked upon a seven-month world tour to take advantage of the co-incidence that an international Bar conference and a seminar upon the conversion of brackish water into fresh were being held simultaneously in Cologne. From Germany they travelled to Athens where, whilst visiting the Acropolis, they were confronted by a demonstration protesting the continued British occupation of Cyprus, which Sheila commented upon when interviewed by a *West Australian* reporter on her return: "I didn't feel so proud of my British passport during that half-hour".[43]

By the end of the 1950s Sheila was generally regarded as being one of the leading legal practitioners in Perth, yet she was not accorded any of the usual rewards of official recognition for excellence in the law. Three of her contemporaries had been elevated to the Supreme Court Bench and another three had been appointed Queen's Counsel. No one in official circles ever approached Sheila to enquire if she was interested in accepting these honours. All the appointees during that period were male and, in the prevailing attitude of that time, it would have been unheard of to award such a high honour to a woman.

42 Hon Alan Barblett, from a personal interview.

43 *West Australian*, 5 October 1958.

Although Sheila's daily practice was of great social value it relegated her to the category of a quiet achiever rather a shining forensic virtuoso. The principal daily newspapers at the time had a policy of not publicising matrimonial cases or the names of counsel involved in them. This sort of publicity was left to the *Mirror* which was scorned in respectable circles. The cases which got most coverage in the daily press and on radio were the sensational criminal trials, the important civil matters involving high awards of damages and the occasional constitutional argument involving the conflicting rights between the State and the private citizen or between the State and the Commonwealth.

The legal profession tended to regard matrimonial law as second rate and few matrimonial cases were reported in the *West Australian Law Reports.* The prospect Sheila faced, approaching the end of her third decade in practice, was to spend the rest of her days listening to the complaints of abused and neglected women and battling for them in the courts – primarily in the lower jurisdictions. However socially necessary it may be, such work is harrowing and mind-numbing. Professionals exposed to it over a long period of time often become emotionally exhausted. In recent years sociologists have invented the expression "social worker burn-out" to describe its effect. Eventually such work ceases to be challenging and becomes a burden.

In 1960 Sheila sold her practice, on generous terms, to Geoff Hammond to assume the position of full-time Secretary of the Law Society of Western Australia and administrator of its Legal Aid Scheme. The first morning of the take-over was a shock to Geoff. A queue of mournful women waited outside his door when he arrived at the office. Fortunately, Veronica Kviesis arrived and helped him to cope. He soon engaged a junior solicitor to handle the bulk of the matrimonial work and ultimately benefited financially from his greatly enlarged practice. Together with the rest of the profession he was also to benefit from the greater efficiency of the Law Society and the development of the Legal Aid Scheme.[44]

Sheila gave a number of reasons for withdrawing from private practice. To Mrs Kviesis she said that constant standing in court was too much of a strain for her back and she could not carry on.[45] She

---

44 Geoff Hammond, from a personal interview.

45 Veronica Kviesis, from a personal interview.

gave a similar explanation to her step-son, Neil Kenworthy.[46] In a 1970 article in a public service journal, *Land Social Survey*, the reason she gave was that she "was getting too old".[47]

Both these explanations seem improbable. In 1960 she was only 50 years of age and at the height of her professional powers. Neither her age nor her back condition prevented her from later resuming practice in the matrimonial courts as a salaried employee of Geoff Hammond from 1970 until 1980 after retiring from the Legal Aid Scheme.

On two other occasions she gave a more likely explanation. In her Anzac Day talk to schools some time in the 1960s, she said:

> All these experiences have made me realise how very important it is for everyone to be of service to other people. So when the time was reached when all the lawyers in Perth, wishing to be of service to others, founded a Legal Aid Scheme to help poor people who had need to go to law I went to work as a lawyer with that scheme as indeed I still do.[48]

The following was her recollection in her *Oral History*, in 1982:

> I continued to practise alone . . . and the practice grew and grew until it became really more than I could manage and . . . at that stage the Law Society for the first time was going to engage a professional person as its Secretary to administer the Legal Aid Scheme and to do the work of the Law Society. And I went there and I did that for five years. . . I think that would have been 1960 to 1965.[49]

The reasonable inference to draw from these two statements is that it was neither age nor ill health that caused her to sell her practice. The Law Society's decision gave her an opportunity to employ her outstanding organising talents to serve both the legal profession and the underprivileged on a grand scale, as distinct from bogging away at the coal face. It presented her with the challenge she needed and she accepted it with enthusiasm.

---

46 Neil Kenworthy, from a personal interview.

47 John O Giles, "Go See Sheila!" (September 1970) *Land Social Survey*, pp 25-27.

48 Anzac Day address: manuscript of a speech in possession of Mr & Mrs Neil Kenworthy. The year of broadcast is not known.

49 C Shervington, *Sheila Mary McClemans: Oral History Memoir*, by courtesy University of WA archives, p 12.

7

"OUR GREATEST ACHIEVEMENT"

The Law Society of Western Australia was incorporated in the year 1927. In that year there were only 153 practising lawyers in the State and the Law School was still in the process of formation. The Great Depression of the 1930s and the out-break of the World War in 1939 had a retarding effect so that by 1950 practising lawyers numbered only 166 and law students 74. More rapid growth occurred during the immediate postwar years and by 1960 the numbers had swelled to 246 and 106 respectively.[1]

Like all professional organisations, the first pre-occupation of the Society was to care for the needs of its members and to foster a sense of cohesion and fellowship amongst them. Convivial meetings, dinners and similar functions have always played an important part in the life of the Society. These were not merely occasions for recreation. In their informal atmosphere professional problems were shared and discussed, cases were sometimes settled between opposing solicitors and, for the young, there was much that could be learned about law and procedure from older practitioners who became more approachable as the wine flowed.

An organisation dedicated to the general interests of a profession which is obliged by its nature to interact with the problems of the community must inevitably involve itself with wider issues. From its inception, the Society was concerned with legal education and fostering the infant Law School. Its founding president, Sir Walter

1 The records of practitioners have been obtained from the Western Australian Law Almanacs for the appropriate years. The student enrolment numbers were kindly supplied by the UWA Planning Services.

James KC, was one of the part-time lecturers the profession provided to help Professor Beasley, the School's only full-time lecturer. Constantly occurring anomalies in the law obliged the Society to become involved in law reform. The desperate conditions of a large section of the community, impoverished by Depression and War, emphasised the necessity for an adequate legal aid scheme.

These problems were Australia wide and in 1933 a conference of State law bodies in Sydney instituted a national body, the Law Council of Australia. For many years, funds were so low that both the Law Council and the States bodies had to make do with part-time voluntary executives. In Western Australia it was usually the lot of an energetic younger practitioner to act as executive officer under the title of Secretary, making use of the facilities of his own firm.[2] Although general elections were held annually, there was a convention that a senior practitioner would hold the post of President for two years at a time. Many presidents were eventually rewarded with a place on the Supreme Court Bench.

In the immediate postwar years, the Honorary Secretary was the Honourable Ian Medcalf AO, QC. It is a measure of the finances of the Society that Medcalf was paid an honorarium of 30 shillings weekly for his services. During his term and largely as a result of his initiative, the Society set up what was to become a very successful superannuation scheme for the profession, entitled Law Trusts (Inc). When he was succeeded in the secretaryship of the Society by one of his junior partners, Ian Stephenson, Medcalf remained on the Council of the Society taking particular responsibility for Law Trusts, law reform and legal aid.

In its early history, Western Australia had little provision for the legal representation of the poor. It inherited from England a system whereby a person facing a capital charge would be assigned a lawyer at the door of the court – known as a "dock brief" – but which, by 1928, was described by the conservative legal spokesman and former Attorney-General, TAL Davy MLA, as having "fallen into desuetude".[3] In civil matters, the rules of the Supreme Court had some machinery for legal assistance known as *in forma pauperis* but

2 Ian Medcalf QC, from a personal interview

3 WAPD Vol 80 NS(1928) 2184.

these the Labor Minister for Justice described as "so hampered by the conditions that very little use is made of the rules of court that enable poor people to gain the advantage of legal aid".[4]

These descriptions of the inadequacy of the prevailing provisions for legal aid were contributed during the parliamentary debates over the introduction by the Collier Labor Government of the *Poor Persons Legal Assistance Act* 1928 (WA). This Act expressed the divergence in views in the legal profession as to the direction a legal aid scheme should take. The conservative majority has always favoured a scheme which placed emphasis upon the work being done by private practitioners, paid (if they are paid at all) from a State-subsidised fund at somewhat less than the standard professional rate. More radical practitioners favoured a service provided by a government agency employing a salaried professional staff and financed from general revenue – similar to State public health services.[5]

The Collier (Labor) Government of the day seems to have placed a two-way bet when it enacted the *Poor Persons Legal Assistance Act* because it provided that the Act should be administered by a committee appointed by the Law Society or by the Public Solicitor when that official was appointed by Parliament. The conservative Opposition, through Mr Davy, expressed some apprehension about the nationalisation of the legal profession and opposed the appointment of a Public Solicitor on grounds of economy. He assured Parliament that the Law Society committee would administer the scheme through a voluntary committee and save the cost of employing a Public Solicitor.[6]

In the event a Public Solicitor was never appointed. His role seems to have been assumed unofficially and in an honorary capacity by WF Sayer KC on his retirement from the office of Solicitor General in 1930. Claiming that he could not in conscience collect his pension without working for it, he dispensed poor persons'

---

4 Ibid, 2028.

5 S Armstrong, "Labor's legal aid scheme. The light that failed" in RB Scotton and H Ferber (eds), *Public Expenditure and Social Policy in Australia* Vol 11, Longman Cheshire, 1980; L Powell & F Regan, "Legal Aid: Reflections on Costs. Lawyers and the future" (1988) 9(4-5) *Legal Aid Clearing House Bulletin.*

6 WAPD Vol 80 NS 1928, 2026 and 2185.

assistance almost until his death in 1943 at the age of 83. An example of his service to indigent litigants was the subject of the following news item in the *West Australian:*

> SIX SUCCESSFUL PORTIAS
>
> Six of ten successful divorce petitioners in the Supreme Court yesterday were women, who proceeded without benefit of legal pleaders. The wronged wives . . . conducted their own cases in a masterly manner. Witnessing this exhibition of forensic skill, as one petitioner after another induced Mr Justice Wolff to snap her matrimonial bonds, occupants of the spectators' gallery could scarce forebear to cheer. One of the reasons for the petitioners' success was that they had all received expert "coaching" behind the scenes from Mr WF Sayer, KC, who, since his retirement from the post of Solicitor General after many years of distinguished service to the State, has devoted much of his time to the assistance of poor persons.[7]

The value of Sayers' contribution was publicly acknowledged in a speech to a municipal conference by the Minister For Works, Mr A McCallum MLA:

> we owe much to our old friend, Mr WF Sayer KC. He is one of those men who cannot stop working. Although he is retired on pension, he asked for accommodation at the Crown Law Department . . . because he feels he cannot accept his pension unless he earns it.[8]

After Sayers' death, the *Poor Person's Legal Assistance Act* was administered by a Crown Law Department clerk. When Justice Henry Wallwork was an articled clerk it was one of his duties in the Department to administer the scheme for a brief period.[9] It was a scheme which was poor by name and poor by nature. A minute amount of public revenue was allocated to it and the clerk in charge worked at other duties as well. The maximum payment to a practitioner assigned to a case was £8 to defend a wilful murder case (in 1928 the male basic wage was about £4 a week). Ian Medcalf remembers that Sir Francis Burt, before his Supreme Court appointment, took a Poor Persons' wilful murder appeal to the Privy Council in London.

7 Undated clipping in the author's possession.

8 Undated clipping in the author's possession.

9 The Honourable Justice Wallwork, from a personal interview.

Under the Act he would have been entitled to £7 for his brief fee which included all preliminary work. He accepted reimbursement of his air-fare but charged no fee.[10]

To qualify for assistance under the *Poor Persons Act*, a claimant's total assets had to be less than £50 and the claimant's income for the previous 12 months had to be less than £4 weekly. Even in the poverty stricken Depression days, few males were poor enough to qualify. The beneficiaries were mainly deserted or widowed women. It can readily be seen that average citizens had little access to the courts unless they were prepared to risk ruin.

The Law Society was never happy with this position but the Depression and the World War postponed any hope of improvement. Postwar there was much hope that the position would improve. In the United Kingdom the sweeping social welfare measures, introduced by the Attlee Labour Government, included legal aid provisions which were envied by lawyers and litigants alike in Australia and the debate over the way to go resumed.

Harry Alderman QC, then President of the Law Society of South Australia and a Member of the national Law Council, visited Western Australia in the 1950s and addressed members of the profession on the subject of Legal Aid. In his address he warned of the threat of government control of legal aid which seemed to be threatened by the appointment of a Public Solicitor in New South Wales and urged the Law Society of Western Australia to take steps to enter the field and ward off this socialistic menace.[11]

The Council of the Law Society of Western Australia took his advice and decided to appoint a committee, as originally envisaged by the Act, to administer the scheme and to seek a greater financial contribution from the State Government. After much debate the government decided to supply sufficient funds to administer a legal aid scheme and pay disbursements but not to pay lawyers' fees for work done for claimants. The Society considered that this was at least a start and decided to employ a full-time executive secretary to administer the scheme and assume the growing burden of administering the affairs of the Society itself.

10 The Honourable Ian Medcalf, from a personal interview.

11 Ibid.

It was this joint position which Sheila applied for and to which the Society appointed her with grateful enthusiasm on 1 July 1960. No one is more capable of assessing her value as an executive officer in the general affairs of the Society than Ian Medcalf who has made available a wealth of material from his own personal files relating to committees on which he served attesting to the quality of her service.

One example is a letter dated 18 July 1960 – a little over a fortnight of her taking up the position – in which she presents a list of the contributors to the Law Society Superannuation Fund together with her calculation of their entitlement to the annual profits with the comment:

> I have worked out a distribution of the profits payable to participants in the fund, as at 30th June 1959. As you will see from the enclosed list, the working out involves halfpennies and leaves for carrying forward a small sum. I myself think this is not the proper way to do it and that the entire amount should be distributed each year, but if I make adjustments it will mean that various investors will get a penny more than their entitlement, whilst some will get a penny less. I would be grateful if you would check that I have approached the working out in the correct way and if you would confirm that I should adjust the amounts payable, so that there is no carry forward. . .[12]

In Medcalf's assessment, this was a typical example of her being able to assume responsibility for quite a complex project, make an immediate assessment of the most efficient way to handle it and act accordingly, yet at the same time to refer it to the sub-committee concerned for approval so that there could be no suggestion of autocracy on her part. The Honourable Justice Wallace was a President of the Society during Sheila's term of office. His recollection is that Sheila's approach would usually be "I'm sure you are concerned with how the society can deal with this matter. . .", from which he would know that Sheila was already embarked on tackling that particular matter and that it was exactly the right course to follow.[13]

---

12 Archival files in possession of the Honourable Ian Medcalf.

13 The Honourable Robert Wallace, from a personal interview.

When questions of law reform were raised at the Society's Law Reform Committee Sheila was always able to provide a concise explanation of the point by reason of her profound general knowledge of the law and the preparation she would put into researching the matter. This, in Medcalf's opinion, was of great value to the committee members, all busy practitioners giving their own time to the Society's business after office hours. Medcalf's summation of her work was that "Sheila was an exceptional character, a very dedicated person who gave a life of service without thought of reward and was a wonderful inspiration and example to her profession".[14]

The Law Society's Legal Aid Scheme did not officially get under way until July 1961. During the intervening year, Sheila took over the Poor Persons' Legal Assistance files from the Crown Law Department and attended to them as well as looking after anyone who came in off the street seeking aid. Leo Wood has provided an amusing account of Sheila's assignment to him of one of these backlog files:

> It was a murder. Eric Edwards reckoned it was the best case I ever won.[15] My star case. I can't remember the name I've got a bugger of a memory for names. It was a case of a man who smothered his wife with a pillow and he made a confession saying he had smothered her because she was abusing him and screaming at him till he couldn't think. And he just grabbed the pillow and the blankets and piled them on top of her to shut her up.
>
> The police found her dead and when they found her she was laid out like she was in the morgue with a nice clean white sheet. Someone had obviously gone in and tidied the whole scene up. It turned out it was the bloke's mother. Thought she should look nice for the police when they found her.
>
> Darcy was the judge. He was like a lunatic. You know he used to be a Crown Prosecutor and he was determined to stitch this bloke up. I used the defence in the Code that the bloke was entitled to use reasonable force to shut this woman up because she was screeching at him and he had no intention to kill. Darcy was so keen to nail him

14 The Honourable Ian Medcalf, from a personal interview.

15 Eric Edwards, who, as Professor Edwards, succeeded Professor Beasley as Dean of the Law School, is the author of several leading textbooks on Evidence and the Criminal Law in Australia.

that he addressed the jury for three hours and made the mistake of keeping them shut up over the weekend so he could do it. I finished on the Friday afternoon and half of them were asleep then.

Everything militated against the Prosecution because by the time Darcy had finished his three hours on the Monday he'd put them all off to sleep. They came back with a total acquittal – not even a manslaughter. The Associate told me after that Darcy was so furious that when he got back to his chambers he pulled his wig off and threw it down on the floor. He didn't believe my bloke because the police found condoms in his pocket and they reckon he had another tart in tow and that's why he killed her but they couldn't prove it.

Any way Darcy says to his Associate "I'll get that bugger Wood yet". But he never did. The very next case I had before him he collapsed and died in the middle of it. I won that one too.

When I reported back to Sheila she said: "Now the usual fee for this is four guineas but there is provision for a special fee for six guineas for special work and skill. Put in a detailed report and claim that". Well six guineas was six guineas in those days, it'd pay your bloody rent for a couple of weeks. So I went back to the office and spent the afternoon drawing up a bill to look good and charged the special fee of six guineas.

I came down flat out next morning and put it in. Just as I was going out the door Sheila said: "You won't be getting any money you know Leo". I said "Why not?". She said "Have a look at this". She showed me the Poor Persons' Legal Assistance bank book she'd taken over from Crown Law. There was a balance in it of one shilling – just enough to keep the account alive.

I said "What the hell did you put me through all this trouble preparing this account for?". She said "Statistical purposes. We've got to be able to quantify our work".[16]

Following this transitional period the introduction of the new scheme was heralded on 30 March 1961 by a generous report in the *West Australian:*

16 Leo Wood, from a personal interview.

A WOMAN LAWYER OUTDATES A MEANS TEST

> The familiar face of Perth lawyer Sheila McClemans has been missing from the Law Courts these past nine months. She has a new job as solicitor administering the Law Society's Legal Aid Scheme.
>
> "One thing this job has taught me is to count my blessings. I've developed a great admiration for the courage with which people of limited means face their difficulties."
>
> The scheme, which comes into operation on July 1, gives assistance on a different basis to the old *Poor Persons' Legal Assistance Act.* The former Act precluded all persons with assets over fifty pounds or earned an amount equal to the basic wage over the past year. This means test is quite unrealistic now. The new scheme is flexible and every application is treated on merit. Of the 691 applications dealt with already the biggest number are in the matrimonial sphere and women outnumber men.
>
> At present the scheme is only able to assist to a limited extent. Miss McClemans interviews clients to decide if their case warrants referral to the Legal Aid Committee or whether free advice from her must be the limit of assistance.
>
> Cases which are taken to court are farmed out to the 235 practising lawyers. As payment is according to means, in most cases there is no payment and the lawyers often work for no fee.
>
> "Members of the profession are very good about taking these cases. They feel that anyone deserving assistance should receive it regardless of whether they can afford to pay."
>
> So far Miss McClemans has been too busy dealing with applications to take any cases herself. The Western Australian scheme is patterned upon the South Australian scheme which has been in force for 10 years and has aroused interest in many countries.

Preparatory to the institution of the new scheme, Sheila selected her staff, a typist and a clerk whose wages consumed most of the government grant for administration costs. The job of the clerk was to interview applicants for aid and take a statement from them before referring them to Sheila for advice. A competent clerk can save a great deal of professional time by getting to the heart of the matter and extracting the essence from a long and often rambling tale of woe.

For this post Sheila approached her old friend, Jim Smythe, whom she knew was due to retire from the position of Chief Clerk to the Married Person's Relief Court in May 1961. No one could be better suited for the post. Jim had spent half a lifetime interviewing the battered wives who had come to the courts for help. It was not part of the official duties of court staff to listen to the problems of the public and offer basic advice but a sense of common humanity had developed a tradition of delegating to the Assistant Clerk the duty of doing so. When the Married Person's jurisdiction was taken away from the Court of Petty Session in Beaufort Street and set up as a separate court, the Chief Magistrate, Frank Taylor MC, SM specially selected Jim for the post of Chief Clerk.

On Jim's retirement from that post, the Council of the Law Society wrote him two successive letters, dated 26 April and 8 May 1961, both signed by Sheila. The first expressed the appreciation of the profession for "the co-operation which you have at all times extended towards them". The letter also invited him to a party in his honour at 5:15 pm on Friday, 19 May. Jim had no doubt that the party was Sheila's idea, it being the sort of gesture that was typical of her. The second was strictly a business letter offering him the part-time position of Clerk to the Legal Aid Committee from 10:00 am to 4:00 pm week-days at a salary of £15 per week.

In addition to interviewing legal aid claimants, Jim's work included attendance at the meetings of the Law Society's Legal Aid Committee to which Sheila would report with her recommendations as to who should be granted aid. He used to marvel at Sheila's ability to judge the merit of each applicant and to recommend those worthy of aid. She was always very fair but also extremely shrewd with a keen nose for applicants who had no merit. Sheila was also very good at judging her fellow practitioners. Although she had a high regard for the profession generally, she did not hide her scorn for those who would ask "what's it worth?" when invited to join the legal aid scheme and then reject the invitation when told no fees were paid.[17]

17 Jim Smythe, from a personal interview.

Over the next few years, Sheila's activities received further favourable press attention. The now defunct *Week End News* of 8 November 1962 published the following eulogy by Roger Locke:

> WOMEN IN PROFILE
>
> Lawyer Sheila McClemans' job is to listen to peoples' legal problems as Secretary of the Law Society's Legal Assistance Scheme. It is easy to see why she is so successful. She has a pleasantly relaxed manner in conversation.
>
> Perhaps it is the way she half turns in her chair, props her arm along the back and rests her head on her hand. Whatever it is somehow, without really trying you find yourself doing most of the talking.
>
> When she does talk she doesn't embroider her conversation with waving hands or legal phrases. She talks in an unhurried but deliberate sort of way that suggests she would be quite unflappable.
>
> A colleague said. "She never gets heated. She has too good a brain. Emotion never interferes. Everything she tackles or discusses is done logically".
>
> She is extraordinarily competent and has the charm and sense of humour to match. Out of her office she becomes Mrs FM Kenworthy, a bright scintillating personality highlighted with a sharp rapier like wit. But she is not a dominating personality. She has a natural charm which draws people towards her.

Another important role Sheila played in the expanding activities of the Law Society was organising what is now called Continuing Legal Education (CLE). In all modern industrial societies the law is in a constant state of change. Lawyers are obliged to keep up with changes in the law, if not by their sense of professional duty to their clients then certainly by their fear of actions for negligence. It is often difficult for the busy practitioner to do this. Weariness from a day of tension in office or court and the social demands of family and friends induce a reluctance to pick up a law book for a quiet evening's reading.

In common with most professional bodies, Law Societies endeavour to promote study of the law – recapitulating what may be forgotten as well as learning about recent developments – by means of conferences and seminars. The Law Society of Western Australia in its early days made a practice of having a guest speaker talk upon some aspect of the law at monthly general meetings. Postwar, the Society began to hold regular country conferences and, in 1957, hosted the national Biennial Australian Legal Convention of the Law Council of Australia. While conferences and conventions are enjoyed by those attending for the social events associated with them, their fundamental purpose is legal education and the learned papers presented at them eventually make their way into legal journals. The *Australian Law Journal* has for years published the principal papers delivered to the Biennial Convention.

The immediate postwar years saw a massive increase in the amount of new taxation law. State and Commonwealth governments were forever amending their revenue Acts to tap fresh sources and to counter measures which cunning taxpayers and their professional advisers had devised for the avoidance of taxation. Traditionally, lawyers had been conservative about manipulation of the law for purposes of tax avoidance. Legal education and tradition had a strong ethical basis and the attitude of most lawyers of the old school was that there was something rather immoral about looking for deficiencies in the law to enable wealthy men to avoid paying their just and lawful taxes. Taxation law generally was held in such low esteem by the profession that nothing was taught about the subject at the Law School of Western Australia for the first 25 years of its existence.

Lawyers tended to take the passive role of advising clients against activities which might breach the law rather than taking the initiative to lead them along paths which would achieve lawful tax-avoidance. This was an attitude which irritated commercial men. At a Law Society meeting in the 1950s the guest speaker was a rising Perth accountant named Charles Court. On the subject of taxation law he made the complaint, "You lawyers are always telling us what we can't do. You never tell us what we can do. You are not positive thinkers".[18]

This criticism was not true of all lawyers and many ingenious means were devised by some of them to reduce the incidence of taxation. Once practices were developed which would save clients

18 From the author's personal recollection, as a member of the audience. Charles (later Sir Charles) Court eventually entered politics as the successful Liberal candidate for Nedlands and was State Premier from 1974 until his retirement in 1981.

money, solicitors risked actions for damages for negligence if they omitted to advise their clients accordingly, however much they may disapprove of the morality of such practices.

It became imperative for lawyers to learn about taxation law and to keep up with the latest developments in that law. The appointment of a senior practitioner Eddie Nicholson to lecture on tax at the Law School in 1953 was a recognition of this need. Whilst this appointment might ensure that future generations of lawyers would start their careers with some knowledge of taxation law it did nothing to counter the dangerous lack of knowledge on the subject amongst the profession at large. This aroused the concern of a visiting American Fullbright Law Professor, Willard H Pedrick, who, after consultations with an equally concerned Eddie Nicholson, delivered a paper on the subject to the 1957 National Convention of the Law Council of Australia which was later published in the *Australian Law Journal*.[19,20]

Professor Pedrick compared the attitude of United States lawyers to taxation law with that of Australian lawyers. He advised:

> Until the 1930s, the tax field did not count for much. . . There were few lawyers who professed to know anything about taxes, little was published on the topic, bar associations did not interest themselves in the subject and the law schools did not teach it.[21]

All this changed, however, with the proliferation of taxation legislation engendered by Roosevelt's New Deal programme followed by the World War.

American lawyers realised they could not afford to abandon this field to other practitioners not only for their own sake but for the sake of their clients who would in the long run be poorly served if their advisers on taxation law did not have legal training. Another danger to the clientele lay in the fact that taxation had invaded so many fields that lawyers could not safely draw business documents, divorce settlements or even a will without considering and advising upon the taxation ramifications which may be involved.

---

19 The Honourable Justice Robert Nicholson, from a personal interview.

20 Willard H Pedrick, "Tax Practice and the Legal Profession" (1957) 31 *Australian Law Journal* 267.

21 Ibid, 269.

Taxation courses became part of the curriculum in United States universities and some States made them compulsory for Bar examinations. Even this was not enough – as Professor Pedrick observed:

> By the time a legal profession schooled on tax matters in law schools could have replaced the then incumbents of the profession the field would have passed into other hands and the recapture process cannot be easy. Moreover training in the tax field is not something which, once taken, is over and done with like a diphtheria inoculation. The tax field is law in motion with a vengeance. This then is an ideal field, indeed an essential field for what is called continuing legal education for the practising profession.[22]

This was a seminal passage for Australian lawyers. It was probably the first time most of them had come across the expression "continuing legal education". Professor Pedrick then went on to consider the position in Australia, with some diffidence, appreciating that the dangers of doing so as a guest in another country called for "a high order of statesmanship and perhaps some fleetness of footnote as well".[23] In a well-documented survey – in the preparation of which he had probably been assisted by Eddie Nicholson – he showed that Australian tax lawyers were in the position United States lawyers were 20 years before. To remedy the situation he urged the Australian legal profession to foster the study of taxation law by developing programmes of continuing education in the field of taxation because as he put it: "No practitioner could possibly read all that is published in the tax field and in any case it would be difficult to imagine a worse fate. As literature it often leaves something to be desired".[24]

Professor Pedrick's paper proved to be something of a hit at that conference. It would not have been easy to win general acclaim for a paper on taxation law – particularly one that was critical of the Australian legal profession. It says much for his charm and wit that he was able to do so. Perhaps its impact was softened by a now legendary anecdote he recounted at one of the Convention's less formal occasions:

---

22 Ibid, 271.

23 Ibid, 267.

24 Ibid, 272.

> In the years before the burgeoning of law in the taxation field many US lawyers used to bring their secretaries to legal conventions and call them their wives. Today, having regard to the principles of tax-deductible expenditure, they bring their wives and call them their secretaries.[25]

Professor Pedrick' s urgings were heeded by the profession in Australia and, in 1960, a taxation seminar was held at the University of Sydney led by Justice Else-Mitchell of the Supreme Court of New South Wales. Dr Ross Parsons, who had been a colleague of Pedrick and Nicholson on the staff of the Law School of Western Australia before leaving to take a post at Sydney University, attended this seminar and wrote to his successor, Eric Edwards, enthusing about it. Inspired by this letter, Edwards suggested to Nicholson that they approach Professor Beasley and the Law Society to hold a Law Summer School on the subject of taxation at the University of Western Australia as a pilot project for future years.[26]

This was a very attractive idea because the University of Western Australia had pioneered the idea of holding annual Adult Education Summer Schools upon its campus. In those days the Supreme Court of Western Australia observed a long summer vacation which eased the pressure upon practitioners at that time of the year. Professor Beasley was enthusiastic and he, in turn, approached Francis Burt QC, who was then President of the Law Society, requesting the Society's assistance to organise a school early in 1961.

The Law Society responded with equal enthusiasm despite the fact it would have to bear the burden of raising the money to pay for the enterprise because the University then – as ever – was having financial problems. When Burt QC suggested that a bank account be opened named the "McClemans – Edwards Summer School Account", Beasley vetoed this on the ground that the University could not accept any financial obligation. The account vas then opened under the name of the "Sheila McClemans Summer School Account", Sheila being then the Secretary of the Law Society and the person upon whose shoulders most of the Law Society's contribution would be loaded.[27]

---

25 The Honourable Brian T O'Dea, from a personal interview.

26 Emeritus Professor Eric Edwards, from a personal interview.

27 Ibid.

Justice Else-Mitchell accepted an invitation to lead the School. It gave a great boost to the project to have Justice Else-Mitchell as leader. He was well known both in professional and academic circles as the writer of the leading Australian text-book on Hire Purchase Law – a subject which was then bedevilling grass-roots practitioners perhaps even more than taxation law.

The initial Western Australian Law Summer School, held in February 1961, got much prominence in the local press and was hailed as the first of its kind in Australia. It was a considerable success both financially and for its contribution to professional knowledge. It became an institution which attracted as leaders or speakers many famous lawyers and academics. Over the years it has been a meeting ground for the finest legal minds in the nation. It endured for 30 years, until superseded by an annual CLE course of lectures and seminars interspersed throughout the year.

Although the University supplied no money to the school, it helped in many other ways, providing accommodation, secretariat staff, printing and postage of papers and a Vice-Chancellor's Dinner to reward the voluntary paper givers from the ranks of the profession. Although for the first two years the main physical burden was accepted by the University, much detail had to be attended to by Sheila. All the financial arrangements, fund-raising, banking, disbursement and ultimate accounting were her responsibility. The informal social functions, the liaison between the Law School and the Society, meeting and accommodating visiting speakers were all part of her brief.

Not least, the idea of the Summer School had to be sold to the rank-and-file of the profession so that there would be a respectable attendance. Sheila looked after this aspect also, by telephone calls, individual letters and buttonholing of members at Law Society functions. All of this activity was superimposed upon her day-to-day work load from the Law Society and the Legal Aid Scheme. Once established, the Law Summer School became an annual responsibility for her which progressively increased as the University unloaded the bulk of the secretarial work upon the Law Society.

The Law Society's role in fostering the social intermingling of its members was another aspect of Sheila's duties which she performed magnificently and in which her husband Frank played a great supporting role. At all important occasions the President and his wife would welcome the guests as they arrived but Sheila and Frank always stood in the second rank to take over as the President welcomed more recent arrivals. They were a tall, distinguished looking couple and visually dominated most gatherings. Because Frank had a law degree and did much legal work in his department he was always at home with lawyers.

Sheila always ensured that no-one felt lonely on these occasions. She would make a point of singling out young practitioners and their partners and introducing them around. No party was ever dull with Sheila there to infuse it with her wit, charm and intelligent conversation.

Most Law Society functions tended to be male dominated – particularly the High Court Dinner which wives did not attend unless they also happened to be legal practitioners. According to Joan Heenan, Sheila was insistent that women practitioners attend these functions to break down the male insularity. At the High Court Dinner, Sheila made a point of introducing women practitioners to all the visiting Justices.[28]

Sheila also involved herself in the personal problems of members. When Sir John Lavan's first wife died, she telephoned him to ask how he was managing his household and offered the services of her cleaning lady, advising him that, "She doesn't like working for men as a rule, but she'll work for you if I ask her to".[29]

An elderly bachelor solicitor lived with his French mistress for many years and was very coy about her, never bringing her to functions or introducing her to his legal colleagues. The sad result of his embarrassment was that the poor woman did not know to whom to turn when he died. Sheila sought her out at home to present her with quite a substantial cheque from her late partner's Law Trusts entitlement. She continued to console her with visits from time to time thereafter.[30]

The increasing numbers of women practitioners who began to use the Supreme Court Robing Room complained that there was no

---

28 Joan Heenan, from a personal interview.

29 John Lavan, from a personal interview.

30 The Honourable Ian Medcalf, from a personal interview.

convenient toilet for them and that some of the male practitioners used to undo their flies ostentatiously to tuck in their shirts and use unnecessarily coarse language in their presence. Sheila prevailed upon the notoriously parsimonious Crown Law Department to install a separate robing-room with ensuite toilet in the Supreme Court building for female counsel.[31] Sheila also made a point of advising young female practitioners on matters of court dress which was much appreciated because there was no one else whom they could approach.[32]

Sheila's primary responsibility, however, was always the Legal Aid Scheme. By 1965 the annual number of applicants for legal assistance had exceeded one thousand and the limited space allocated to the Society in the Supreme Court building became inadequate. Fortunately, in the gardens adjacent to the Supreme Court, there was a decaying old stone structure designed and built in 1836 by the State's first Civil Engineer, Henry Revely, a close personal friend of the poet, Percy Bysshe Shelley. For many years it housed the Colony's first Supreme Court, presided over by its first Chief Justice, Sir Archibald Burt.[33]

For the first half of the 20th century, the Old Court House was occupied by the State Industrial Arbitration Commission which moved to larger premises in the 1950s. Notwithstanding that it was Perth's oldest surviving building, built by the State's first official architect, the government of the day announced plans to demolish it in the interests of "Progress". The Law Society led popular agitation to save it and campaigned to have it leased to the Society as its headquarters, combined with the office of the Legal Assistance Scheme. Sheila played a prominent part in this agitation and, when it succeeded, she supervised the restoration of the building, insisting its rusty iron roof be replaced with she-oak shingles to conform with its original design. She also requisitioned a hoard of old colonial furniture from the government stores to furnish it. Amongst the furniture was a massive desk which had originally belonged to Sir John Forrest and which had a distinctive bay at the rear which,

31 Moira Rayner, from a personal interview.

32 Shirley Offer, from a personal interview.

33 The history and design of the Old Court House is described by Ray and John Oldham in their book, *Western Heritage*, Paterson Brokensha Pty Ltd, 1961.

according to legend, was especially designed to accommodate his large paunch.[34,35]

Securing a permanent home for the Law Society was one of Sheila's last acts as Secretary of the Society. In 1965 health problems, particularly her back condition, and a desire to spend more time with her family made it imperative for her to reduce her work load and to resign as full-time Secretary. The position of Secretary was assumed by a Fremantle solicitor, Loris Wood. Sheila continued to act as part-time Assistant Secretary for some years, concentrating her efforts upon the Legal Aid Scheme.

A leading court reporter, Caroline Pummer, reported in the *West Australian* of 5 June 1965:

> This week West Australians have lost the services of an outstanding woman lawyer who in the past 5 years has dealt with more than 10,000 applications for legal aid. Of that number Miss Sheila McClemans has brought more than 6000 to completion. The cases have ranged from domestic squabbles to murder. She has resigned for health reasons. . .
>
> Miss McClemans has enjoyed her work with the Legal Aid Scheme which she says is helping to meet a great need in the Community. Her words indicate a vital side of her personality, apart from her knowledge and efficiency – her sympathy kindness and sense of humour – which are quickly apparent.
>
> Besides being Secretary Miss McClemans worked hard as a member of the Law Reform Committee. She is still a member of the Canteens Trust Fund Committee and a member of the Parole Board. Miss McClemans plans to continue these interests and attend Adult Education programmes. Most of her time, however she will devote to her home and husband. In private life she is Mrs Frank Kenworthy.

Sheila's work as Assistant Secretary after her retirement from the full-time position in June 1965 was concerned with the setting up of

34 Loris Wood, from a personal interview.

35 The Old Court House is now the Perth Headquarters of the Francis Burt Law Centre, a community education project sponsored by the Law Society and financed from the Public Purposes Trust Fund created under the *Legal Contribution Trust Act* 1967 which also provides that the Trust money may be used for research into law reform and for legal education.

a new scheme which would ensure that practitioners actually got some payment for the work they did. The Law Society reasoned that, if it could show the government figures proving that tens of thousands of dollars were donated by the legal profession annually by way of unpaid legal work, this might have some persuasive effect towards a subsidy for payment of fees. This was the reason Sheila was obliged to ask busy practitioners like Leo Wood to render detailed accounts of their work with no hope of payment, for statistical purposes.

By 1960 the United Kingdom was spending £6 million annually of taxpayers' money on the fee-paying legal aid scheme instituted by the postwar Labor Government. By contrast, the grant made by the Western Australian Government in 1960 was £6,000, solely for administrative purposes, no money being allocated to the payment of practitioners' fees which were all donated as part of the service.

State governments always responded to pleas to follow the British example by pointing out that, as the Commonwealth Government effectively controlled the national finances and had assumed major responsibility for social services, the legal profession should look to the Commonwealth for additional legal aid funds. In 1962 the Commonwealth Government announced that it was considering granting financial assistance in matters involving Commonwealth law, but this never proceeded beyond discussion stage.

When the vague promise of Commonwealth funds evaporated, the Law Society devised a new scheme which would make use of the idle funds tied up in solicitors' trust accounts throughout the State and which did not earn interest. All legal firms in general practice have trust accounts holding money collected on behalf of clients and which, for various reasons, cannot be paid out immediately. A typical and prolific source of trust account money is the deceased estate. There is always a delay between death and the time when the proceeds of the estate can be legally disbursed. During all this period the solicitors for the estate collect money on its account in dribs and drabs from all kinds of sources.

At any given moment millions of dollars lie unused in the total trust accounts of the legal profession. The banks find this very useful because there is no barrier against them drawing upon this vast reservoir of money to lend out at interest to their clients. The solicitors holding the money on account are not permitted to lend their clients' money out at interest because it is not theirs to lend.

The Law Society proposed an Act of Parliament which would require all solicitors holding trust accounts to pay a proportion of the money in those accounts into a statutory fund to be known as the Legal Contribution Trust Fund. The interest from the Fund would be accumulated and made available to finance a Legal Aid Scheme which would actually pay practitioners a reasonable fee for work done. A secondary purpose of the Fund would be to reimburse clients who may be defrauded from time to time by the theft of trust account monies by dishonest solicitors or employees.

The proposal met with considerable opposition from some members of the profession – notably those who had banks as clients. It was also opposed by some conservative members of the Legislative Council, who claimed that it was unethical to skim off the interest from other people's money. Those who put forward this argument ignored the fact that the banks had always skimmed off the interest from other peoples' money – including money deposited in solicitors' trust accounts. The bank-lobby practitioners were out voted at a lively general meeting of the Society and the opposition of the Legislative Council members was overcome after much persuasive lobbying by Ian Medcalf.[36]

The *Legal Contribution Trust Act* became law in 1967 but Sheila advised against paying out claims for solicitors' fees until a sufficient amount accumulated to withstand the demands likely to be made upon the Fund once legal aid work became profitable. Sheila also persuaded the Society to take out insurance cover to protect the Fund against heavy pay-outs incurred through fraudulent defalcation. Although she had the highest regard for the great majority of practitioners, Sheila knew from her long experience in practice that the profession harboured its share of potential villains.

Sheila's wise counsel was soon vindicated. Within two years of the proclamation of the *Legal Contribution Trust Act*, a practitioner was struck-off and gaoled for the theft of many thousands of dollars of clients' money. The Law Society was very relieved to be able to

36 The Honourable Ian Medcalf AO, QC, from a personal interview.

announce that all the clients had been reimbursed from the Legal Contributions Trust Fund. The Fund remained intact because the Society was able to call upon its insurers to make good the loss. By 1971 the Fund was large enough to bring the new scheme into full operation, special features of which were:

1. The scheme could afford to pay an administrator who operated separately from the Law Society and in separate premises provided by the State.
2. A Legal Advice Bureau was established to dispense basic advice for a nominal charge.
3. Duty solicitors financed from the Fund and operating on a roster system were supplied to the two Perth Courts of Petty Sessions.
4. Practitioners whose clients were granted legal aid were paid a reasonable fee.
5. A duty counsel hand-book was produced for which a number of practitioners, experienced in criminal law, wrote helpful notes on problems likely to be encountered in courts of Petty Sessions.

There was no set means test for the new scheme. Applicants were assessed on the basis of two criteria – whether they had means to pay and whether their case had legal merit. If a client had some available means, a fair contribution would be asked for. If the client succeeded and recovered costs, those costs would be refunded to the scheme.[37]

The new scheme was a considerable advance upon those which had operated previously and represented a significant contribution to the social service structure of the State. Many years after its establishment Joan Heenan recalls reminiscing upon the history of the Law Society with Sheila who described the institution of the Legal Aid Scheme as "our greatest achievement".[38]

37 Loris Wood, from a personal interview.

38 Joan Heenan, from a personal interview.

8

"NOW I CAN REST IN PEACE"

Six year's withdrawal from full-time professional employment appears to have restored Sheila's physical health sufficiently to enable her to resume practice. In 1971 she joined Geoff Hammond's firm as a salaried employee. In her *Oral History Memoir*, Sheila refers to her decision to do so as follows:

> I began to think I had become too closely involved with Legal Aid. . . I decided I would go back into private practice and I joined Hammond. Fitzgerald and King and remained there until 1980 when I retired. In that time I actually did maintain my interest in Legal Aid [and] served on various Legal Aid committees. . .[1]

The Legal Aid committees to which Sheila refers were really sub-committees consisting of small groups of practitioners who agreed to donate their lunch hours assessing legal aid applications. This became necessary to cope with the great increase in applicants for aid which occurred in 1972 when lawyers began to get paid for legal aid work. Before that date most applicants for legal aid had either come to the Society's office direct, without first approaching a solicitor, or had been rejected by their own solicitor because they could not afford to pay.

If a destitute person went to a solicitor for help in former days, the solicitor would either act for no fee out of goodness of heart or simply send the pauper away on a "no pay no work" basis – depending on the solicitor's social conscience. One hard-nosed firm of matrimonial lawyers, being reluctant to send clients away but even

1 C Shervington, *Sheila Mary McClemans: Oral History Memoir*, by courtesy University of WA archives, p 13.

more reluctant to work without payment, adopted a practice of lending their poorer clients sufficient money to pay their fees in advance. They would then charge the clients interest at the current bank rate until the loan was repaid. Pending repayment the loan would be secured by a bill-of-sale over the client's meagre household goods.

Many clients, turned away from private solicitors' offices because they were not able to pay, would eventually present themselves at the Law Society's Legal Aid office where, providing their claim had some merit, they would be assigned to one of the solicitors who had agreed to be placed on the Legal Aid list. That solicitor would not be paid for work done but at least he or she would not be asked to do non-paying work until his or her turn on the roster came around again.

Although the Law Society's pre-1972 scheme was essentially a means of spreading the burden of charitable work among the more charitably minded members of the profession, the well publicised fact that there was a Legal Aid scheme in existence gave the poor some assurance that they would be looked after if their cause was just. Much valuable service by way of advice and reassurance was rendered at the Legal Aid office itself by Sheila, Loris Wood and Jim Smythe who would often solve minor problems without the necessity of referring them to private solicitors for action.

Once practitioners actually began to get paid for legal aid work, the whole scene changed. Most of those who would have nothing to do with the old voluntary scheme became enthusiastic supporters. No longer were clients turned away on a "no pay no work basis". They were made welcome and invited to complete an application for legal aid. That done the solicitor would make an application to the Committee on their behalf. This process necessitated the enlistment of the voluntary sub-committees which had the task of assessing the *bona fides* of the applicants for aid – both as to the merit of their cause and the size of their income and assets.

The Society's policy was to make legal aid available to anyone who had a reasonable case yet found the cost of justice too high. Aid was not restricted only to "poor persons". The Society was aware of a general complaint that access to the law was only available to the very rich or the very poor and did what it could to improve this situation. If a client had some capacity to pay but would be ruined by the total potential cost of a court action, aid would be granted on the basis that a contribution was made by the client which would be held in trust by the Society.

If the client was refused legal aid by the sub-committee, some practitioners would simply withdraw, sometimes even on the eve of a trial. This practice earned the barely disguised disapproval of Murphy J in the leading legal aid case of *R v McInnis*.[2]

The clients were not the only people who needed assessing, however. The sub-committees were also faced with the need to check the bills of costs submitted to the Society by solicitors for work done, some of which were exorbitant. The fund would quickly have been milked dry if all bills had been paid as submitted.

Sheila's authoritative hand was very much needed for the first few years of the new scheme to back up the sub-committee members who had to sit in judgment upon the demands of their peers. The author, who was a member of one such sub-committee, found it quite embarrassing at times to have to argue with fellow practitioners about the merits of their client's case and the value of work done, which some took as a reflection upon their competence and their honesty.

As all bills were calculated on a rate and time basis, it would be necessary to assess both the amount of time taken and the quality of the work. If a practitioner took two days to conduct a trial which should have been finished in one, that practitioner was either incompetently slow or deliberately dragging out the trial to bump up the fee. Only personal experience would enable one to make a fair judgment on the issue. It was always a relief to hear Sheila say: "I agree with Lloyd – he should have done the job in half the time".

On the other hand no one would dispute the matter when Sheila said – as she more often did: "Let's be fair now, there was a lot of finicky detail to be done and Mr X would have been a difficult client – I'd have hated to try to cope with him as a witness. I think that's a reasonable bill".

The explosion in drug-related crime in the early 1970s posed an increasing threat to the Society's limited legal aid funds. Sheila led a

---

2 *R v McInnis* (1979) 149 CLR 575.

school of thought amongst those administering legal aid which considered that the Legal Aid fund was not set up to assist organised crime. She developed a policy in which aid would only be assigned to drug traffickers if they pleaded guilty and needed counsel to make a plea in mitigation.

Those opposed to this policy would point out that State and Federal governments had enacted laws imposing penalties of up to life imprisonment upon those found guilty of drug trafficking and that it was most unjust that impecunious drug dealers should be denied aid to defend themselves. The answer to this was that, if the Mafia did not look after its own, the taxpayer should not be called upon to do so and that the limited legal aid dollar should more properly be spent on young first offenders or ordinary battlers unable to afford to present some just claim or defence to the courts.

Sheila and her supporters maintained this policy and defended the legal aid funds against the financial threat of the demands of organised crime for years. After the establishment of the Legal Aid Commission in 1976, there was a change in policy and many thousands of dollars were paid out annually in the defence of professional criminals, mainly for drug-related offences. The High Court of Australia has signified its approval of this more liberal policy in the case of *Dietrich*, holding that the right to a fair trial is a "fundamental prescript of the law of this country" and that accused persons charged with serious criminal offences must be provided with counsel except in exceptional circumstances.[3]

The reasons for the establishment of the Legal Aid Commission are complex and require a brief historical exposition. When the Whitlam Labor Government came into office in 1972 with great promises of vastly improved social services, those involved in legal aid had high hopes of the increased funding from Commonwealth sources, which had been promised then withheld in 1962. These funds were indeed provided by the Whitlam Government, but not in a manner which suited the majority of lawyers.

The Labor Government made it clear that it favoured setting up a "store front" organisation of salaried employees to dispense legal aid, in contrast to schemes administered by Law Societies in which

3 *Dietrich v The Queen* (1992) 177 CLR 292.

private practitioners sought money to pay themselves for looking after their own clients.[4] It decided this for two reasons, the first of which was that the existing Law Society legal aid schemes were clearly inadequate to satisfy the full demand for legal aid services within the community.[5] Second, a salaried "store front" scheme would be much more approachable by the community and keep a tighter rein on costs, it being the experience of legal aid schemes elsewhere that salaried services are much less costly than services which rely in the main upon the private profession.[6]

The Commonwealth was faced with a major problem in funding legal aid, in that all law passed by the Federal Parliament must be based upon one of the limited powers of the Commonwealth Constitution. There is no general power in that Constitution to legislate with regard to legal aid. Whilst its law officers were pondering how to find a constitutional base for a national legal aid scheme, there was a section of the population in desperate need to whom the Commonwealth could give immediate help.

Pursuant to a referendum in 1967, which amended s 51(xxvi) of the Constitution, the Commonwealth was given the power to make special laws in relation to the Aboriginal people. Crime statistics showed that the number of Aborigines in gaol at any time was grossly disproportionate to their actual numbers in the population as a whole. There was, in addition, a vast body of anthropological and sociological evidence proving that Aborigines did not get a fair deal from the police or the lower courts – particularly from racist Justices of the Peace who regularly dealt with them in rural areas when magistrates were not available.

The Whitlam Government took immediate steps to establish an Aboriginal Legal Service (ALS) in every State, controlled by elected committees of Aborigines and staffed by salaried lawyers. In Western Australia, none of the lawyers employed by the ALS was Aboriginal because there were no qualified Aboriginal lawyers – in

---

4 S Armstrong, "Labor's legal aid scheme. The light that failed" in RB Scotton and H Ferber (eds), *Public Expenditure and Social Policy in Australia* Vol 11, Hale & Iremonger, 1980, p 221.

5 R Sackville, *Law and Poverty in Australia* (2nd Main Report October 1975), Commission of Inquiry into Poverty, pp 17-18.

6 Ibid, pp 31, 37.

fact in 1972 few Aborigines had tertiary qualifications of any kind. Aboriginal para-legal field officers and secretarial staff were recruited from the ranks of the few Aborigines who had struggled to attain some degree of literacy in the face of official neglect and unofficial racial prejudice. Overall supervision of the ALS was exercised by the Commonwealth Department of Aboriginal Affairs (DAA), which in 1989 became the Aboriginal and Torres Islander Commission (ATSIC).

Although he realised he was on dubious constitutional grounds, Whitlam's innovative Attorney-General, Senator Lionel Murphy QC, grasped the nettle and, in 1974, established a salaried legal aid service in each State entitled the Australian Legal Aid Office (ALAO) which set up a number of "store front" offices throughout Australia to dispense legal aid and advice to needy persons on the basis of a means test. Initially, the work of the salaried staff was limited mainly to an advisory minor litigation role, major court work being briefed out to the private profession. The ALAO was welcomed by the public but not by the majority of lawyers who, fearing socialisation of the legal profession, traditionally opposed government-controlled legal-aid schemes.[7] In Western Australia, professional opposition to the scheme was exacerbated by States-rightist suspicion of anything emanating from Canberra.

Sheila disapproved of both the ALS and the ALAO, it being her opinion that the proven model of the Law Society's scheme was the best and Federal monies should be channelled into those schemes in each State by way of an annual grant, rather than being used to create another national bureaucracy. She expressed her disapproval of ALAO many years afterwards in her *Oral History Memoir* when explaining the need to establish the Legal Aid Commission:

> There was at that time and had been since the Whitlam Government an Australian Legal Aid Office. It was not thought to be functioning terribly well and commissions in the various states were thought to be the answer to this. . .[8]

---

7 S Armstrong, "Labor's legal aid scheme. The light that failed" in RB Scotton and H Ferber (eds), *Public Expenditure and Social Policy in Australia* Vol 11, Hale & Iremonger, 1980, p 222.

8 C Shervington, *Sheila Mary McClemans: Oral History Memoir*, by courtesy University of WA archives, p 15.

This is hardly a fair summation either of the ALAO in operation or the circumstances of its demise. The ALAO had functioned quite well, given the restrictions placed upon it by the Commonwealth Constitution and the hostility of the legal profession. It was so popular with the public that the conservative Opposition never attacked it publicly nor did it seek a mandate for its cessation in the 1975 post-dismissal election which established the Fraser Liberal Government.[9]

Sheila's disapproval of the Aboriginal Legal Service was expressed quite bluntly when told that the author had accepted the position of in-house counsel to that Service. "I strongly disapprove!" was her comment, "It's a waste of your talents. . ."[10]

Professional opposition to the ALAO soon generated a legal challenge which underlined its delicate constitutional position and the necessity of restricting itself to limiting aid to "federal people".[11] "Federal people" were defined as people having a "federal interest" such as pensioners, ex-service personnel, clients involved in matters involving Commonwealth law and all others who could be brought under its *aegis* by some tenuous connection. Significantly "federal people" included matrimonial clients because the Commonwealth had entered that field on 1 February 1961 with the proclamation of the *Matrimonial Causes Act* 1959.

From 1974 to 1976, three separate legal aid organisations existed in Western Australia – the Law Society Scheme, the ALAO and the ALS. The Law Society Scheme was still restricted to its small grant from the State Government plus the annual interest from the Legal Contributions Trust. Its funds still had to be carefully husbanded by limiting aid to the meritorious needy and strictly monitoring practitioners' bills of costs to curb the avaricious.

Sheila shrewdly pointed out that, if the Scheme had no access to Commonwealth money, it should restrict itself to State matters and send "federal people" off to the federal organisations. This was not appreciated by many practitioners because the ALAO and the ALS

---

9 S Armstrong, "Labor's legal aid scheme. The light that failed" in RB Scotton and H Ferber (eds), *Public Expenditure and Social Policy in Australia* Vol 11, Hale & Iremonger, 1980, p 237.

10 From the author's personal recollection.

11 *R v Bannister; ex parte Hartshorn* (1975) 5 ACTR 100.

both operated on the basis of in-house lawyers who could take over the matter from the client's lawyer and conduct it without fee.

The author still recalls the fury of one solicitor who applied for a sizeable grant to travel to Carnarvon to conduct a Summary Relief case for an Aboriginal woman. Aid was denied on the basis that the client should be referred to the ALS, who would conduct the case without charge. This policy led to allegations of "racial discrimination" and "refusing the right to the lawyer of the client's choice". Although Sheila was always sympathetic to the role of the private practitioner and the desirability of a client having a lawyer of personal choice, she considered it her duty to protect the fund, the primary aim of which, in her opinion, was to provide legal aid to the needy and not to create a milch cow for private lawyers.

After the Whitlam Government was dismissed by Sir John Kerr in 1975, the powerful lawyers' lobby persuaded the Fraser Liberal Government to abandon the ALAO in favour of making Commonwealth legal aid grants to the States to be administered by State Legal Aid Commissions dominated by representatives of the legal profession. The lead was given by the conservative government of Western Australia where a *Legal Aid Commission Act* was passed in 1976 although, owing to administrative problems, it did not come into full operation until 1978.

The Western Australian Legal Aid Commission was virtually an amalgamation of the Law Society Scheme and the ALAO. Funding for the Commission came from the former State grant, the proceeds from the Legal Contribution Trust, and Commonwealth grant money made available by the dissolution of the ALAO.

Sheila took an active part in the setting up of the Commission and upon its formation was appointed one of the Commissioners. She did not, however, enjoy her service with the Commission as much as with the previous scheme, as her comments in her *Oral History Memoir* indicate:

> when it became the Legal Aid Commission it had to stop being quite as informal as it was while the Law Society administered it and I was sorry. I thought the informality and the spirit in which it was done was a very good thing. It became more regimented when it became the Legal Aid Commission. That's not to underestimate the value of

> the work that is done there, it's good work and it fills a great need. It just is different.[12]

Despite being a made a Commissioner, Sheila did not relinquish her hands-on approach to legal aid. She remained on one of the lunch-hour voluntary sub-committees of practitioners, assessing applications and bills of costs, for several years after the Commission came into operation. Being at the same time in private practice in the matrimonial field, she continued to represent legal aid assignees in court until she retired from practice in 1980. By retiring at that time she was spared the problems which the escalating cost of paying private lawyers, and the stiffening reluctance of governments to pay, imposed upon the Legal Aid Commissions throughout the nation. At the time of writing, these problems have reached such a point of crisis that one critic, at least, predicts the inevitable collapse of the system.[13]

A revealing sidelight on Sheila's return to private practice in the 1970s comes from Alan Barblett who, for some years before becoming Chief Judge of the Family Court of Western Australia, was Lecturer in Family Law at the Law School. He recalls that Sheila sought permission to do a refresher course in Family Law because she felt out of touch, not having been involved in court work for ten years. She attended at 8:00 am for two mornings a week for the whole academic year and never missed a lecture. The penetrating questions which she asked greatly enriched the year – both for Alan and his students.

> Every one of them would have made a good examination question. It was really quite remarkable that a senior practitioner of her standing – an expert in her field would go back and do a whole year's course at the age of 65.[14]

A possible reason for Sheila's return to the Law School may have been the change in divorce procedure brought about by the Commonwealth *Matrimonial Causes Act* 1959, which came into

---

12 C Shervington, *Sheila Mary McClemans: Oral History Memoir*, by courtesy University of WA archives, p 13..

13 L Powell and F Regan, "Legal Aid: Reflections on Costs, Lawyers and the Future" (1988) 9(4-5) *Legal Aid Clearing House Bulletin* 67.

14 Alan Barblett, from a personal interview.

operation in 1961, a year after she had taken up her post with the Law Society. Whilst she was fully aware of the provisions of the Act, having personally protested to Attorney-General Barwick about some of its terms, as described in Chapter 4, and later having written an explanatory paper on it when the Bill was first introduced, she had not presented any cases in court under its provisions before returning to practise.[15]

When the morning lecture finished, Sheila would catch a bus to Perth and start her day's work. It would usually be a long day, few lawyers can leave the office sharp on 5 o'clock with mail to sign and clients to see whose own working hours often make late afternoon appointments imperative. If she spent a day in court, answering the accumulated telephone messages alone would be likely to fill the rest of the afternoon. For at least two lunch-hours a week, she would be required to sit in on a legal aid sub-committee meeting, her only reward for which was a free round of sandwiches.

The 1959 Act brought a new concept into the law for Western Australian divorce lawyers, namely the power of the court to order settlements of property as part of its provisions for maintenance upon granting divorce decrees. The previous State Code of 1945 did not have this power. Alan Barblett ascribes his elevation to the post of Chief Judge of the Family Court of Western Australia to the fact that an early Law Summer School devoted some of its programme to considering the new *Matrimonial Causes Act* 1959. There was universal ignorance on the subject of divorce property settlements and he was allocated the responsibility of researching the subject and writing a paper on it. At that time in his professional career, he was a conveyancer and had very little to do with divorce. The paper made him an instant expert on divorce settlements and from that time onwards he was embroiled in what began to be known as "family law", becoming one of the State's leading practitioners in that field.[16]

It is likely that the complicated subject of property settlements induced Sheila to do her refresher course. As would be expected she soon became an expert in the subject herself. Knowledge of

15 The paper is in the Law Society archives, the date and occasion for its delivery are not known.

16 Alan Barblett, from a personal interview.

settlement law became an even more important feature when, in 1976, the Family Court was established pursuant to Lionel Murphy's revolutionary *Family Law Act* 1975 (Cth). This dispensed with the concept of fault and attempted to lay down guidelines for the court in dividing the family property on dissolution of marriage.

One innovation was the provision in s 79(4)(b) that credit should be given for a spouse's role as a "home maker" when totting up each party's contribution to the family assets. Previous law had tended to be unfair to a wife who had simply stayed at home to look after the family while the husband went out to work and earned the money which paid for the family property. "I paid for it all. Why should she get any of it?" the typical husband would argue after a marriage break-up. This was an argument which carried much weight with the courts steeped in a legal tradition of male property rights.

Making bold use of the provisions of the "home maker" concept, the Full Bench of the Family Court under Chief Justice Evatt established what was called the "equity is equality" principle which pushed Australian family law a long way towards the European community of property concept. Sheila had long been an advocate of this principle as can be seen from her contribution to the 8th Triennial Conference of the Australian Federation of Women Voters, described in Chapter 6.

Sheila acted as counsel in one of the leading cases in which the Family Court established the "equity is equality" principle, the 1978 case of *Pothoff* which Sheila argued on appeal before the Full Bench of the Family Court in Perth.[17] Ironically, in this instance, Sheila acted for the husband and argued against the application of the rule in the particular circumstances of the case. Sheila's argument was unsuccessful and the wife's share was increased. It is indicative of Sheila's professionalism that she did not put her own philosophical views before her duty to her client.

Six years later the High Court of Australia overturned the "equity is equality" principle in the case of *Mallet*, but that was a bit late for Mr Pothoff.[18] It was also only of academic interest for Sheila, she having retired in June 1980. Sheila told Patsy Adam-Smith that

---

17 *Pothoff v Pothoff* (1978) FLC ¶90-475.

18 *In Marriage of Mallet and Mallet* (1984) 156 CLR 605.

she retired "on the day I broke my back".[19] This alarming description is not amplified in Adam-Smith's text. In her *Oral History*, Sheila merely says "in 1980 I retired".[20] Neither friends nor family have any record of any traumatic incident precipitating her retirement. It must, therefore, be assumed that this was Sheila's rather dramatic way of expressing the fact that her old chronic ailment eventually wore her down.

In a letter to the author on the point, Geoff Hammond wrote:

> Sheila was always the last to complain of any disability. I cannot ever remember her being absent a day for her back or any other reason. Obviously she must have suffered a lot with her back but this was never advanced as a major reason for her leaving. . . I gathered she felt the strain of being on her feet in a long case and decided it was time to retire.[21]

Simultaneously with her full-time employment, both in private practice and with the Law Society, Sheila had important positions in three government bodies – the State Parole Board, the Commonwealth Council on Discrimination and Employment and the Services Canteens Trust Fund Regional Committee, the last two of which she chaired.

The Parole Board was the creation of the *Offenders Probation and Parole Act* 1963. It was introduced into Parliament on 5 September 1963 by Sheila's one-time rival for the Cottesloe seat, the Honourable Ross Hutchinson. Mr Hutchinson pointed out that there had been no significant penal reform legislation during the whole 130 years of the State's existence apart from the creation of a somewhat ineffectual body known as the Indeterminate Sentences Board in 1918. The penal system did little or nothing to rehabilitate prisoners:

> Instead of Fremantle Prison being a bulwark of community social protection . . . it is little more than a common meeting place for criminals and social derelicts who actually infect the casual offender, the weak, and the mentally and morally retarded: and as hundreds of these pass through prison life back into the outside world, the

19 Patsy Adam-Smith, *Australian Women at War,* Thomas Nelson, 1980, p 251.

20 C Shervington, *Sheila Mary McClemans: Oral History Memoir*, by courtesy University of WA archives, p 13.

21 Geoff Hammond, from a personal interview.

> infection spreads and criminal incidents occur in community life in other parts of the State . . . a great body of both short and long-term prisoners remain neglected and unassisted.

Commending the success of probation and parole legislation in Victoria and Tasmania, he described the provisions of the proposed Bill as follows:

> It comes in two main parts . . . a system of probation with a view to reducing the number of persons committed to prison. The second deals with the release of prisoners on parole . . . the setting up of a new board to replace the Indeterminate Sentences Board . . . directed to keeping the offender within the community but under adequate and proper supervision. One of the main objects of the Bill is to assist in the reform and rehabilitation of those offenders who are reformable.[22]

Sheila was one of the original members of the Board whose first chairman was fellow Modern School graduate, Mr Justice Negus. Justices Lavan, Jones and Smith succeeded him in turn. Sheila served under all four until she was retired from the Board in 1984. When Sir John Lavan became chairman on the death of Justice Negus in 1969 it was the practice of the Board to allocate male and female parolees to separate committees. Sheila worked on the female committee and Sir John recalls her work as being "very painstaking and of great value to the board".

Ivan Vodanovich, a Master of Laws with a Diploma in social work, came to Western Australia in 1974 to take up the position of Senior Parole Officer towards the end of Sir John's chairmanship. He first met Sheila at a meeting of the Parole Board and had frequent contact with her thereafter through the Law Society and Crown Law Department as well as in the course of Parole Board business. Shortly after his arrival, the Board abandoned the policy of separate male-female committees and he recalls that Sheila voluntarily took on a greatly increased workload by adding a number of male parolees.

According to Ivan it was a heavy workload which, of necessity, included a lot of homework. Each board member received papers relating to up to 60 parolees several days before the monthly Board

22 1063 WAPD 847.

meeting. They would have to read through the documents before the meeting and bring the papers with them to the meeting; the physical burden of these papers was often literally quite heavy. If one worked full time like Sheila, the cases would have to be studied at night.

Ivan remembers that Sheila had great empathy for individual cases, which she had to balance against her sense of responsibility for the safety of the public. One case, which worried her greatly, was that of Darryl Beamish a deaf-mute serving a sentence of life imprisonment (commuted from a death sentence) for the wilful murder with sexual overtones of a young woman, in her own home. He had been convicted solely on the basis of dubious confessional evidence.

There was much public disquiet about the case and many lawyers were far from satisfied of Beamish's guilt. His appeal counsel, Sir Francis Burt, always maintained a private conviction that he was innocent. A prominent academic, Professor Brett, wrote a book proclaiming Beamish's innocence and heavily criticising the proceedings both in the jury trial and the appellate courts which had condemned him unjustly to many years in prison. Doubt of Beamish's guilt intensified when a psychopathic multiple murderer, Eric Edgar Cooke, the last person executed in Western Australia, confessed to the crime. An appeal on the ground of fresh evidence failed in the Court of Criminal Appeal, which found Cooke's "confession" opportunistic and wholly incredible.

Sheila, wearing her legal aid hat, had arranged representation for both Beamish and Cooke at their trials. She was thus fully conversant with the background to Beamish's case and the doubt surrounding it when it came to her as a parole application some ten years later. The Board eventually released Beamish on parole but he was later convicted of subsequent offences whilst on parole and returned to prison for breach of parole. Self-appointed "Law and Order" advocates attacked the Board on Beamish's first parole and repeated their attack when he was re-paroled some years later. Happily Beamish married and lived a blameless life thereafter but it was a worrying time for Sheila for the seven years of supervision that followed the second release, lest she have the anguish of yet another victim on her conscience. Sheila's agonising over her Parole Board decisions is confirmed by her old friend and confidant, Veronica Kviesis, who believes that Sheila found it the most exacting of all her work because she had such concern for the people involved and found it extremely difficult to sit in judgment upon them.

As a board member, Ivan Vodanovich found her:

> Very conscientious, perceptive and self-assured. She was also very acceptive of changes to the more liberal policies the Board adopted under Bob Jones and even more so under Howard Smith. Another feature was her popularity with the Parole Officers. She was so straight with them and had such sense a wry sense of humour she was a great mixer at all our staff socials.[23]

The Honourable Ian Medcalf was Attorney-General in 1979 when Sheila reached the retiring age of 70. At the time Sir Charles Court was Premier of the State and he had very strong views that all persons in public office should retire at that age – a rule he observed himself in 1982. Ian recalls that Sheila was so valuable to the Board that the Chairman, Justice Jones, persuaded Sir Charles to allow her to continue in office. In all, her tenure on the board was extended nine times. In 1984, the Burke Labor Government terminated her services and appointed an entirely new Board of its own preference.

Perhaps the Burke Government bestowed a fortuitous kindness. Ivan Vodanovich remembers that in her final years Sheila's back was so bad that the Board had to provide her with a special chair so that she could cope with the Board's five-hour sittings and transported her and her heavy files to and from the Board's City office. Notwithstanding her dismissal and her failing health, the Board still called her in on a number of occasions for the next two years on a consultancy basis. On her retirement, Sheila had the distinction of being the Board's longest serving member.

Sheila's appointment as Chairwoman of the Western Australian Committee of the Commonwealth Council on Discrimination in Employment and Occupation was made in November 1976. Other members of the Committee were Paddy Troy, Secretary of the Painters and Dockers Union, and Ruth Geneff, Secretary of the Clothing Trades Union.

The Act at that time had no penal provisions and the function of the Committee was merely persuasive. Nevertheless, Ruth Geneff

---

23 Ivan Vodanovich, from a personal interview.

recalls that Sheila achieved remarkable results simply by calling in alleged offenders and lecturing them sternly whenever a case of discrimination could be established. Ruth was particularly impressed by Sheila's efficiency and business-like approach to problems. Everything that came before them was dealt with and cleaned up within the limits of the Committee's powers – there was no such thing as a "too hard" file.[24]

Sheila served upon the Regional Committee of the Services Canteens Trust Fund from the date of its formation on 1 January 1948 until its dissolution on 31 October 1986. It was undoubtedly the area of her social work that was dearest to her heart. The fund was created by the Commonwealth *Services Trust Funds Act* in 1947 to administer and distribute the profits of the war-time service canteens, plus some miscellaneous relief funds and schemes. The object was expressed to be:

> to compensate the distress suffered after World War II by members of the Australian Armed Forces and their dependants by providing education schemes for dependants, and welfare for widows and orphans.[25]

The first Chairman of the Regional Committee was the distinguished airman Sir Norman Brearley, whom Sheila succeeded in the chair for the last ten years of the Fund. It was originally planned that the capital of the fund and accrued interest from time to time be wholly expended by 1977, but it was ultimately extended to 1986. The Trustees were particularly concerned with widows and orphans requiring welfare relief; special assistance was given to children with disabilities.

The total sum transferred to the Fund, nationally, (converted into dollars but not 1992 value) was $11,090,910.00. By the end of 1986, throughout Australia, the Fund had assisted 40,000 ex-service personnel, 32,000 widows and orphans and 2750 children with disabilities. During the same period, the educational component of the Fund had assisted 70,000 children with a total of 146,500 grants.

---

24 Ruth Geneff, from a personal interview.

25 The Western Australian Office of the Australian Archives kindly supplied the author with a computer print-out summarising the objectives and history of the Trust Fund from which the material cited in this work was collated. Additional material was helpfully supplied in personal conversations with John Limb and Dave Spencer.

John Limb, who was Secretary of the Regional Committee from 1956 to 1986, estimates that approximately $1,000,000 was distributed in relief alone in Western Australia.[26]

Dave Spencer, Perth's Bailiff for many years after the War, supplied an example of the sort of work that the Committee did. Whenever he seized goods for non-payment of debt from people, who plainly had no means of paying, he would ascertain if they had ex-service connections. If so, he would refer them to the Committee and hold the warrant pending payment from the Fund. Many a poor household was saved its few sticks of furniture in this way.[27]

In the education field John Limb well remembers a gifted youth from a needy ex-service family who went to University on Commonwealth Assistance to Students scholarship. The student social life overwhelmed him to the detriment of his studies and he failed first year. He was refused further Commonwealth Assistance by reason of his failure. His widowed mother applied to the Trust Fund Committee, which, with great understanding, granted him assistance to repeat First Year. The lad went on to obtain three degrees and become a distinguished public servant.

The Regional Committee met fortnightly of a lunch hour at the Swan Barracks in Irwin Street, Perth. Members were sent a précis of each application some days in advance. As there were often as many as 30 applicants at a time the caseloads were heavy. John Limb recalls Sheila as being very warm-hearted with a tendency to be over generous to applicants. Because of her legal training she brought a valuable oversight to the meetings which she seldom failed to attend. She often brought her own applicants to the fund, battered and deserted wives or ex-WRANS down on their luck.[28] When she became the Secretary of the Legal Aid Committee, she found many more destitute people to refer to the Trust Fund for bread-and-butter help. "Let's hope that will solve their legal problems", she would say to Jim Smythe on assigning a case. "In the meantime these people have to live. I suggest we refer them to the Canteens Trust Fund for assistance".[29]

---

26 Ibid.

27 David Spencer, from a personal interview.

28 John Limb, from a personal interview.

29 Jim Smythe, from a personal interview.

Like all other members of the Regional Committee, Sheila served in a purely voluntary capacity. She regarded her work with it as something special because it was an ex-service organisation and because her special responsibility on it was to represent all ex-service women and their families. She worked on the Regional Committee until the last years of her life when her health was rapidly failing. When the fund was wound up, she wrote to one of her closest friends: "Now I can rest in peace".[30]

For her outstanding services to Law and the Community, Sheila was awarded the Queen's Silver Jubilee Medal in 1977 and appointed a Companion of the Most Distinguished Order of Saint Michael and Saint George in the 1978 New Year Honours. These decorations, with their citations, repose in the Naval Museum at *HMAS Cerberus*.

The community bestowed these rewards in recognition of Sheila's outstanding contributions in many fields. Sadly lacking, however, were those honours usually accorded the members of the profession to which she gave special service. It is important to examine the factors and conditions responsible for this omission. As observed in Chapter 6, there came a time in Sheila's life when, had she been a man, she could legitimately expect to have been asked if she was interested in an appointment as a judge, yet she was passed over. This was during the years immediately before 1960 when she decided to quit private practice to administer the Law Society. In the course of researching this work the author put the question directly to her most distinguished living contemporary, Sir John Lavan, as to why this didn't happen. After some thought, he replied: "I suppose it didn't occur to anyone to do so. People didn't think in terms of women on the bench in those days".[31]

That is an assessment which few practising lawyers of that time would dispute. In any event it is supported by historical fact. The first Australian female judge, South Australia's Dame Roma Mitchell, was not appointed until 1965. Her appointment was the subject of an interview with Jon Faine on the ABC programme *The Law Report* in January 1991, from which the following extract is taken.

30 Mary Howard, from a personal interview.

31 John Lavan, from a personal interview.

> FAINE What do you think the reaction of your contemporaries would have been if they could have looked forward and seen that a woman would be appointed to the Supreme Court of South Australia in due course?
>
> MITCHELL Well my own reaction was one of absolute surprise, so I suppose theirs would have been similar. When in fact I was appointed the Attorney, who was Don Dunstan, asked me if I would have lunch with him at Parliament House. That sounds naive but it really didn't occur to me that that was what he wanted to talk to me about. . . I still didn't think anybody would appoint a woman judge.[32]

Dame Roma Mitchell was almost an exact contemporary of Sheila's, having been admitted to practise in 1934, one year after Sheila. Like Sheila she specialised in court work in a State where there was no division between solicitors and barristers and, at that time, no independent Bar. Despite the absence of an independent Bar, practitioners were from time to time appointed Queen's Counsel from the general profession, the only qualification necessary being a general reputation as an outstanding advocate. Sheila certainly came within this category and so did Dame Roma. The only difference was that South Australia was prepared to grant recognition of this quality and did so by appointing Dame Roma Queen's Counsel in 1962. It was the first Australian State to award this honour to a woman.

Dame Roma's appointment as Queen's Counsel occurred under a conservative government so it cannot be argued that that her later judicial appointment was due fortuitously to the advent in office of a Labor Government with a notoriously avant garde Attorney-General, Don Dunstan. The greater probability is that South Australia, the first State to grant female suffrage and to admit women to practise law, was following an honourable historical tradition.

Western Australia could easily have become an honourable second to South Australia by honouring Sheila with an appointment, either as silk or a judge – if only to the District Court, which it established in 1969 and to which it appointed another of her contemporaries, the Honourable RE Jones, as one of its initial four judges. Again it appears that nobody gave it a thought. In the matter

32 Jon Faine, *Taken on Oath*, Federation Press, 1992, pp 5, 6.

of female appointments, Western Australia ultimately finished a very bad last, appointing its first female District Court judge in 1983, its first female Queens Counsel in 1997 and its first female Supreme Court judge in 1998.

Busy as she was with her professional work and her extra-mural committees, Sheila responded frequently to requests to talk to all kinds of groups. Her Anzac Day address to children has been quoted at some length in Chapter 2. Her contributions to the Women's Service Guilds and the Federation of University Women are noted in Chapter 6. The *West Australian* of 8 August 1962 reported:

> LAWYER TELLS OF WOMEN' LEGAL RIGHTS
>
> Some problems connected with women's property rights were described yesterday. . . Infant health sisters attending a refresher were told by Miss Sheila McClemans that vexed questions of this sort had given rise to a line of decisions called "Palm Tree Justice". . . Property in law had become a big difficulty in recent years because of the contributions brought into marriage by women. . . Young couples pooled savings to buy land, houses and furniture. When thing went well no one bothered to put in writing whose possessions were whose but this made trouble when things went wrong. . .

Amongst a bundle of her papers in the possession of the Law Society there are miscellaneous notes for other lectures on various aspects of the Matrimonial Law; the history of the Law Society; Legal Aid – all unfortunately undated. One intriguing document is the text of a speech delivered at Wesley Church, Perth, on its 100th anniversary, which concludes:

> We do better to look to see what we find in today's women which has been passed on from those who came to this church 100 years ago, and which we cherish. I think that on the whole we find honesty of purpose, integrity and the will to leave their part of the world a better place than they found it, and the recognition of forces for good, as typified by religious faith, which transcend personal issues.
>
> The past never dies. It is part of our present, and will be a part of those who come after us.
>
> If we, in the present, and those who come after us, can serve each other and this community in which we live with the same faith,

> dedication and courage, as did the women who first sat in this Church, we will do well.[33]

Also amongst the papers are short histories of a number of former notable Western Australian lawyers prepared for the Canberra National Memorials Committee. These include a lengthy paper on Sir Archibald Paul Burt which was published in *Early Days,* the journal of the Historical Society of Western Australia Vol 6 Part 5 (1966), and her biographical note on Enid Russell which was published as an appendix to Russell's *History of the Law of Western Australia*, referred to in Chapter 2.

In May 1982, a number of women lawyers under the leadership of Vivien Payne founded a body named Women Lawyers of Western Australia, believing that the Law Society did not concern itself with a number of matters of particular interest to women.[34] Sheila did not approve of this move, explaining her attitude in her *Oral History Memoir* as follows:

> I have never been interested in forming a Women's Lawyers Association. I have just felt that we're lawyers and as such we are part of the Law Society if we wish to be such and that's enough. We have no separate interest to serve.[35]

Some may question whether Sheila's attitude to Women Lawyers indicates that she was anti-feminist. Certainly those associated with her on legal aid committees knew that she was strongly opposed to some of the more extreme propositions of contemporary feminism – such as the right of lesbians to raise children. In the 1970 article, "Go See Sheila", she proclaimed "I am not a feminist . . . I do love people".[36]

Sir Francis Burt has gone on record as saying of Sheila: "She was not a feminist as that word is now understood. She was conscious of no 'rights' which had been denied to her".[37]

---

33 The Wesley Church was founded on 10 April 1887. This address would therefore have been given on or about 10 April 1987.

34 The formation of the WLWA is reported in *Brief* Vol 12, 8, May 1982, 10.

35 C Shervington, *Sheila Mary McClemans: Oral History Memoir*, by courtesy University of WA archives, p 18.

36 John O Giles, "Go See Sheila!" (September 1970) *Land Social Survey*, pp 25-26.

37 Obituary by Sir Francis Burt, *Brief* Vol 15, 5, July 1988, 8-9.

This opinion would seem to be supported by Sheila's own statement in her *Oral History Memoir*:

> I was never prominent in a movement for women's rights. I just have always felt that women were people. You made the most of yourself. I don't like having to fight for women's rights and things like that.[38]

This statement may express Sheila's feelings at the time it was made, in October 1982 when she was 73 years of age and in failing health, but it does not accord with historical fact. In the late 1940s and early 1950s, Sheila played a prominent part in the State's leading feminist organisation, the Women's Service Guilds, and made a number of public pronouncements in support of the advancement of women's rights, all of which is detailed in Chapter 6. The whole of her working life, including her naval service was devoted to the needs of women and their social advancement.

The *Oxford Dictionary* defines feminism as "Advocacy of extended recognition of claims and achievements of women; advocacy of women's rights". In the 1950s Sheila was clearly a feminist by that definition. Although there is no record of her ever having made a further public pronouncement on the subject since the 1951 Declaration of Equality, which she sponsored at the Ninth Triennial Conference of the Australian Federation of Women Voters, her whole life thereafter indicates that she never abandoned that position.

Sheila was, however, a woman of her time and her feminism was essentially that of the first wave whose work was done on the achievement of formal political and economic equality, with the granting of the right to jury service in 1957 and the acceptance of the principal of equal pay by the Arbitration Commission in 1969.

Like many first wave feminists, Sheila was politically conservative; she was also steeped in conservative religious principles. For these reasons, she was opposed to reforms which the second-wave feminists considered essential, such as no-fault divorce. For these reasons also she was bound to reject the militant philosophy and tactics of the second-wave feminists, impatient to make political

38 C Shervington, *Sheila Mary McClemans: Oral History Memoir*, by courtesy University of WA archives, p 18.

and economic equality a reality and to eliminate the many unwritten conventions of discrimination by which men continued their position of domination over women.

The Women Lawyers of Western Australia was a product of the second wave. There are things that women lawyers need to discuss and to promote that men would be unlikely to listen to: the heresy that women should be granted silk and appointed to the Bench, for instance; how to counter sexist language; how to deal with physical sexual harassment; the economic "glass ceiling" which restricts most professional women to a lower wage than men. The mere mention of such matters at a Law Society meeting dominated by men would be likely to lead to a shouting match.

Sheila's own attitude to such matters was expressed in her *Oral History Memoir*:

> No, no, I was never aware of any discrimination because I was a woman. If there was any it didn't come close enough for me to be aware of it. I was always treated by the men in the profession as just one of them. . .[39]

It is likely that many women lawyers would regard these observations with disbelief. It is certainly contrary to the public expressed experiences recounted by the women lawyers interviewed on *The Law Report* on 12 August 1997, by Justice Gaudron at the inauguration of Australian Women Lawyers on 20 September 1997 and by Justice Wheeler in her lecture at Edith Cowan University on 31 July 1998, all of which are summarised in Chapter 1, fn 1.

With respect, Sir Francis assumes too much when he speaks of Sheila's inner feelings. What must any outstanding lawyer, scholar and nationally acclaimed wartime commander feel when contemporaries and juniors with no greater ability are appointed judges and made Queens Counsel yet she is not – simply because she is a woman? She would have to be a saint if she were not deeply resentful.

How did Sheila feel about being passed over for legal recognition? It is unlikely that anyone living knows the answer. It is unlikely that anyone ever asked her. Why should they? After all, nobody asked if she wanted to take silk or go on the Bench. The

39 Ibid.

family says she bitterly resented being refused pre-selection for the Cottesloe seat. It would indeed be strange if she did not resent the deeply wounding, albeit quite unconscious, discrimination imposed upon her by the profession which she loved.

It would also be unlikely for Sheila to disclose her inner feelings to anyone but her closest family because Sheila always insisted that she was a very private person and kept her private life private. As mentioned in Chapter 5, many practitioners who knew her for years by her professional name were surprised to discover she was married. She was always a very proud person and would never think of complaining or lobbying on her own behalf.

Sheila would not have approved of anyone writing her biography, yet she would be the first to say that others, as prominent in the law and public life as she was, should have their life's work recorded for posterity as a duty to history. For this reason, the author is prepared to risk her posthumous disapproval. On the other hand, Sheila's private life is not part of history and she left little record of it, perhaps intentionally. It is therefore only touched upon in this work to emphasise her humanity, to record vital facts and, in conclusion, to touch upon the final years when she was no longer a public person.

Ada McClemans died in 1955 and the Canon in 1960. Both are remembered in buildings and scholarships at Christ Church Grammar School, which several of their grandsons attended, the most famous of whom being the yachtsman, Jon Sanders, who thrice circumnavigated the globe and was acclaimed national Sportsman of the Year.

When Frank retired in 1965, he and Sheila relinquished the departmental house in King's Park for a home of their own on a steep river front block at Salter's Point, with a grand view across the Canning to the Darling Ranges. Their garden was landscaped by John Oldham who had worked with Frank to create the hillside parks overlooking Frank's last great dam at Serpentine. At the same time, they bought a unit at Shoalwater Bay with no telephone so that Sheila could occasionally escape the demands of legal practice. Salter's Point proved too far from other members of their family and they moved, finally, to the western end of Waratah Avenue,

Dalkeith, where the wide windows of their pleasant light-filled home overlooked Freshwater Bay.

Frank and Sheila had no children of their marriage. However, Frank's two children, Neil and Lesley, lived with them as a family until each was old enough to leave home. Sheila spoke from personal experience when she dealt with the subject of working mothers in her oral history interview:

> CS: I suppose (the increase in serious juvenile crime) could go back to the fact that there are a lot more latch key children and a lot more working mothers?
>
> SMcC: . . . I have read various bits of research which indicate that the working mother is a much better proposition than the one who doesn't work . . . some research in Melbourne I think has come to that conclusion. So I don't think it's necessarily the question of the working mother, she is rather an interesting person often, more interesting than if she stayed at home all day. But it depends on what arrangements you then make for the children.[40]

As well as the Kenworthy family, Sheila had an affectionate life-long relationship with her nephews and nieces, the children of her four sisters. Although Sheila was not initially in favour of Jon Sanders' circumnavigations, it was a particularly proud day for her when he did a special lap of honour for her around Freshwater Bay, on his return from his first world journey, and she stood on her balcony to salute him.

In addition to their families, Sheila and Frank gained much pleasure from their many friends from a wide spectrum of life – law, engineering, the University, the armed services (particularly the Navy), charitable and service organisations and the Australian-American Association in which Frank was particularly active.[41]

Neil Kenworthy treasures a tape-recording of a speech by Frank, toasting Professor Fred Alexander at a Vice-Chancellor's dinner on 30 September 1975 to honour the 50th anniversary of his appointment to the Chair of History at the University of Western Australia. In his speech, Frank recalled that both Sheila and he read history under Fred over 40 years before. Professor Alexander himself,

40 Ibid.

41 Neil Kenworthy, from a personal interview.

shortly before his own death, recalled that dinner and made the point that his friendship with the Kenworthys was so close they were one of five couples invited to that exclusive dinner. Asked for a brief comment upon Sheila, he replied with the dry thoughtful deliberation one might expect from a nonagenarian historian, "She was an extremely able woman who made an important contribution to the society in which she lived".[42]

Both Kenworthy children agree that they were a devoted couple and that Sheila was heart-broken when he died. It was really hard for anyone who knew them to accept the fact that they were no longer together. To visit their house was to enjoy collective warmth – Sheila witty and stimulating, always with something of importance to discuss, Frank, quiet, kindly, good humoured tending to sit back but occasionally joining in with some significant contribution. One always went away feeling enriched by sharing their minds and the joint affection they bestowed upon their visitors.

Frank's death in 1976 came at a very busy time for Sheila with the transition from the Law Society Legal Aid Scheme to the Legal Aid Commission, on top of all her other work. She did not let her grief show to those who worked with her. It is probable that she deliberately sublimated it in her work and kept on working until her failing health forced her to quit full-time employment.

Ivan Vodanovich, who lived nearby, used to drive Sheila to and from Parole Board meetings and would lend her books from time to time from the Board library. He got the impression that, whilst she was obviously very lonely in that grand house, she was determined to keep going. Although she was never keen to discuss her private affairs she dropped her guard occasionally. On one occasion when he was carrying her files for her, she remarked, "The body may be failing but the mind is sharp".

On another she told him of a startling incident which obviously worried her. She had awakened one night at home. It was full moon and the whole house was lit by moonlight, streaming in through the panoramic windows. She could clearly make out the figure of a strange man standing by the door of her room. Sheila reasoned that if she screamed or became agitated in any way he might panic and do

42 Professor Alexander, from a personal interview.

something drastic. Calmly she demanded in her most authoritative Chief Officer voice: "What are you doing here?". The man did not answer but simply moved away out of sight. To give him time to get away Sheila lay in bed for a while then went looking around the house. She found a pile of household goods near the front door but no intruder. She heard a car start outside and looked through the window to see two men drive away. Fortunately, they had taken nothing. She wondered whether it could be a parole board client. Ivan assured her it was more likely to be someone working on a building site next door who had seen easy pickings in a house occupied by a woman on her own. Parolees would have more to lose than gain by burgling Board members' homes.

She was obviously shaken by the incident, not frightened but outraged at the invasion of her privacy. However, she put it behind her philosophically: "Well its over now. The past is past. What matters is the present and the future". It was a saying Ivan often heard her use in her Parole Board work and thought it particularly appropriate.[43]

A less traumatic invasion of Sheila's privacy was reported to Loris Wood who often visited her both at home and in hospital in her last few years. The house next door was owned by a *bon-vivant* who worked in the television industry and was the scene of frequent parties which lasted through the night. Normally these goings-on did not worry Sheila because her house was substantial, air-conditioned and well insulated against noise. One summer morning, however, she arose at dawn to give the roses in her front garden a good soaking. She was confronted by a late-model European Convertible, with hood rolled back, parked on her nature strip. In it was a naked couple who had obviously placed a literal interpretation on the function of a nature strip and was still joined in post-coital slumber. This spectacle offended Sheila's strait-laced, High Anglican susceptibilities. She filled a bucket with water, walked out onto the nature strip and doused them with it: "That's what we do to dogs round here!". She admonished them.[44]

---

43 Ivan Vodanovich, from a personal interview.

44 Loris Wood, from a personal interview.

Sheila's old friend and former secretary from her Fremantle days, Constance Morgan, moved into Goldsmith Road, only three streets away from Sheila's home at Waratah Place. Knowing that Sheila did not have a car and could no longer walk without the aid of a stick, Constance offered to take Sheila shopping. Sheila declined, preferring, as ever, to be independent. She had an arrangement with a local taxi driver who would call regularly at a set time, take her to the local shopping centre, wait patiently for the half-hour it took her to do her shopping and drive her home.[45]

The first time Sheila visited Constance at Goldsmith Road she enquired, aggressively: "I hope this is not one of those No-Smoking houses?" Smoking was one of the few activities Sheila became aggressive about. She had been a smoker all her adult life and did not take kindly to the growing public health campaigns against it. Legal Aid committee meetings were a torment for non-smokers. If Sheila was present, she would smoke at least three cigarettes in a lunch-hour. She never asked if anyone minded and nobody dared to object.

Justice David Anderson remembers entertaining Sheila and his former partner, Hugh Guthrie MLA, at a private dinner party. Sheila ridiculed incipient attempts by the Australian Medical Association to reduce cigarette smoking.

> They showed us some of their propaganda on television the other night – you know those post mortem shots of a nice "healthy" non-smoker's lung alongside a gnarled old lung with bits falling off it supposedly belonging to a smoker. They said, "there you are – that's what happens to you if you smoke, it'll kill you". What they didn't point out was that the owners of both lungs were dead! Nor that not smoking hadn't saved the other chap from whatever killed him.[46]

Sheila's defiance of health warnings was a worry to her friends, particularly in her last two years when she developed a chronic asthma which audibly worsened from day to day, requiring frequent hospitalisation. Her wrinkled face was a living anti-smoking advertisement. When Geoff Hammond visited her in hospital for the last time, her doctor came in and shook his head to see her smoking: "Sheila", he scolded her, "here we are doing all we can to keep you

45 Constance Morgan, from a personal interview.

46 David Anderson, from a personal interview.

alive and you're doing your best to kill yourself". Unrepentant Sheila replied: "I've been smoking for 60 years and nobody's going to stop me now".[47]

She died two days later, on 10 June 1988. Dr Elphick sadly recorded the causes of death as "asthma, cigarette smoking and carcinoma of the lung".[48]

There were long lists of death notices in the daily press in the days following her death, from her sorrowing family, her many friends and professional acquaintances and the clients she had served so well. There were no graveside speeches because, at her own request, she was cremated privately at Karrakatta cemetery with only her local Anglican priest in attendance. *West Australian* chief court reporter, Margot Lang, wrote an obituary in the edition of 14 June. Her former secretary, Dr Josephine Hawkins, remembered her in the August 1988 issue of the Newsletter of the Australian Federation of University Women.

Although Sheila did not wish to have any memorial ceremony, her Naval friends, who had watched her failing health with increasing concern, would not allow their Chief Officer to pass out from life without a final parade. An unofficial ceremony was held at *HMAS Cerberus* on September 21 1988, which was reported by Iris Purnell in a special newsletter sent to all branches of the Ex-WRANS Association.

Iris explained that Mary Howard had visited Sheila not long before she died and Sheila had asked her opinion regarding arrangements she should make for her decorations and the naval portrait painted in England during the Victory celebrations. Mary suggested that she bequeath them to the Naval Museum at *Cerberus*. Sheila's executor, Geoff Hammond, had written to advise that this had been done and Mary organised a memorial ceremony to encompass the official delivery of these important relics. Twenty-one ex-WRANS who had served at wartime *Cerberus* attended; together with Commander Caton, representing the Naval Officer in Charge, and a number of other officers; serving WRANS and museum staff. Mary handed over the relics; together with a donation of $400.00 from the

47 Geoff Hammond, from a personal interview.

48 Death certificate of Sheila Mary McClemans.

Ex-WRANS Association and made a short speech. Her final words of tribute to her old friend were:

> For myself I can only repeat what I wrote in the special *Vale* edition of the "Ditty Box" of the NSW Ex-WRANS Association that I felt Sheila's life was best summed up in the obituary notice which was published in the WA Newspaper at the time of her death from her close legal friends and associates. It stated –
>
> > "She always demonstrated great wisdom in her counselling; depths of compassion and understanding to all who consulted her; her service to the community as a legal practitioner; as a law society executive; as a naval officer during World War II; as a member of the Parole Board – are but a few of her outstanding abilities and achievements – A truly great Australian lady – Now at rest".[49]
>
> We were indeed honoured to have known her and served with her, and can now be particularly happy and satisfied she will be remembered in this museum – in an area where we also had the privilege to serve and which meant so much to her.[50]

In July a special valedictory issue of the Law Society's monthly magazine, *Brief*, contained a scholarly tribute by Sir Francis Burt which concluded:

> I suppose that at the end of the day, it was, for lawyers, her professionalism which was her most outstanding attribute and it was that uncompromising and uncompromised professionalism which was the true source of her capacity to lead and to influence. She served the law and through the law she served ordinary men and women with an unswerving devotion. Such material rewards which came to her were mere by-products which in no way influenced her in what she did. And I am sure that at the end of her professional life she still saw herself as a debtor to her profession. And we are indebted to her.[51]

49 Mary Howard's quotation was from a death notice published in the *West Australian* by the firm of Hammond Fitzgerald and King.

50 Mary Howard supplied the text of her valedictory speech in a personal letter to the author.

51 Obituary by Sir Francis Burt, *Brief* Vol 15, 5, July 1988.

Bibliography

Adam-Smith, P, *Australian Women at War*, Thomas Nelson Australia, Melbourne, 1980

Alexander, F, Professor, *Campus at Crawley*, University of Western Australia Press, Perth, 1963; *Four Bishops and Their See*, University of Western Australia Press, Perth, 1975

Allen, JA, Rose Scott, *Vision and Revision in Australian Feminism*, Oxford University Press, Melbourne, 1990

Aveling, M *Westralian Voices*, University of Western Australia Press, Perth, 1979

Bevege, James, and Shute, *Worth Her Salt*, Hale & Iremonger, Sydney 1982

Cowan, P, *A Unique Position*, University of Western Australia Press, Perth, 1980

Curtis-Offer, M, *WRANS*, Naval Historical Society of Sydney, Sydney, 1975

Davidson, D, *Women On The Warpath*, University of Western Australia Press, Perth, 1997

Davidson, R *High Jinks At The Hot Pool*, Fremantle Arts Centre Press, Fremantle, 1994

Faine, J, *Taken on Oath*, Federation Press, Sydney, 1992

Hasluck, P, *Mucking About,* University of Western Australia Press, Perth, 1994

Hobbs, V, *But Westward Look*, University of Western Australia Press, Perth, 1988

Mackinolty, J and Radi, H (eds), *In Pursuit of Justice*, Hale & Iremonger, Sydney, 1979

Miller, C, *Season of Learning*, Fremantle Arts Centre Press, Fremantle, 1973

Oldham, R and Oldham, J, *Western Heritage*, Paterson Brokensha Pty Ltd, Perth, 1961

Pedrick, IFH, "Tax Practice and the Legal Profession" (1957) *Australian Law Journal* 267

Powell, L and Regan, F, *Legal Aid: Reflections on Costs, Lawyers and the Future*, Legal Aid Clearing House Bulletin, 1988

Rischbieth, B, *March of Australian Women*, Paterson Pty Ltd, Perth, 1964

Russell, EM, Robinson, FM, Nicholls, PW, *A History of the Law in Western Australia,* University of Western Australia Press, Perth, 1980

Sanders, DL, *Six for Heaven*, Hodder & Stoughton, London, 1952

Sharp, P, O'Hara L, *A Goodly Heritage*, Anglican Parish of Claremont and Edith Cowan University Publication Services, Perth, 1992

Scotton, RB and Ferber, H, *Public Expenditure and Social Policy in Australia*, 1980

Shervington, C, *Oral History Memoir of Sheila McClemans*, UWA Archives

Stewart, N, *As I Remember Them*, Artlook Books, Perth, 1987

Street, J, *Truth or Repose*, Australasian Book Society, Sydney, 1966

Woods, MV and Bisset, WW, *The History of the Western Australian Association of University Women 1923-1973*, self published, Perth, 1973

General Index

Index of Cases

Index of Statutes

Commonwealth

Western Australian